THE BUSINESS OF COMMON LIFE

The Business
of Common Life

Novels and Classical Economics
between Revolution and Reform

DAVID KAUFMANN

THE JOHNS HOPKINS UNIVERSITY PRESS   BALTIMORE AND LONDON

The Johns Hopkins University Press
2715 North Charles Street
Baltimore, Maryland 21218-4319
The Johns Hopkins Press Ltd., London

LIBRARY OF CONGRESS CATALOGING-IN-PUBLICATION DATA

Kaufmann, David, 1958–
    The business of common life : novels and classical economics between
revolution and reform / David Kaufmann.
        p.   cm.
    Includes bibliographical references and index.
    ISBN 0-8018-4930-6 (alk. paper)
    1. English fiction—19th century—History and criticism.   2. English
fiction—18th century—History and criticism.   3. Literature and society—
Great Britain—History.   4. Economics in literature.   5. Business in
literature.   I. Title.
PR868.E37K38   1995
823.009′355—dc20   94-12392
A catalog record for this book is available from the British Library.

Contents

Preface

In the end, *The Business of Common Life* turns out to be a study of liberalism. This is both an interesting and dangerous topic. Liberalism has not fared well in the literary-academic world over the last two decades, and it came under serious attack during the 1980s from leftist professors and conservative politicians. I have little truck with the newest Right, as I hope will have become very clear by the conclusion to this book. But we academics make a mistake when we reduce the liberal catechism to the works of Locke, Hobbes, and Kant, or when we follow Anthony Arblaster and take individualism, whether possessive or not, as the sole teaching of liberal theory.[1] Autonomy is, to be sure, a potent ideal and one whose energies are still vital, as anyone involved in the debate on abortion can tell you. But the ideal of autonomy does not exhaust the normative base of liberalism. J.G.A. Pocock and a number of other students of Georgian Britain have shown that the eighteenth century was marked by the vigor and heterogeneity of its political languages, and liberal theory made use of quite a number of them. In many ways, we would do well to heed Ian Shapiro's argument that Hobbes and Locke are in fact best understood in (and, in some ways, when left to) their seventeenth-century context.[2]

To construct a history of liberalism one really should read the eighteenth-century answers to Locke and Hobbes in, amongst others, Hutcheson, Hume, and Adam Smith. Such a history would also require, as I will argue, reading novels. The "liberal" eighteenth century meditated on the problems of distributive justice in a supposedly self-regulating market which neither Locke nor the civic republican tradition could really begin to address adequately. On the other hand, those who came from the Neoplatonic, Shaftesburian, and moral-sense schools could. But it will not do merely to add Scottish philosophy and maybe a dash of Cambridge Neoplatonism to the liberal curriculum, for we have to give due importance to the influence of Newton and of Deism as well. Nor can we assume that the influence of these ideas was local to metropolitan Britain. Many of the radical theoretical and social changes Gordon S. Wood ascribes to the American Revolution did not leap full blown out of the circumstances of the American situation, but had been intimated, if not actually discussed, in "liberal" philosophical, theological, and economic texts in Britain.[3] The Americans had to describe and justify a political system based on a commercial market society. Like the British Whigs they drew from, they had to find a good vocabulary to legitimate commercial modernity.

Legitimation is, as Austen would say, a "hard word," a bit of the social scientist's lexicon. Weber makes much of "the generally observable need of any power, or even of any advantage of life, to justify itself."[4] Brute force (*Macht*) is never quite enough to assert power or advantage. Rather, the more efficient form of domination (*Herrshaft*) rests on the acquiescence of the less advantaged or less powerful. It must provide an account of their "interest . . . in obedience"; it must compel their belief.[5] Sometimes personal affection can do the trick: a charismatic leader can manufacture obedience merely by virtue of that charisma. But more often than not, legitimation requires an appeal to what are presented as transpersonal norms, either of rationality or tradition.[6] In many cases justification only has to ape the forms of accepted rationality to be convincing.

Liberalism, then, is a way of describing and legitimating a market society, and because it bases its individual acts of legitimation on invoked and thus discussable norms, it is always open to attack. It is particularly vulnerable when it attempts rigorous philosophical justification. As I hope to show, the "liberal tradition" is only a tradition in that its participants try to solve similar problems, not (as with many traditions) because the solutions are the same. It is a network of competing imperatives. *My* chief interest will be the conflict between commutative rights and distributive justice. The eighteenth century made this conflict central when it described "happiness" as the proper goal of social life. Of course, the concept of happiness has a venerable history, and Locke and Hobbes did try to reduce human motivation to pain and fear, pleasure and glory. But that all-important abstraction "happiness," with the emphasis not on Aristotelian contemplation but Mandevillian material satisfaction, seems to belong peculiarly to Georgian and especially late-Georgian British social thought.

I am particularly queasy about generalizations, as much out of a sense of professional training as of theoretical commitment. So I will focus in this book on some novels and some economic debates as a way of investigating the richness and the impossibility of liberalism. As my first chapter will argue, political theory does not have a lock on the discussion of political problems. In fact, political theory does itself a terrible disservice when it ignores the discourses that, like it, play the apparently necessary game of legitimating modernity.

Acknowledgments

Any form of historical research requires chunks of free time and easy access to good facilities. In my case, these were provided by the National Endowment for the Humanities, which helped me kick off this work with a summer research grant at Yale University and enabled me to begin to finish it with a summer seminar at Johns Hopkins University. The Commonwealth Center at the University of Virginia presented me with strenuously stimulating company, searching criticism, and constant conversation. I cannot thank Ralph and Libby Cohen enough for the opportunities the Center provided in the semester I was there. I owe a debt of gratitude as well to Hans Bergmann, then chairman of the English Department at George Mason, who helped make it all possible.

I am not disingenuous when I stress my luck. No one who writes about the ideology of free markets as an ideology (normatively true and empirically false, in Andrew Arato's brilliant formulation) can be blind to the sheer number of privileges and contingencies that have to coincide before one is able to benefit from the market's scarce resources. Unfortunately, as material resources become even scarcer, especially at large state universities, every winner in the zero-sum scholarship lottery succeeds at a direct loss to many others whose projects are no less interesting and no less important. Markets are rarely free in any practical sense for the small intellectual entrepreneur, and I can only hope my book proves to be useful: hence, at least, my recourse, wherever possible, to readily available paperback editions — the kind most of us own and teach with.

If I have benefitted in a number of material ways in the past few years, I have also been very fortunate in the intellectual help I have received. Professor Wolfgang Iser's timely and incisive intervention turned my series of potentially interesting insights into a much more coherent project. Jerome Christensen helped me think closely about liberalism, and my anonymous reader at Johns Hopkins provided the most telling and trenchant criticism I have ever enjoyed. I owe more than I could begin to acknowledge to the intelligence and friendship of Adrienne Y. Donald, Ian Duncan, and R. E. Livingston, who have taught me enough to be called my mentors, if they were not already my friends.

Beyond the moments of gut-wrenching anxiety and the short stretches of boredom, this book was actually fun to write, in large part because of my friends in Washington and New York: Stephen Collins, Marianne Conroy, Pearl Ehrlich, Jim Hyde, the other Kaufmanns (Jenney, Peter, Sarah, Rachel, and Didders), Liz Koch, Kelly Schoen, Paul and T. D. Squassoni, and Orrin Wang. Donald Seelig's interventions were invaluable and brought me through. And I cannot do proper justice to Sharon Squassoni, whose intensities and grace are my greatest source of light.

It is customary to thank one's parents or one's children in the acknowledgments to a first book. I have no children, and my debt to my parents is witnessed by every page. This said, I would like to dedicate *The Business of Common Life* to two aunts: Florence Tritt, whose gentleness and decency are a constant inspiration; and the memory of Sandra Schoenberg Kling, who died as I began my research and who provided me with my first article on the Frankfurt School those many years ago.

1

Dialectics, Systems, and Context

There is an odd convergence in late Georgian culture that has generally escaped notice. In the first three decades of the nineteenth century, political economics became a center of concerted intellectual activity and debate. In this same period, the novel as a genre achieved newfound critical status. In short, economic theory and narrative fiction in prose both became objects of and media for considerable and respectful discussion. Of course, both fields had been well theorized by the mid-eighteenth century.[1] But at the moment when Revolution, foreign war, constitutional reform, Catholic emancipation, and restrictive import duties were the most important issues, novels and political economics reached new levels of achievement and regard.

A brief outline of the case at hand. Although Dugald Stewart, Adam Smith's biographer, began his lecture course on economics at Edinburgh in 1799,[2] the first economics course at an English university was taught by Pryme at Cambridge in 1816. As James P. Henderson has shown, Pryme's struggle to establish economic theory at the university was a significant moment, not only in the institutionalization of economics, but in the history of educational reform.[3] The first chair at Oxford (the first chair in the subject) was not established until 1825. John Ramsay McCulloch was appointed to the chair at the new London University in 1827.

As Biancamaria Fontana has argued, the *Edinburgh Quarterly* was an important vehicle for disseminating the principles of economic theory, but the *Edinburgh* was merely one outlet amongst many.[4] Jane Marcet published the first "familiar" explication of economics in 1814; James Mill and McCulloch followed with their drier primers of Ricardian orthodoxy in the early 1820s. Economic theory was also promulgated, as in the eighteenth century, through pamphlet wars over bullion, the Corn Laws, and matters of taxation, and these struggles were very important for the formulation of both Thomas Malthus and David Ricardo's theories. Political economics found its way into compendia of useful and important knowledge. The *Encyclopaedia Britannica*, showing its true *Edinburgh* colors, ignored Malthus (because of his guarded defense of protectionism)[5] and commissioned McCulloch to compose a major explication of political economics in 1823. If the economists made their mark in print and at a university, they also brought their debates forward in other, equally public, places. When Ricardo entered Parliament in 1819, he made concrete and official the relations between the actual institutions of politics and the work of those economists (himself included) who had sought to influence the policies of Liverpool's ministry since its inception.[6] There has always been some debate about the extent of Ricardo's ascendancy, and historians have recently made strong claims for the important influence of figures as diverse as the Whig statesman Henry Brougham[7] and the prominent Evangelical preacher Thomas Chalmers.[8] A better sign of the rather heated diversity of economic thought at the time however, is the foundation of the Political Economy Club in 1821, as a stage for oral debate on questions that the members brought forward. Henderson has made a nice case for seeing the Club, not as a manifestation of Ricardo's strength, but rather as a means for undercutting that strength. Establishing a club signaled an attempt to get important economic discussion out of Ricardo's notoriously hospitable, though intellectually confining, dining room and thus to free it by locating it on relatively neutral territory. With Ricardo's death in 1823, Robert Torrens and Malthus, two friends and intellectual opponents of the late Member of Parliament, became the de facto ranking members of the club.[9] The debates and conflicts in the club continued through the 1820s, and the rump Malthusians (including Malthus himself) centered at Cambridge University were influential in the vote in 1831 to create a statistical society to provide material for a non-Ricardian, historical and inductive, economic and moral science of the state. The Statistical Society of London was duly formed in 1833.[10] And it is perhaps not too glib a point to note that the proliferation of institutions and debates continues to this day. The growing importance of economic theory and the ongoing high-cultural supremacy of poetry in the so-called Romantic period have overshadowed the newfound authority that began to be accorded to novels at the same time. Nevertheless, the recent and invaluable work of Michael Munday and Ina Ferris has alerted us to the close and—more importantly—respectful attention paid to the novel in the periodical press of the first twenty years of the nineteenth century.[11] Of course, such attention is harder to collate and summarize than the influence of a Ricardo, a Malthus, or a Smith. Journalists and reviewers did not begin from first principles. Rather, they developed principles in the sheer process of producing their reviews. While more reconstructive research on the reviews needs to be done, I would like to suggest that we also pay attention to another interesting phenomenon of the period. The fashion of publishing collections of "established" novels in uniform libraries, which thus created a canon, seems to have started with Anna Barbauld's fifty-volume *British Novelists* in 1810; it went on to include Sir Walter Scott's *Ballantyne's Novelists's Library* (which ended unsuccessfully in 1824) as well as Coburn and Bentley's Standard Novels Series which produced the 1831 text of *Frankenstein* that is in most common use today.

This concatenation of details presents some problems, not solutions. It indicates that the cultural and critical fortunes of political economics and the novel seemed to improve markedly at the same moment. We are thus prompted to ask how should the fortunes of these disparate spheres be understood to coincide? In other words, can we find a mediation between the two? How can a study do justice to a genre that is so adamantly heterogeneous and to a field of research and thought that, as I have indicated above, was so bracingly fractious? How should one limit the field of this study while making claims that are expansive enough to be interesting?

My brief historical digest also raises, if somewhat obliquely, another set of questions. If the field of political economics was so rich in the first three decades of the nineteenth century, why are so many of its thinkers forgotten now? Why is there a canon of so-called classical economists (a canon that consists of Smith, Ricardo, Malthus, and Mill)? The short answer is simple, though rather tau-

tological: Smith, Malthus, and Ricardo defined the central problems of the field we now call economics, even if their suppositions
and claims have proven to be untenable. But such an answer merely
defers the issue, for we must ask why it is that professional economics has organized itself around *these* problems? One could propose
to address this issue through an institutional history of Anglo-
American economic theory from the eighteenth through the twentieth centuries, and such a history would be invaluable. In this
study, however, I want to push the question in a different direction.
I want to ask why these problems were and remain so compelling,
so apparently urgent. By framing the issue this way, we must look
at the vagaries of taste: Why is it that *Frankenstein* and the novels of
Austen still command such wide readerships, while the works of
Scott, so much more important in their time, are of merely antiquarian interest?

We can be led in this regard by one of Theodor W. Adorno's
more arresting dicta: "Taste is the most accurate seismograph of
[lived, bodily] historical experience."[12] The rather clumsy addition
of the words in brackets—for which I, not the translator, am to
blame—is meant to signal some of the complexity of the term
Erfahrung in English. *Erfahrung*, in the work of Benjamin and
Adorno, betokens a less alienated, more integral form of knowledge that transcends the atomization of more impoverished modern notions of experience.[13] Taste, in this formulation, is not
merely the expression and sign of class bias, although it is certainly
that. Rather, if we tease out Adorno's figure, the shifts in historical
Erfahrung, in the subterranean substance of historical life, are
recorded best in the medium of taste. Taste, which is a bodily metaphor transposed into the spiritual and thus which includes both
realms, serves as a sensitive register of situated, historical experience. Taste, then, will be a guide not only to conditions of domination but also to felt needs within those conditions and the aspiration to overcome them.

Taking my lead from Adorno and Jürgen Habermas (whom I
will play off against the systems-theorist, Niklas Luhmann), I will
argue in the chapters that follow that "classical" economics (Smith,
Malthus, Ricardo, and Mill) and certain historically important novels (Radcliffe's *The Italian*, Scott's early Waverley novels, Shelley's
Frankenstein, and Austen's last two works, *Persuasion* and *Sanditon*)
constitute parallel contributions to the project of framing, express-

ing, and suppressing the needs generated by the development of British commercial modernity.

Here is a guide to my argument in this book. The material success of Britain's commercial revolution after 1688 and the shift in social organization that this success entailed helped develop new means of self-description and self-justification. Not surprisingly, this project required the establishment of new normative benchmarks. The particular genius of the eighteenth-century jurisprudential defense of the commercial and the modern is that it provided a coherent theory of history which placed, as its proper end, the happiness of those fortunate enough to be born in those latter, that is modern, days.

Of course, happiness is a slippery word, and even if only understood in purely material terms, it presents a problem. While the promise of a secure secular happiness in a commercial world will necessarily include protections for private property and contract, it also seems to imply a satisfaction of basic needs. And achieving this satisfaction can destabilize the principle of private property. To put this another way, we can say that eighteenth-century "happiness" required the balancing of two very different, and sometimes conflicting, notions of justice: the commutative and the distributive.

Adam Smith's resolution to this tension was extremely elegant. Following Hutcheson and Hume, he argued that the economy was best understood as a system of interlocking and interdependent spheres that distributes the material means to happiness, not according to equality or desert (as in the Aristotelian and Thomist traditions), but according to an individual's participation and situation within the system. Because an economy free from distributive regulations is inherently more efficient than an economy intent on distributing social goods equally or fairly, it will raise everybody's standard of living. Under Smith's system of "natural liberty," the inequities of a class society will still exist, of course, and the poor will always be with us. But they will be better off—that is happier than under any other system. Thus, if you have a free market based on the inviolability of private property, economic growth will fulfill the material claims of the population more effectively than traditional distributive solutions ever could.

Smith's system depends on constant growth. Its ability to meet the objections of its detractors weakens in periods of economic stagnation and depression. This raises the question of what should pick up the market's slack when an economy slips? A good part of the so-called Revolution debate in Britain produces two differing and equally coherent answers. While both Burke and Paine argue that the public sector should pitch in, they disagree over the definition of the public sector. They therefore reopen the discussion about the validity and the reach of distributive claims, a discussion which renders the differentiation between the spheres of life more important, as we shall see in the third chapter. Furthermore, the arguments about who is responsible for what goods and what ends in the modern world lead to an interrogation of the very project of legitimation itself (chapter 2). And this interrogation gives rise to important definitional conflicts over the nature and gender of citizenship, that is, of participation in the market and the polity (chapters 4 and 5). Classical economics and novels have a large investment in these issues, but their mode of investment is different in each case. And this difference makes a project such as this book's — limited though it is to a small group of texts and issues — problematic because it pulls the study in opposite directions. On the one hand, this project generates totalizing claims about "culture" with unsettling ease. On the other hand, the particular novels and the economic debates we will look at construct separate constellations and focus attention on specifics. How then should one mediate between ambition and tact?

If we accept, however provisionally, Adorno's aphorism about the historical truth of taste, then we might also want to pay due attention to the recent prevalence in the Anglo-American literary academy of dialectics. In an odd way Hegel, however modified by Sartre and Lacan (through Kojève), by Derrida and De Man (through Heidegger), by Marxism, or by feminism and postcolonial theory (with their constitutive fascinations with the notion of the Other), has returned as the philosophical repressed to a culture that developed positivism in order to get away from him. Dialectics, which Hegel called the "orderly, methodically cultivated spirit of contradiction,"[14] have proven to be useful as a way of thinking about the complex and the nonidentical at a time when such thinking has become an important part of reconceiving the limits and legitimacy of literary studies in Anglo-American universities.[15]

There are, of course, a number of styles of dialectical thought. The grimly proper dialectics of Lukacs are remarkably different from the principled refusal of sublation and reconciliation one finds in Derrida. In the discussion that follows, I will outline a version of dialectics that should seem very familiar in its scruples and undigestably foreign in its terminology and designs. I will start with Adorno,[16] correct him with Niklas Luhmann, and correct Luhmann in turn with Habermas. The reader who has no patience with this rather Teutonic thicket can skip the next section of this chapter with full approval of Adorno who wrote: "Performance legitimates method, which for that reason keeps its suppositions in abeyance."[17]

I

How can one cultivate "methodically" the "spirit of contradiction" that is dialectics? We can begin by treating with suspicion anything that seems either self-evident or immediate:

*There is nothing
self-evident
about
culture*

> According to Hegel, there is nothing between heaven and earth that is not *"vermittelt"* [mediated]. . . . Those allegedly elementary qualities of immediacy always appear already categorially formed, and thus the sensory and the categorial moments cannot be clearly distinguished from one another as "layers". . . . Immediacy always already contains something other than itself—subjectivity—without which it would not be "given" at all, and by that token it is already not objectivity.[18]

Thought cannot naively celebrate the immediate, for the immediate is immediate only to someone who already has a conception of the immediate and can thus say reflectively to him- or herself, "This experience I am having is unreflective, immediate." In other words, as soon as epistemology admits the perceiving subject, there is no such thing as a given object on its own. The subject's mental categories have to have always already situated it, thought it.

But the object is not gobbled up by the imperialism of the subject's categories. If it were, knowledge would constrain itself to a self-laudatory and self-limiting narcissism: Adorno sees this tendency in all noncritical, that is, nondialectical, modes of modern rationality. Critical knowledge, such as it is, has to derive from a confrontation with specificities:

> The central nerve of the dialectic as a method is determinate negation. It is based on the experience of the impotence of a

criticism that keeps to the general and polishes off the object being criticized by subsuming it from above. (*Hegel* 80)

Determinate negation is, as Hegel maintains, not an abstract skepticism that destroys everything from an external, formal viewpoint. Dialectics are not nihilism. Rather, they arise from thinking about the mediated object itself. They free that object from the false circumscription by the formal tendency of the percipient's mind.[19]

Determinate negation signals the mind's acknowledgment of objective complexity. Nothing is simple. Nothing exists on its own, not even thought. Just as subject and object are mutually implicated through mediation, so are all objects and subjects and all the categories of thought. The following quotation is perhaps Adorno's clearest distillation of the sociohistorical dimensions of dialectics:

> The universal is always also the particular and the particular the universal. By analyzing this relationship, the dialectic gives an account of the *social force field* in which everything individual is socially preformed from the outset and at the same time nothing is realized except in and through individuals. The categories of the particular and the general, the individual and society, cannot be put to rest any more than can those of subject and object, nor can the process that takes place between them be interpreted as a process that retains their individual identities: *the contributions of the two moments—indeed, what those moments actually are—can be discerned only in historical concretion.* (*Hegel* 45; emphasis added)

If one shifts terms from the epistemological to the sociological as Adorno does here, then one can say that while the social determines the individual (person, work of art, etc.), the relation between the particular and the social can only be seen in particular historical cases. In other words, neither term—the individual and the social—is given license to supercede the other. Furthermore their mutual determination and negation will make their relations volatile and processual. For while historical concretion sediments a constellation of social relations at a certain time (*ND* 163), history does not end with that concretion. Instead, that concretion takes on a historical life: it becomes implicated in a new set of constellated relations. And so on.

Adorno's stress on social labor makes individuals and their creations practically interchangeable. This gives those creations a special dignity and underscores Adorno's point about the sociohistorical determination of human individuality. Nevertheless, the bulk of Adorno's extensive work was devoted to the critical scrutiny of philosophical, literary, and musical texts. It is appropriate, in a project such as my own that deals only with texts — many of which are literary — to turn our attention to Adorno's suggestions about the dialectical, sociohistorical analysis of art.

Adorno's "Theses on the Sociology of Art" is a short, polemical essay that is stridently clear about its intention to critique what Adorno took to be the prevailing winds of art sociology in the early 1960s. Adorno argues against the prevalent tendency to fetishize quantitative empiricism. He also inveighs against the concomitant positivist fascination with the distribution and the reception of individual works:

> According to the meaning of the terms, the sociology of art consists of *all* aspects of the relationship between art and society. It is impossible to box it into any one area, even into the social effect of art works. For this effect is itself only a moment in the totality of that relationship. (*OL* 94; emphasis added; see also *ISM* 199)

Art's reception is not to be ignored nor are the conditions of its distribution. But, for Adorno, the sociology of art cannot rest there. It cannot do without aesthetics, without concentrating on the specificities of a given work.

Adorno claims that we need to determine the quality of a work. It is important to note that he uses the term "quality" (*Qualitaet*) and not "value" (*Wert*). We would do well to remind ourselves that by using this word, he points back to Aristotle: "By quality I mean that in virtue of which people are said to be such and such."[20] Quality never rests with the dichotomy of good and bad. In fact, it does not even have to include it. According to the same chapter of Aristotle's *Categories,* substance can have contrary qualities at the same time. To be able to discriminate qualities, one has to know how to look. One has to learn to pay attention to the thing in question and distinguish its features.

Adorno worries about the specificities of a work because he wants to save sociology from falling into the homogenizing abyss that administered society and its handmaid, the culture industry, guard with such jealousy. The danger presented by quantification and by the worship of the chart and the verifiable fact is that these tools flatten out distinctions in order to plot data points. They permit the replacement of the faculty of judgment with a reflexive form of memory, a mere bland familiarity. Positivism attempts to render immediate the relationship between the universal and the individual by asserting "the false identity of the general and the particular" (*DE* 121).[21] It is both the agent of abstraction and the servant of the exchange principle. This principle, which enables one to reduce all particulars to a single denominator, appears here as the very basis of alienated and alienating knowledge.

Accordingly, a sociology that pays attention to aesthetics as well as reception, which looks at the qualities of works, cannot be value-free (*OL* 100–101). It has to be critical or else it would betray the negation at the heart of dialectics, and thus reproduce the merely existent by taking it as ossified law. But Adorno, who wants to mediate between aesthetics and social science, has to argue on two fronts. Against traditional aestheticians, he claims that value is not transhistorical. Against crude relativists, he argues that value is not completely situational. So Adorno gives Kant a historical twist. He maintains that every judgment of predicative logic assumes values and critiques that cannot be abstracted from that judgment at the time it is rendered. Each predication looks like a concept (the subjugation of a particular to a universal law) but is not and therefore only names a particular (*OL* 99). In this way, he recasts Kant's famous definition of art as "purposefulness without a purpose," that is, the appearance of conceptual form without the closure that form entails. As we saw above, according to Adorno's lights, you cannot presuppose values or else you will miss the particular. But if you try to be value-free you will merely allow the unarticulated valueless "values" inherent in an exchange society to achieve the status of a natural law. You need to follow the route of determinate negation.

This difficult tug-of-war between the demands of the universal and the claims of the particular leads Adorno to place a great stress on mediation. It is no coincidence that he ends his *Introduction to the Sociology of Music* with a chapter on the subject. In his "Theses" Adorno argues that music sociology should not end with discussing distribution nor with considerations of the "position of art in society." Instead it should seek to recognize "how society objec-

tifies itself in art works" (*OL* 102), that is, how the universal subjects itself to the particular:

> The ideal sociology of art would be to bring into line objec-
> tive analyses — that is, of the works — analyses of the struc-
> tural and specific mechanisms that produce both impact and
> effect, and analyses of those subjective findings that can be
> recorded. They must mutually illuminate each other. (*OL* 96)

Along with attempting to determine the "position of art in society,"
the sociologist of art should play aesthetic analyses of individual
objects against the subjective receptions of these works. Adorno's
ideal is the investigation, not only of the ways the object is used by
society, but also of the ways that the object uses and transforms
"society" within itself. Hence his aestheticism. He respects what
he always recognizes as the *fictive* autonomy of the realm of art in
spite of its illusory quality. Aesthetic freedom constitutes a negative moment in an unfree world.

According to Adorno, this fictive autonomy is a fact of a history
that cannot be ignored. Following Weber, he argues that the division of labor and the rationalization of activity that mark capitalist-
Western modernity lead to the conceptual and institutional separation of different spheres of reason, production, and distribution.
Such separations are always false if taken as absolutes because they
are all bound together within a common horizon called society and
thus depend quite strongly on each other. Although the sphere of
art and art itself have developed their own rationality, their autonomy is also a lie in that they exist in and feed off the very society
from which they are understood to be free. In a society based on
illegitimate domination, the supposed independence of art is an
effective falsehood for the critical theorist. The illusory autonomy
of art allows the sphere of the aesthetic and single aesthetic works
an Archimedean distance from society, a conceptual distance
which allows the art work to figure possibilities of mundane reconciliation. The reconciliations in art works are always suspect in that
they can be criticized either as ideological or utopian. But their
mere existence reveals the disjunctions in the "real" world that the
"real" world cannot or will not heal. They stand as an ever-fixed
mark which we have not hit, but cannot abandon.

We do not have to accept Adorno's emphatic version of aesthetic
truth, his resolutely aestheticist point that the individual work is

only a cipher of reconciliation and not a means of achieving it communicatively. We can follow Albrecht Wellmer in factoring back into the equation the notion that the work exists not merely for itself but for others as well. It forms part of a communicative circuit. This has important implications for our understanding of art and its relation to its "beyond," the utopian transformation of the social:

> But the *beyond* of art, to which it points and to which it is related, is . . . the social life process itself as it can be *affected* by aesthetic experience. Understood in this way, aesthetic experience, by illuminating our life praxis and our self-understanding, by pushing back the boundaries of muteness and inarticulate silence, and by making accessible the hidden depths of our lives to ourselves, *is*, as Adorno thought, the presence of a utopian perspective.[22]

The work of art, by making visible what is kept secret, by granting expression to that which the social would mute, serves an important, if limited, social function. It asks us to pay close attention to the untapped but utopian semantic potential of all works, even those which seem to affirm the enforced silences of social domination.

There is a good deal of dignity in this project, but there are also a number of well-known difficulties. Adorno's vision of the sociology of art is part of his defense of modernism, and therefore needs to assume that art aspires to a condition of autonomy from something called society. It needs the notion of *l'art pour l'art*, which is (if you bar the example of the Schlegels) a mid–nineteenth century phenomenon and really does not take hold until the *fin de siècle*. What do we do with works that appeared before this, with works that were not considered autonomous by their authors or their readers? Is there another definition of aesthetic autonomy that we can draw upon? Furthermore, how do we conceptualize that complex *outside* of the work, the social whole that includes but keeps separate the field of artistic production?

Adorno's polemical intent, his desire to save modernism and Hegelian Marxism at the same time, cause him to stress vertical differentiation, that is the separation between high and low art. His commitment to high art leads him to define aesthetic autonomy as a freedom from society. But we can read Weber in another way to note that rationalization is also a horizontal phenomenon, the division of the world into separate spheres of knowledge and activity which, ideologically, are understood as having different methods but equal value. And these spheres will be subdivided into smaller spheres or systems to manage better the terrifying chaos of the empirical world. Thus art will differentiate itself from natural sciences and the novel will differentiate itself from its sister arts. To conceptualize this "horizontal" differentiation, and to substitute it for the vertical differentiation of "autonomous art," I will have recourse to the systems theory of Niklas Luhmann. In this way, I shall try to follow Zuidervaart's reconstruction of Adorno:

> To locate cultural phenomena in a "context of problems" is to avoid both the narrowness of technical historiographies and the imprecision of global philosophies of history. To evaluate the contributions of cultural phenomena within their context of problems is to avoid both the positivism of merely descriptive accounts and the idealism of strongly prescriptive accounts. To argue for the legitimacy of such evaluations is to take issue with the historical relativism of poststructuralism and the historical dogmatism of orthodox Marxism.[23]

By invoking the problematic theories of Luhmann, I want to expand Zuidervaart's "context of problems" to include not only questions of material, procedure, and technique but other and just as relevant cognitive and social considerations.

II

Luhmann's sociological theory begins with an inversion of what it sees as an outmoded humanist model. Sociology should not study the relations of parts to wholes, of individuals to groups, and groups to society. Rather than start with individuals' actions and their intentions as data, Luhmann suggests that we concentrate on the very medium of social interaction and cohesion—*communication*—and the meaning horizon within which that communication takes places—the *system*.[24] In other words, sociological reflection has to concentrate on the conditions of possibility as well as the determining boundaries of what appears to us as meaningful action. Action thus becomes a matter of secondary interest because it is merely an effect of the system that precedes and dictates it.[25]

Luhmann means "meaning" in a specific way. He understands it as a prelinguistic intentionality within the system, a context of possibilities waiting to be actualized and not already actualized.[26] This notion he derives from Husserl:

> [E]very conscious process is, in itself, consciousness of such and such, regardless of what the rightful actuality-status of this objective such-and-such may be . . . Each . . . conscious process . . . "means" something or other and bears in itself, in this manner peculiar to the meant, its particular *cogitatum* . . . The house-perception means a house — more precisely, as this individual house — and means it in the fashion peculiar to perception; a house-memory means a house in the fashion peculiar to memory . . . and so forth.[27]

As meaning is an orientation, a preverbal act of attention and delineation, it cannot be transferred or transmitted. Meaning precedes communication.

A system organizes meaning for a purpose, and here cybernetics reveal their importance in Luhmann's scheme. For Luhmann, a system is a way of conceptualizing, analyzing, and solving problems through a complicated series of binary choices. He describes three different types of problem-solving systems: interactive (face-to-face relations which are very time-consuming); organizational (where larger groups cohere through the individuals' successful fulfillment of entry criteria, such as certification for teaching); and society (the widest set of mutually accessible communicative relations).[28]

In "modern" societies, organizational systems (such as political economics) are no longer articulated according to segmentation (equal clans or tribes) or stratification (unequal distribution of function and importance along hierarchical lines), but according to functional differentiation:[29]

> Functional differentiation organizes communication processes around special functions to be fulfilled at the level of society. Since all necessary functions have to be fulfilled and are interdependent, society cannot concede absolute primacy to any of them.[30]

The importance of the implications here cannot be stressed too strongly. In societies organized according to function, no single system is central. They are all necessary, interdependent, and still very independent. Each does something different and no single one can do it all:

> [F]unctional differentiation is possible only through the *rejection of redundancy*. Functional systems cannot step in for, replace, or even simply relieve one another . . . [After the eighteenth century, the] old, multifunctional institutions and moralities are, therefore, dissolved and replaced by a co-ordination of specific codes to specific systems that distin-guishes modern society from all those before.[31]

Luhmann's vision of the system is positively Prussian in its efficiency. No functions are repetitive. Redundancy is, as he says, rejected.

An important result, according to Luhmann, of advancing func-tional organization is that modern societies become increasingly "centerless," and increasingly unable to represent themselves to themselves in their totality:

> As long as society was differentiated according to center/ periphery or rank, positions could be established where it was possible, as it never has been since, to represent the system's unity, i.e., in the center or at the apex of the hierar-chy. The transition to functional differentiation destroys this possibility when it leaves it to the many function systems to represent the unity of society through their respective sub-system/environment differences and exposes them in this respect to competition among themselves while there is no superordinate standpoint of representation for them all.[32]

No organizational system can represent itself as a synecdoche for society as a whole. It cannot claim a universal validity for its own organization of meaning. To maintain that a discourse is indeed foundational is to misrecognize the limits of that discourse, and to misunderstand the functionally differentiated organization of soci-ety. So although discourse systems are thrown into competition with each other in modern society because each has to argue for its own legitimacy, no discourse system can actually know itself. A system can discuss itself, can "become a topic within itself as a sys-tem within an environment," but it cannot know its boundaries exhaustively.[33] In this way, its self-thematizations, its self-descrip-tions, will always be partially blind. A system can gain insight into another system by applying its own peculiar organization of meaning. It can thus get to know another system's boundaries and blind-spots, but not its own.[34] Even though each system needs to legiti-mize itself in terms of the total system's needs, it will always get those needs wrong, because it will never be able to account for itself—and therefore for the totality that includes it—at all accur-ately. Its insights will always by necessity be local. Its observations will taste of its self-description. A system therefore always speaks to "society" but cannot speak for it.

If we want to render a proper account of Luhmann's usefulness for us, we will have to concede that his insistence on nonredundant functional differentiation within a common horizon allows us to begin to understand the articulation between the novel and politi-cal economics, the relation in difference that binds them together and keeps them apart. But we should remain aware of the other implications of his thought. His notion of the centerless society, his assertion of the self-referential autonomy of organizational sys-tems, his location of meaning in intention, all restate as cold fact Weber's rather tragic thesis that we are increasingly caught in the iron cage of instrumental/systemic reason, where we can only argue means and never ends.[35] Luhmann gives organizational and social systems a rather frozen positivity, a sheer existence and alien will. The antihumanist tendencies of this line of thinking make a pow-erful contribution to the ongoing critique of the philosophy of the subject. And in his acerbic comments on the social movements (ecological, feminist, and student), Luhmann reminds us forcefully of the essentially conservative systemic constraints on radical thought and action.[36] Furthermore, his strictures against synecdoche re-mind us of the dangers of economism, biologism, and the overex-tension of any given discourse's methods and insights. But in the course of these valuable warnings, he also makes the autonomous system into a fetish, and counters one spectral agency (the subject) with another (the system). In other words, he demystifies the au-tonomy of the subject and goes on to create a brilliant, totalizing, and rather gothic myth about the omnivorous rationality of sys-tems and communication.[37]

One can thus counter Luhmann from a number of different the-oretical angles, the two most obvious being provided by Bourdieu and Habermas. With Bourdieu we can argue that the relative autonomy of systems is a good heuristic device but a dangerous model because we live in a matrix of conflicting discursive systems. Accordingly, the legitimation of the hegemony of any discursive regime will entail the active suppression of all other discourses and dialects. Bourdieu's account of "symbolic violence" thus effectively deconstructs Weber's distinction between domination (*Herrschaft*) and power (*Macht*), between consensual subjugation and brute force. All systemic differentiation involves subordination and therefore all legitimation will require violence.

More important for our purposes, however, is Luhmann's most engaged and sympathetic antagonist, Habermas. The duration, complexity, and abstraction of their more than twenty-year debate cannot be rehearsed here. I *do* want to reiterate one aspect of Habermas's more recent account of Luhmann. Because Luhmann locates meaning as a prelinguistic possibility, and because his phenomological reduction of communication to intention performs an end run around hermeneutics, he denies single or collective agents any access to the creation of meaning. Systems always preexist those who communicate within them. It is a brilliant move, but like most examples of "rigor," a counterintuitive one. The history of economic thought, as Keith Tribe has shown and as this study will demonstrate, was not completely pre-given, but was also the product of arguments about what precisely should be understood as meaningful.[38] Following Habermas, can we not ask if systemic intention always precedes meaning or is collapsible into meaning? Might there not be cases where conflicts within as well as between discourse systems create new intentions and orientations? By defining communication through reduction to systemic intentions, Luhmann secures a field for sociology but falls into the trap of all phenomenological reductions: a system can only see what it has defined as visible and its limits are dogmatically reinforced.[39]

Luhmann's theory discounts all attempts to reach metalanguages and metameanings. But he also claims that all systems compete for place and recognition in that spectral totality known as society. For this to be the case there has to be a common language of legitimation, of norms into which individual system claims can be translated in order to be judged. Otherwise there has to be a virtual center, such as Habermas imagines, towards which and in the name of which each system makes its claim. There is thus either a translating mechanism in society or something akin to the category (though not necessarily the reality) of a public sphere for the competition between systems to have any meaning. Although I have doubts about Habermas's idealizations of speech acts and life worlds as horizons of intersubjectively derived meaning, I do think that we can accede to his point that in acts of communication, the communicator assumes a *virtual* center and/or a shared—if only as a projection—horizon of linguistically recoverable meaning that transcends the boundaries of a given organizational system.[40]

In other words, Luhmann might not take his notion of "society" seriously enough. There has to be, by his account, a level of communicative organization that transcends almost all subsystemic limitations, otherwise there could be no such thing as a social system in the first place. While society can be understood by Luhmann to be the sum of the differences between systems, he is reluctant to allow organizational systems the higher levels of communicative integration that his theory in places seems to demand.[41]

In the light of these objections, I think we can put Luhmann to good use, provided we keep certain modifications in mind. His notion of a developing nonredundant functionalism allows us to see how both the novel and classical economics could become increasingly important discursive organizational systems in the early nineteenth century without being reducible to each other. It helps us understand how both could become necessary and different at the same time. Necessary, because novels and economics were both contained within a common, *virtual* horizon of meaning and therefore within a common and *real* horizon of problems. In this way they tend to cover similar ground. Different, because novels and economics organized their fields of study, limited their questions, and framed the range of their answers in specific and particular ways. Furthermore, as they are necessary and different at the same time—they are articulated within a more or less functionally organized social system—they are caught in constant competition with each other and with other organizational systems, which all want recognition/attention for their own endeavors. They also seek the always quixotic privilege of representing the unrepresentable, that is, for serving as the synecdoche for the ever-elusive totality of the society in which they operate. In short, the tendency towards the functional organization of society makes legitimation and self-description constantly urgent necessities.

But these arguments are only interesting when tested against specific historical concretions. Accordingly, I want to end this chapter by looking at one attempt to legitimize the dignity of the novel and one attempt to define and defend what we have come to know as the discourse of "classical" economics.

III

In many ways John Stuart Mill was born to be the great apologist for, and critic of, classical economics. The son of James Mill and the student of David Ricardo, Mill was tutored from a painfully early age in the principles of the new science. Not surprisingly, he became a combative partisan for Ricardian principles by his early twenties.

In January 1825, he published a spirited defense of these principles against an anonymous reviewer in the Tory *Quarterly Review* who had maintained that Ricardo's followers were not the true heirs of Adam Smith. Mill was more than happy to reclaim this heritage:

> Happily, the old and orthodox faith was not left altogether destitute, for our author [Ricardo] remained. It was reserved for him to carry back the science to its fountainhead — to restore the legitimate rule of Adam Smith, or, as he afterwards expresses it, of "Adam Smith and Mr Malthus."[42]

Mill is playing a rather sophisticated game here. He maintains that Smithian doctrine is a faith already established, and that Ricardo is the defender of that faith, a defender whose line of descent runs directly from Smith to Malthus. Mill thus elides the argument over free trade between Malthus and Ricardo (to which we shall return in chapter 4), a rift that had caused, as we have mentioned above, an irrevocable breach between the Whig Malthus and the Whig literary establishment of both the *Edinburgh Review* and the *Encyclopaedia Britannica*. Mill wants to claim a common front between the Malthusians and the Ricardians, thus making Ricardo the touchstone for "proper" political economy.

Perhaps Mill knew that it was Malthus himself—banished as he was from the pages of the *Edinburgh*—who had written the article in the *Quarterly*. In any event, he professes not to. In fact, he claims that the *Quarterly*'s attack is a "grave piece of raillery" which pillories Malthusian arguments by parodying not only their logic but Malthus's own rather misty style.[43] Thus Mill indicates that Malthus's objection to Ricardo's belief in the efficacy of international trade does not belong in the field of political economics at all. Malthus's article is not economics, Mill implies, but a joke played out in the style of economics.

Having thus used a fine piece of legerdemain to create the illusion that political economics consists of an unmixed bloodline and unanimous belief, he goes on to argue that political economics is a science because it has made three great discoveries since Smith: Malthus's principle of population, the theory of rent worked out by Malthus and Ricardo, and Ricardo's notion of comparative advantage.[44] As these principles will play an important part in the story I have to tell, it is worth explaining them—however briefly—here.

The principle of population (which we will discuss in greater detail in chapter 3) is as elegant as it is notorious. Put most simply, it maintains that population will always follow and yet grow faster than the production of food. The more food, the more babies. With more babies, the amount of food available to any given individual will either remain constant or, more probably, decrease. Thus economic growth will not translate easily into improved living conditions. In fact, population presents an iron limitation to individual and collective well-being.

This rather dismal conclusion was a product of the debates of the 1790s. In a similar way, the doctrine of rent was the product of a later historical debate between Malthus and Ricardo on the cultivation of marginal lands towards the end the Napoleonic Wars. Rent is "that portion of the produce of the earth which is paid to the landlord for the use of the original and indestructible powers of the soil."[45] The notion of rent presupposes that land is not cultivated by its owner, but by an independent agricultural capitalist who employs labor to work that land. When demand for agricultural products overreaches the capacity of the most fertile land, less productive tracts have to be cultivated. They, in turn, will yield less at a greater cost to the capitalist and the consumer. In short, the returns diminish as all the nation's land gets cultivated. The least productive land will pay the least rent. The most productive will pay the highest. But in the three-way division of income between landowner, capitalist, and labor, the increase in rent (and a stable or increasing price of labor which is keyed to the price of food) means that the capitalist's profits will decrease proportionately. Profit and rent, capitalist and landowner are at odds with each other. And, what is worse, the decline in profits leads to a decline in investment and growth.

This rather dystopic horizon of what economists call "the stationary state" derives from a simplified model of economic relations, a simplification that Schumpeter called "the Ricardian vice." For Ricardo, there is only one product (grain), one input (labor), and demand for the product is constant.[46] Malthus disagreed with this reductionism. He argued that demand should be taken as a variable as important as supply, and that the conflict between capital and land was not as insoluble as Ricardo's *Principles* might indicate. But, as Mark Blaug has pointed out on more than one occasion, Ricardo's theory of rent was taken to its extreme for polemical purposes. His use of the stationary state was "at most a useful device for frightening the friends of protection."[47] The stationary state was in part a cautionary tale, a bogeyman to scare those who, like Malthus, sought to defend standing investments in marginal lands by retaining high import tariffs on grain. Ricardo, on the other hand, wanted to create a world market which would permit the capital of each country to move quickly to the most profitable areas of local production, thus providing goods to be traded against other necessaries from other countries. By "discovering" the principle of comparative advantage, Ricardo sought to influence policy. He used as an incentive an attractive picture in which the people of every nation would be able to obtain the greatest number of goods as efficiently—that is, as cheaply—as nature could possibly allow.

Mill's confident claim that these three "truths" constitute the incontrovertible postulates of Ricardian economics thus co-opts Malthus's authority (as the author of the principle of population) while discarding Malthusian heresies. Interestingly, Mill's argument defends Ricardo against Malthus, but it does not provide a defense of political economics as a field. That is, Mill maintains the legitimacy of Ricardian doctrine while ignoring the legitimacy of political economics as a whole.

Mill wants to justify the authority of Ricardian orthodoxy while assuming that the reader will require no justification for the claims of economics. In short, he arrogates the authority of science to Ricardo's followers, but does not show *how* political economics can claim to be a science in the first place.

Mill proposed such a legitimation in an article entitled "On the Definition of Political Economy," which was written between 1831 and 1833, although he did not publish it (in the *London and West-*

minster Review) until 1836.[48] Mill begins this piece with the paradoxical but ultimately unexceptional claim that the "definition of a science has almost invariably not preceded, but followed, the creation of the science itself" (310). A science, then, begins with practical observations, and does not account for itself, does not rationalize itself until it has already been established. Then, and only then, according to Mill, can it ground (or rather, re-ground) itself on first principles. It submits itself to reductions. It limits its field of observation and the reach of its claims. Thus political economics, to be a science, has to forgo the pleasures of normative prescription: "Science is a collection of *truths*; art, a body of *rules*, or directions for conduct. . . . Science takes cognizance of a *phenomenon*, and endeavours to discover its *law*; art proposes to itself an *end*, and looks out for *means* to effect it" (312). Political economics is not an art. It cannot suggest moral ends. It is not a system of practical *rules*, but a list of natural tendencies.

Not only does economics necessarily bracket moral considerations, it must also perform other acts of logical reduction. It is concerned with the laws that "regulate the production and distribution of wealth" (313, 318) in a society. It defines wealth as "all objects useful or agreeable to mankind, except such as can be obtained . . . without labour" (314). Thus political economics will not interest itself in the distribution of water or air except in those places where water or air can only be obtained by labor.

Political economics further distinguishes itself from the physical sciences by concentrating on the production and distribution of wealth "so far as they depend upon the laws of human nature" (318). It is thus a "moral" science in that it concentrates on the psychological reductions that reveal "human nature." But it needs to limit the variables within its enabling fiction of that essential human nature:

> It does not treat of the whole of man's nature as modified by the social state, nor of the whole conduct of man in society. It is concerned with him solely as a being who desires to possess wealth, and who is capable of judging of the comparative efficacy of means for obtaining that end. It predicts only such of the phenomena of the social state as take place in consequence of the pursuit of wealth. *It makes entire abstraction of every other human passion or motive; except those which may be regarded as perpetually antagonizing principles to the desire of*

*wealth, namely, aversion to labour, and desire of the present enjoy-
ment of costly indulgences.* (321; emphasis added)

"Man" for the political economist is an animal interested in material gain and given to forms of inertia that can inhibit gain. This
abstract reduction of human activity does not signal stupidity on
the part of the economist but serves as a necessary self-limitation
that the practice of science requires (322).

So political economics fulfills the criteria of a science through a
series of reductive definitions and self-imposed constraints on the
field of its inquiry. It also fulfills the criteria of a mathematical
science through the logic of its method, which is deductive and a
priori. Political economics has to be deductive (unlike the physical
sciences), because you cannot experiment in the human sciences
and therefore cannot pursue controlled, inductive investigations
(327). Instead, the political economist analyzes the state of society
into its constituent parts (desire for wealth, inertia), figures out
their laws, and then reconstructs the whole as a law-governed system (328, 336) from which can be made deductions about the
present and a priori claims about the future.

Mill's Ricardian legitimation of political economics divorces it
from the studies of morality and practical politics, on the one hand,
and physical science on the other. It establishes economics by
differentiating it in a three-way split. Political economics insists on
the rigors of its reductions and its particular specialization. It
understands mankind in a purposefully one-dimensional way so as
to contrast itself to the other human sciences which perform still
other important reductions. In many ways, Mill's two articles
show how Ricardian economics was able to claim that it constituted the whole discipline. Furthermore, both articles constitute a
self-enclosing critique of Ricardian political economics by establishing its "necessary" margins.

At the end of "On the Definition of Political Economy," Mill
restates the contrast between art and science that begins his essay.
Science, he writes, is about laws, the unavoidable constraints on
means and ends. There are no exceptions to laws. What appears to
be an exception is merely the instance or insistence of a countervailing law. In art, however, there are no laws, no necessary natural
restraints on action. There are only rules. Hence art will always
allow exceptions (337–38). If this is the case—or at least was an

accepted idea at the time — then we can begin to understand the problems facing Mrs. Barbauld when she engaged in the defense of the novel. In her introductory essay to *British Novelists*, she could not, or rather did not deduce laws for either the novel in general or the British novel in particular. And yet she had to delimit the field to explain her peculiar claims on her readers' attention.

In "On the Origin and Progress of Novel-Writing,"[49] Barbauld tries to establish the grounds for the legitimacy of the novel in a standard eighteenth-century way. Following Warton, Beattie, Clara Reeve, and Richard Hurd, she constructs a history of the westering of romance, of its translation from the wilds of Arabia ("The East is emphatically the country of invention" [3]) through the superstitious European Middle Ages, to the more sedate, less superstitious and resoundingly modern Britain. Her chronological laundry list of romances, pastorals, and novels is similarly not as haphazard as its initial presentation might suggest because it argues quite clearly for the usefulness of the novel as a form and for the moral superiority of the British novel over its European — especially French — counterparts. (It is worth remembering that *British Novelists* was produced in the middle of the Napoleonic Wars.)

Barbauld begins by acknowledging that her enterprise will not be generally well received: "A collection of novels has a better chance of giving pleasure than of commanding respect. Books of this description are condemned by the grave, and despised by the fastidious" (1). The grave condemn novels because they are written for entertainment (not instruction), and the fastidious worry about their fictive nature. Mrs. Barbauld is quick to protest, however, that fiction presents no moral problems. After all, fiction served as the basis of mythology, and mythological writings such as the *Aeneid* were the staple of higher education and the currency of cultural capital. A novel has no less a claim on serious regard than the *Aeneid*: "A good novel is an epic in prose, with more of character and less . . . of the supernatural machinery" (3). In fact, a novel has perhaps an even stronger claim than the epic, for it is less fictional than its ancient counterpart and contains more instructive truth about people and the world.

The history of the progress of the novel that Barbauld recounts is in large part the story of the ways that the novel divested itself of the supernatural machinery that marked both the epic and romance and thus became "natural." In fact, she singles out Daniel Defoe as the father of the British novel in that he was "the first author amongst us who distinguished himself by natural painting" (37). Nature here seems intimately tied to the notion that probability should be taken as verisimilitude. If we accept the Johnsonian tenet that the advent of the novel marks the recent triumph of probability, Mrs. Barbauld's exclusions from her collection are as telling as her inclusions. To make this quite clear, her introductory essay concerns itself mostly with these exclusions. She censures writers such as Sterne and Brooke for eschewing plot or for constructing plots that are completely improbable (40–44).

Barbauld's narrative thus goes a long way towards eliminating the censures of the fastidious, for it undermines their arguments against fiction on two fronts. Not only can the fictive serve as the foundation for high culture, it can also resemble the truth even when it is not strictly speaking true. How, then, to answer the complaints of the grave? Barbauld wants to maintain that pleasure is a good thing and that the amusement that novels provide is a laudable end in itself:

> Reading is the cheapest of pleasures: it is a domestic pleasure
> . . . the humble novel is always ready to enliven the gloom of
> solitude, to soothe the languor of debility and disease, to win
> the attention from pain or vexatious occurrences, to take
> man from himself. . . . It is pleasant to the mind to sport in
> the boundless regions of possibility; to find relief from the
> sameness of every-day occurrences by expatiating amidst
> brighter skies and fairer fields. . . . (47)

There are thus a number of situations in which unalloyed entertainment is to be valued. But novels are not only sources of amusement:

> The unpardonable sin in a novel is dullness. . . . But it is not
> necessary to rest the credit of these works on amusement
> alone, since it is certain they have had a very strong effect in
> infusing principles and moral feelings. (48)

Novels, when read judiciously (52–53), can instill benevolence and honor (49), as well as prudence and economy, by which Mrs. Barbauld seems to mean "order, neatness, industry," and "sobriety" (50). British novels, she claims, will have few, if any, harmful effects on their readers:

Our national taste and habits are still turned towards domestic life and matrimonial happiness, and the chief harm done
by a circulating library is occasioned by the frivolity of its
furniture, and the loss of time incurred. Now and then a girl
perhaps may be led by them to elope with a coxcomb . . .
but she will not have her mind contaminated with such
scenes and ideas as Crebillon, Louvet, and others of that
class have published in France. (58)

If one accepts the condemnations of the grave and the fastidious,
one cannot take moral or epistemological exception to modern
English novels, with their emphasis on domestic life and matrimonial happiness, and their insistence on probable plotlines and
recognizable character types. The progress of the novel has indeed
been a progress, and the form has reached its acme in Georgian
Britain.

So Mrs. Barbauld has established the legitimacy of the British
novel within the field of world literature, but has not established the
claims of the novel against other forms of nonliterary knowledge
beyond arguing for its efficiency as a delivery device for moral education. In the very last paragraph of her essay, Barbauld writes:

Some perhaps may think that too much importance has been
already given to a subject so frivolous, but a discriminating
taste is no where more called from than with regard to a
species of books which every body reads. It was said by
Fletcher of Saltoun, "Let me make the ballads of a nation,
and I care not who makes the laws." Might it not be said
with as much propriety, Let me make the novels of a country, and let who will make the systems? (61–62)

At first blush, this paragraph seems a bit of an anacoluthon, that is,
an argument that lurches away from its initial thesis. She maintains
that novels are worthy of serious consideration because everyone
reads them. Because *everyone* reads them, a set of criteria for judgment has to be developed to guide weaker minds. So far, so good.
But then Barbauld quotes Fletcher, the neo-Harringtonian Scot
who, a century earlier, had argued for strong militias and educational institutions that could counter the decline in public virtue
caused by the modern commercial order.[50] Fletcher's preference
for ballads over laws is telling, for the ballad seems to have a more

fundamental relation to the imaginative life and moral organization of a society than its laws. Laws are epiphenomenal while ballads are basic. Mrs. Barbauld does not retain Fletcher's opposition
of literature and law. Instead she substitutes "system" for the latter
term. In and of itself, her revision of Fletcher's statement is rather
odd. Just a few pages earlier, Barbauld has written:

> No small proportion of modern novels have been devoted to
> recommend, or to mark with reprobation, those systems of
> philosophy or politics which have raised so much ferment of
> late years. . . . In the war of systems these light skirmishing
> troops have been often employed with great effect; and so
> long as they are content with fair, general warfare, without
> taking aim at individuals, are perfectly allowable. (59)

System thus refers to complete, self-contained, or totalizing bodies
of thought. For all its self-restraint, Mill's version of political economics would most likely count as a system for Mrs. Barbauld. By
her lights, the novel can be dragooned into the struggle between
systems and ideologies provided that it does not indulge in ad hom-
inem attack. But according to Barbauld's final paragraph, the novel
and the system are neither necessarily nor easily compatible. The
novel is more fundamental than the system, just as the ballad is
more fundamental than the law. The novel will either have a deeper
effect or it will touch a greater truth than the system can. In the
end, Barbauld argues that the novel deserves greater attention than
the war of ideas (or ideologies) that had played such an important
part of British intellectual and political life over the previous two
decades because novels play a more important role in the moral
education of a people. I would also like to suggest that Barbauld's
contrast between novel and system valorizes the novel precisely
because the "natural painting" which has "more of character" is not
liable nor susceptible to the reductions that systematic thought
must resort to. In short, Mrs. Barbauld's historical account of the
nature of the novel means to show precisely how much more inclusive, flexible, and adequate to the complexity of "truth" the novel
is than its more "rigorous" intellectual rivals. In the end, the fastidious and the grave are wrong in every way. The fictions of the
novel are moral, important, and more truthful than other modes of
thought and representation.

To read Mill in conjunction with Mrs. Barbauld is to indicate that the intuition with which this study began—that there is a relationship between the valorization of the novel and the explosion of interest in political economics in Britain during the later Georgian period—is wrong. While both Mill and Barbauld are careful to legitimize their fields and limit them by distinguishing their objects and methods of attention from the general environment in which those objects and those methods might originally be found, the methods of the novel and classical economics cannot really be more different, a point which is made quite clear by Barbauld's distinction between the novel and systemic thought.

Nevertheless, contemporary accounts of economics go out of their way to maintain that political economics is of great importance to female and "domestic" readers (the main consumers of the novel according to Barbauld's account) because it resembles home economics. James Mill's *Elements of Political Economy* assumes a not uncommon analogy between the home and the state: "Political Economy is to the State, what domestic economy is to the family."[51] If we follow Nancy Armstrong's contention that the novel develops as a way of codifying the separation between the domestic and the economic, the female and the male spheres, then we see in Mill's maxim a way of reasserting the structural similarities between these spheres. In fact, he seems to argue that while they might be separated by gender, gender is a superficial aftereffect. The domestic novel and the masculine world of commerce are not so different after all.[52] The novel and political economics deal with the same problems on different scales.

Mrs. Marcet's *Conversations on Political Economy* goes even further than James Mill. The preceptor, Mrs. B., overcomes her young friend Caroline's antipathy for political economics by pointing out that the subject does not involve "custom-houses, and trade, and taxes, and bounties, and smuggling, and paper-money, and the bullion-committee, etc." Rather, she persuades her charge that the "science of political economy is intimately connected with the daily occurrences of life" and that ignorance of this branch of study "may lead us into serious practical errors."[53] The study of economics then entails the study of everyday life; in this way it is not so different from the respectable project that William Hazlitt ascribes to the "standard novel and romance" which allows us "to examine the very web and texture of society, as it really exists, and as we meet with it when we move into the world."[54]

In "On the Definition of Political Economy," John Stuart Mill objects to this analogy between the supposedly male and female spheres, between the domestic and the commercial:

> The definition most generally received among instructed persons and laid down in the commencement of most of the professed treatises on the subject, is to the following effect: —That Political Economy informs us of the laws which regulate the production, distribution, and consumption of wealth. To this definition is frequently appended a familiar illustration. Political Economy, it is said, is to the state, what domestic economy is to the family. (313)

Mill concedes that the standard definition justly sees political economy as a science, in that it concentrates on the laws of nature and not the prescriptive maxims of conduct. But it misrecognizes domestic economy, which is not a science but an art. Domestic economy teaches the normative rules of prudence, not ineluctable constraints. While the standard definition of political economy is fine, its illustration is not.

Mill's cavil with his father's point is another indication of his desire to distinguish and delimit his area of study, to show how political economics is both different and legitimate. We can thus discern from the florilegium of quotations in these last few paragraphs (and indeed in this first chapter) an interesting double movement in which different discourses relate themselves to each other in order to highlight their particularity and importance. They appeal to what appear to be more or less common criteria (hence Mrs. Barbauld's elegant though diffuse refutation of the fastidious and the grave) and go out of their way to show how they both fulfill similar functions differently and different functions similarly. It is obvious that to collapse the novel into economics (or vice versa) would be a mistake, just as it would be a mistake to claim that they do not share the common horizon that Mill, Marcet, and Hazlitt invoke. Different novels engage classical economics in different ways, just as Malthus's concerns were different from Ricardo's. And yet, in the end, the novelists and the economists were worrying the same problems. We will provide a fuller delineation of those problems in the next chapter.

2

Burke and Paine Meet *Frankenstein:* Novels and Economics between Revolution and Reform

The rights of man were designed to promise happiness even to those without power. Because the cheated masses feel that this promise—as a universal—remains a lie as long as classes exist, it stirs their rage. . . . To those who spasmodically dominate nature, a tormented nature provocatively reflects back the image of powerless happiness. The thought of happiness without power is unbearable, because only then would it be true happiness.
    —HORKHEIMER AND ADORNO, *Dialectic of Enlightenment*

In the previous chapter, I suggested that the early nineteenth-century systemizations of the novel and political economics might profitably be seen as functionally separate responses to similar, if not the same, problems. The answers these discourses would produce could only be, by their very nature, partial and specialized. These limitations—and their compensatory fictions of autonomy—render them both ideological and grant them the possibility of real insight, as they address the "public" which serves as the virtual center of the society they inhabit.

In this chapter, we will begin to fill in the blanks, to put some meat on these abstract, theoretical bones. By reading the 1831 edition of *Frankenstein* in light of *The Wealth of Nations* and the eighteenth-century debates over freedom and distributive justice that culminated in the set-to between Burke and Paine, I will argue that political economics was developed as both a description and legitimation of the commercial order of the Georgian fiscal-military state, but was not successful in reconciling the disparate claims of justice. Political theory, with its interest in the precise boundaries between society and the state, tried to close the gap procedurally, while the novel attempted to tender an ethical investigation of the conflicts raised by the legitimation of its modernity.

I

At the end of his life, Victor Frankenstein offers Walton yet another summary of his life. He has been reckoning up his own moral accounts and he does not really find himself wanting:

> Think not, Walton, that in the last moments of my existence I feel that burning hatred and ardent desire of revenge I once expressed; but I feel myself justified in desiring the death of my adversary. During these last days I have been occupied in examining my past conduct; nor do I find it blameable. In a fit of enthusiastic madness I created a rational creature and was bound towards him to assure, as far as was in my power, his happiness and well-being. This was my duty; but there was another still paramount to that. My duties towards the beings of my own species had greater claims to my attention because they included a greater proportion of happiness or misery. Urged by this view, I refused, and I did right in refusing, to create a companion for the first creature. He showed unparalleled malignity and selfishness in evil. . . . Miserable himself that he may render no other wretched, he ought to die.[1]

Victor's ethical double-entry bookkeeping is quite complex. Having created the monster, he is responsible for its happiness. But this consideration is overridden by two concerns. The monster is evil and is not human. Solidarity with his fellows demands that Victor perform a felicific calculus by which he decides that the good of the many requires the misery of this one individual. But more important, perhaps, than Victor's sense of his species is his conviction that the monster is malignant. On the one hand, he worries about his responsibility for another's happiness; on the other, he constructs a principled refusal to recognize the status of that other's claims in the light of stronger and more binding obligations. And, to top it off, he is firm in his conviction that crime must be punished.

In the end, the monster seems to agree with Victor's verdict:

> I am content to suffer alone while my sufferings shall endure; when I die, I am well satisfied that abhorrence and opprobrium should load my memory. Once my fancy was soothed with dreams of virtue, of fame, and of enjoyment. Once I falsely hoped to meet with beings who, pardoning my outward form, would love me for the excellent qualities which I was capable of unfolding. . . . But now crime has degraded me beneath the meanest animal. No guilt, no mischief, no malignity, no misery, can be found comparable to mine. (259)

The monster, like Victor, sees virtue as the sine qua non of humanity. The monster's crimes have opened an ontological gap between himself and the human race and this gap undercuts his claims for recognition. Nevertheless, the monster, like Frankenstein, wants to exonerate himself. He stakes the legitimacy of his demands for happiness on an invocation of the norms of justice:

> For while I destroyed [Victor's] hopes, I did not satisfy my own desires. They were forever ardent and craving; still I desired love and fellowship, and I was still spurned. Was there no injustice in this? Am I to be thought the only criminal, when all humankind sinned against me? . . . Even now my blood boils at the recollection of this injustice. (259)

The monster's crimes are remarkably chaste. He does not commit them to satisfy his lusts. In fact, the murders he commits are designed to desolate Victor's heart, to reduce Victor to the monster's situation, to force him into sympathy and perhaps identification. They most definitely do not satisfy the monster's desires. The monster assumes that once he is alone, Victor will recognize the monster's feelings, will see how unjust he himself has been. What is more, the monster's crimes are the product of a moral Newtonianism—his reactions are the result of equal and opposite actions. Humans have sinned against him by not recognizing his needs. They have cast him out and so he has behaved as if he were not one of them, not bound by their laws.

The monster's tragedy, of course, lies in the fact that he *is* one of them in what really matters. I appeal to Victor's response to the monster's first eloquent appeal for a mate:

I was moved. I shuddered when I thought of the possible consequences of my consent, but I felt there was some justice in his argument. His tale and the feelings he now expressed proved him to be a creature of fine sensations, and did I not as his maker owe him all the portion of happiness that it was in my power to bestow? (187)

Victor's decision to acquiesce in his creature's demands is based on two interlocking considerations. We have already noted that he is responsible for the monster by virtue of the fact that he has created it. But this obligation is not binding until he discovers that the monster has "fine sensations," that is to say, has a recognizably human soul. Victor seems to accept, if at least temporarily, the monster's argument that he is malicious because spurned (186); that his viciousness is the result of injustice, not basic depravity. The monster is a person and deserves the recognition that one person can demand of another. Victor breaks the agreement to create a female monster when he decides that the monster is, in fact, inhuman—that is, truly monstrous (206-7).

There are thus three conditions that need to be fulfilled before Victor can perform what he is willing to see as his obligation. First, there has to be justice in the monster's argument, that is, it has to appeal to some legitimate transpersonal criterion—the inalienable right to happiness. Secondly, the monster has to show itself to be a "creature of fine sensations"—that is to say, a being of discriminating feelings, presumably like Victor himself. And finally, the monster has to make his plea in the right jurisdiction: Victor, by virtue of his position as the creature's creator, has certain responsibilities that go with that position. It is important to note that in the end, Victor does not argue that happiness is not a right (quite the contrary, in fact), nor that he as creator has no obligations. He merely asserts that the monster, being other, cannot be recognized by this informal court as a claimant, though he will be recognized and condemned as a criminal.

One cannot lay too much emphasis on the language of justice in this novel—*Frankenstein* is obsessed and apparently deeply disappointed with it. The novel's scenes of formal justice make human laws look, as the monster notes (using a fine expression from Paine), "sanguinary" (184).[2] When Justine Moritz is unjustly condemned for the murder of little William, Victor can only invert a commonplace and coin a fierce, if ironic, verdict on the court: "all judges had rather that ten innocent should suffer than that one guilty should escape" (128). Although Victor's father argues that Justine should "rely on the justice of our laws" (123), the laws prove to be the servants of nothing more than blind revenge. Similarly, the De Laceys are undone by the unjust imprisonment of Safie's father and the "injustice of the French courts" (164).

One could therefore argue that *Frankenstein* indicts justice as nothing more than an imperfect mask for sheer resentment. Thus one could produce a rather rigorous Nietzschean reading of *Frankenstein* which would see the novel as the staging of an intricate web of narratives of *ressentiment*. Justice would be shown to manifest nothing more than a weak will-to-power in judicial masquerade. We could gloss *Frankenstein* as a fine commentary on Nietzsche's acerbic observations that justice is nothing more than a drive that dares not speak its name; is just the "development of the drive to revenge,"[3] and at its base is just a frustrated form of a "will to overpower."[4]

Frankenstein shows that such "weak" wills defend themselves against stronger wills through febrile acts of justification. Justification is the order of the day in *Frankenstein*. We would do well to follow David Marshall in seeing the novel as a series of *tableaux vivants* that dramatize the limits of sympathy,[5] although it might be more accurate to say that it consists of *tableaux parlants* that explore the limits of justice. In this light we can begin to understand the urgency of the structure of the novel. The maze of narrative frames— Walton's letters to his sister, Victor's narration, the monster's own tale—all constitute confessions, as Lee Sterrenburg has noted, or rather, justifications.[6] In each tale, the teller attempts to convince the listener and reader that his actions have been legitimate, that is, congruent with norms that the listener or reader could and should agree to. The novel might best be seen as a rather formal essay in forensics, in special pleading.

Nevertheless, the drive for revenge that motivates the novel might not merely signal frustration in the face of the inexorable linearity of time—our Nietzschean reading could make much of Victor's attempt to blame fate for his own sovereign acts, and much of the monster's mere reactiveness. Rather, revenge may mark the conflict between what turn out to be exclusive notions of justice. The monster sees justice in terms of future fulfillment while Victor sees it in terms of present protection. In the end, Victor adheres to the stringencies of commutative justice in the protection of property while the monster argues in terms of distributive justice and the satisfaction of basic needs, a satisfaction that he is owed by virtue of citizenship (as in Aristotle), of common humanity (as in the Christian tradition), or by virtue of living in a certain community that has not yet granted the rights of citizenship to all its members although it exacts responsibilities from them.

Not for nothing, then, can we map Nietzschean thematics onto this novel. Nietzsche's hatred of rights talk, of all forms of liberalism, recasts debates between the commutative and the distributive as a form of pseudo-universalism that hides all-important struggles of individual and collective wills. And here lies the limit of this interpretation. The reading I have attributed to Nietzsche collapses both commutative and distributive justice into the temporary effects of an overarching *ressentiment*. It does not explain why commutative and distributive justice revenge themselves on each other; or why in this text, at this time, they are seen to be so close yet so incompatible.

We might want to take seriously the sense of history that the novel's subtitle proclaims. "The Modern Prometheus" indicates that the figure Prometheus serves as a typological guide to our reading of the book. But Victor is an odd Prometheus—neither the rebellious benefactor of humanity nor the successful fabricator of man. In fact, the modernity of this Prometheus seems to consist in the fact that he cannot be read back into either Ovid or Aeschylus. In a similar way, the epigraph from *Paradise Lost* can be taken as a gloss on the monster's own predicament, as indeed it is. But it also could be applied to Victor's own self-understanding as the victim of an inexorable destiny (86, 90, 93, 221, 244).

Paradise Lost has for good reason been taken as a proof-text for *Frankenstein*[7] and David Marshall has done us an inestimable service by showing how Rousseau's works align with Godwin's, Wollstonecraft's, and Milton's in Mary Shelley's novel.[8] One of the remarkable features of *Frankenstein*, of course, is its insistence on pre-texts, its overt references to Wordsworth, Coleridge, Goethe, Plutarch, Volney, as well as Milton. More remarkable, perhaps, is the way that these writers fail to provide a guide for the novel's present. That "The Ancient Mariner," a text whose strategies of unreadability have been so admirably outlined by Jerome McGann,[9] should be a spur for Walton's own quest (65) is an indication of the difficulties presented by exemplary works for the readers within *Frankenstein*. The monster, though moved by *Werther*, does not know how to situate himself in relation to that novel: "As I read, however, I allied much personally to my own feelings and conditions. I found myself similar yet at the same time strangely unlike to the beings concerning whom I read and to whose conversation I was a listener" (170). So, the monster's discomfort when he reads *Paradise Lost* is not atypical. Rather it constitutes the most concentrated account and most consistent metaphor for the failure of exemplary, typological reading within *Frankenstein*:

> I often referred the several situations, as their similarity struck me, to my own. Like Adam, I was apparently united by no link to any other being in existence; but his state was far different from mine in every other respect. . . . Many times I considered Satan as the fitter emblem of my condition. . . .
> (171)

The point of this, of course, is that *Paradise Lost*, like other received texts, does not present a ready map of experience. The norms its examples body forth are not pertinent guides for behavior or moral judgment.

I would like to submit that such a conclusion should not lead us to claim that *Frankenstein* teaches us that all texts are essentially unreadable. Rather, from the title page on, it seems to argue that at a certain moment, older texts become unreliable and that, in some way, "modernity" entails a break with the past. The temporal structure of past history no longer bounds "a continuous space of potential experience."[10] Rather "the divide between previous experience and coming expectation" opens up so that lived time is "experienced as a rupture, as a period of transition in which the new and the unexpected" continually happens.[11] In the face of such novelty, justification becomes increasingly urgent because there are no moral maps from the past and no hierarchies which provide easy and ready value. To put it in the terms of Luhmann's version of sociology, in a functionally differentiated world, no single discourse, no single system, will provide a chart of reliable values for the whole of society, and yet the existence of "society" as a whole requires that one frames one's appeals within a universalist, normative frame that has not been fully established. The constant requirement that one justify one's actions makes the definition of justice all the more interesting and complex. *Frankenstein* not only stages a strong drama of justification, it sees justification as the scene of a supposedly modern conflict between two norms of justice, the distributive and the commutative.

How then to contextualize *Frankenstein*'s self-presentation? How to account for its account of itself as a text—even an exemplary one—about modernity? It is something of a commonplace now to see *Frankenstein* as a reflection on the French Revolution either directly (Mary and Percy Shelley had read deeply into the Revolution in the year or so before she began writing the novel[12]) or indirectly (Mary reread her parents' books during the same period[13]). Lee Sterrenburg has performed valuable and convincing excavations of Shelley's text to uncover and historicize the language and metaphorics of Jacobin and anti-Jacobin polemics in the novel:

> From the Burkean tradition of horrific, evil, and revolutionary monsters, [the monster] seems to have derived the grotesque features that physically mark him and set him apart. . . . From the republican tradition of social monsters, he seems to have derived his acerbic, verbal critique of poverty and injustice, which serves as his stated rationale for insurrection. As he tells us with pointed eloquence, monsters are driven to rebellion by suffering and oppression.[14]

The monster seems to be unreadable because he marks the crossing between two different polemics. On the one hand he stands for the amoral anarchism of the mob; on the other he stands as a visible and eloquent indictment of social inequity. Similarly, one could see in Victor a Burkean villain of speculative egotism, the prototype of the failed utopian whose revolutionary dreams are masks for personal ambition (97–98). Of course, Victor, like Walton, is nothing if not a misguided utopian—he even dreams (as that greatest of revolutionary utopians, William Godwin, did in the *Enquiry Concerning Political Justice*) of overcoming death through science.[15] Victor, like his creation, is a monster in both Burkean and in Painean terms, for he can be read as both an uncaring aristocrat and a violent revolutionary. As Paine says of the aristocracy:

> Their ideas of *distributive justice* are corrupted at the very source. . . . With what ideas of justice or honour can that man

enter a house of legislation, who absorbs in his own person
the inheritance of a whole family of children, or doles out to
them some pitiful portion with the insolence of a gift?[16]

The fact that one can map onto this text the language and themes
of both Burke and Paine indicates that the two antagonists, like
Frankenstein, rely on and summon forth a complexity of assumption, reaction, similarity, and difference.

Both Burke and Paine see the Revolution as an epochal, if not
millennial, break with the past. Burke adopts the apocalyptic tone
of Richard Price's famous sermon against which he is writing. But
whereas Price utters his *nunc demittis* in praise of the Revolution ("I
could almost say, *Lord, now lettest thou thy servant depart in peace*"),[17]
Burke sees the revolutionary break with the past an epochal catastrophe. After his famous dilation on the events of October 6, 1789,
Burke exclaims:

> Excuse me, therefore, if I have dwelt too long on the atro-
> cious spectacle . . . or have given too much scope to the
> reflections which have arisen in my mind on occasion of the
> most important of all revolutions, which may be dated from
> that day, I mean a revolution in sentiments, manners, and
> moral opinions. As things now stand, with every thing
> respectable destroyed without us, and an attempt to destroy
> within us every principle of respect, one is almost forced to
> apologize for harbouring the common feelings of men. (175)

The highly theatrical or sentimental tone that Burke adopts and
that Paine and Wollstonecraft (respectively) criticize is of course
the negative version of Price's encomium: apocalypse as destruction, not salvation. Burke's single-minded, and to his contemporaries somewhat overheated, opposition to the Revolution derives
from his sense that in a time of universal tribulation, decisions
must be made, sides must be taken.

Paine also sees recent events as the signals of a qualitative historical break, but he takes all this to be the natural product of enlightened progress. Because he opposes Burke's method as well as his
tone, Paine does not strike the apocalyptic note of either Price or
Burke, but he does celebrate the openness of what appears to be a
novus ordo saeclorum, a resolute modernity. He claims at the end of
the first part of *The Rights of Man*, that his is "an age of Revolutions,

in which everything may be looked for."[18] And Paine, the rational spokesman for everything that can be hoped for, takes sides as well. He seeks to justify the Revolution by demolishing Burke's justification of the British constitution.

Burke and Paine understand very well that they are arguing about the legitimacy of England's odd system of government as much as about the legitimacy of France's experiments with popular representation. Burke's fierce defense of the spirit of the gentleman is prompted by his fear that the republican contagion will infect England. Burke writes to his French correspondent: "You seem to me to be — *gentis incunabula nostrae*. France has always more or less influenced manners in England; and when your fountain is choked up and polluted, the stream will not run long, or not run clear with us, or perhaps with any nation" (174). The downfall of French manners will lead to the destruction of the English constitution if the utility of that constitution cannot be fully proven. And it is precisely this utility that Paine attacks when he assails Burke's cherished notion that the Revolution parliament of 1688 settled the constitution once and for all.

Interestingly enough, the language of attack and defense in both cases is not original to the 1790s. The great historical break that Burke and Paine seek to analyze is discussed in what in the period were rather old-fashioned terms. Pocock has noted the importance of the language of the era of Queen Anne to Burke and the language of the Commonwealthmen to Paine.[19] Burke's attacks on the monied interests in France, on "oeconomists and sophisters," on "metaphysical" rationalism, owe much to the Toryism of Pope and the Country Whiggism of Swift. It is not for nothing that Burke suggests that we read "Gulliver's Travels for the idea of countries governed by philosophers" (238n).[20] Paris is a Laputa that anyone can visit.

No age speaks a language that is completely new or completely adequate for its polemical or descriptive purposes. Nevertheless, the insistence on a language that was already dated, on a language that was often ill suited for Burke and Paine's shared allegiance to what they saw as the modern commercial state,[21] is significant. It points to a century-long tradition of political meditation and argument in which the debate on the French Revolution was merely a rather testy episode. In the next section of this chapter, I will reconstruct, as briefly as I can, the outlines of that tradition. I will argue that the functional restructuring of English government and society after the Glorious Revolution included the liberation of a sphere of public debate and thus made legitimation a social as well as a systemic necessity. I will show that the monster's claim for happiness, for distributive justice, is an expression of one of the most vexing problems facing the legitimation of the modern commercial system, and that it was the temporarily successful attempt to settle this problem that made *The Wealth of Nations* such an important book for the self-understanding of Britons in the years after its publication.

II

A remarkable set of reclamation projects over the past two decades has uncovered for us a complex variety of political idioms available in the eighteenth century. The most influential, of course, have been J.G.A. Pocock's study of the Anglo-American appropriations of Machiavellian republicanism (in *The Machiavellian Moment*) and Pocock's subsequent investigations of the mutual determination of republican and jurisprudential theory (in *Virtue, Commerce, and History*). Drawing on this ground-breaking work, H. T. Dickinson, Istvan Hont, Michael Ignatieff, Nicholas Phillipson, and others have mapped out a number of the available positions on the Whig-Tory, Country-City, Radical-Conservative axes.[22] Coming at these questions from another angle (and more bracingly because more polemically), Jonathan Clark has claimed that eighteenth-century English society was rural, Anglican, and aristocratic. Accordingly, he has done much to remind us of the importance of Church, especially High Church, and High Tory doctrine in the period (as have, in different ways J.A.W. Gunn, Ian Christie, and Linda Colley).[23]

The result — and it is an intended one — of all this work has been the displacement of "Lockean" individualism from the center of our accounts of eighteenth-century thought. As Garry Wills has argued (though perhaps too strenuously), even that supposedly most Lockean of documents, the Declaration of Independence, owes less to the author of the two *Treatises* than to the thought of Hutcheson, Hume, Kames, and Adam Smith.[24] Furthermore, the catalogue and range of political languages available in the period have also reminded us of the subtlety and importance of moral philosophy for political theory. If not Locke, then who? And why the efflorescence of political polemics, meditation, and critique?

The sheer volume of political writing after the Glorious Revolution will not look surprising to the historian of the English Civil War. It thus could easily be dismissed as business as usual or perhaps recast as part of a longer continuum of British political practice. However, if we take seriously the work of P.G.M. Dickson, Neil McKendrick, John Brewer, J. H. Plumb, and Pocock himself, we have to argue that in fact the publicity of the public debate on politics from the reign of William and Mary signals a new *function* for the debate, and for publicity itself.[25]

The restructuring of public finance, the establishment of a Stock Market and the Bank of England, the creation of new instruments of credit and the commitment to extensive foreign wars allowed post-Revolutionary England enviable commercial and agricultural growth, while necessitating the imposition of unprecedented taxation in order to feed the ever-increasing governmental administration of national affairs. This large-scale and long-term transformation of the English state and British society had a number of effects. It created (as far as contemporary commentators could tell) new classes of rentiers and economic speculators; it seemed to shift the nation's center of gravity from the landed to the monied interests; it made parliament and the executive stronger than they had been before. It seemed to encourage "luxury" and consumption.

To a number of people, this shift signalled a catastrophe, a fall from virtue into corruption (defined in either Christian or Machiavellian terms). Dynastic arguments over the legitimacy of the Hanoverians shaded over into political arguments about the legitimacy of what Brewer calls, in *The Sinews of Power,* the "fiscal-military" state, or what could also be called Whig-commercial hegemony. Such polemics were greeted by counterthrusts aimed at the legitimation of the new dispensation. And, after the Licensing Act was allowed to lapse, these debates were held in public in a relatively unrestrained press.

Brewer maintains that this public sphere was opened when the Parliament, previously seen as a watchdog over administrative excess, was understood to be an integral part of administration itself and thus its duty to police public finance and policy fled to the press and extramural groups.[26] Brewer dates this displacement to the 1730s, but the work of Gunn and indications in his own book make this date perilously late.[27] Brewer is, in the end, more interested in lobbyists than he is in the press, and not being a historian of Augustan literature, he is perhaps less attentive to the tendencies of the arguments we find in Addison, Steele, Pope, Defoe, and Swift than he is in what appears to be a more recognizable structural change in political life. But it would be a mistake to imply from Brewer's discussion that the press of the early eighteenth century was a literary training ground for future political debate, and thus to follow Habermas's earlier work.[28] Rather, we can argue that the press from the early years of the new order filled the functional gap between political appeals to "the people" and restricted direct representation in Parliament; between the executive's need to explain taxation and war and the "public's" need to respond.

Thus we can see the opening of the public sphere in the 1690s as a structurally mandated aspect of British liberty in an age of constitutional monarchy. It led to vigorous debate and to the clash of different concepts of normativity and rationality. For the purposes of this discussion, I am less interested in dynastic considerations than I am in the monster's claim to happiness; a claim that both Burke and Paine would recognize as a political one, to the extent that they agreed that happiness was the end of government. M. M. Goldsmith has argued that we see Mandeville as a pivotal figure in the important shift away from virtue towards happiness as the chief goal in life.[29] As Goldsmith defines virtue in civic republican terms (a predicate of arms-bearing, property-owning males dedicated to the common good), he is trying to solve Pocock's problem: How is it that the prevalence of the language of Harrington as a way of delegitimizing the Whig order was superseded by the language of natural law which succeeded in supporting that order?

It might be churlish to quibble with this leading expert on Mandeville, but we might well want to see Mandeville not only as a man who was instrumental in overcoming an ideology of virtue but rather one of the great satirists on the side of commercialism. What is so stark about *The Fable of the Bees* is its insistent presentation of the paradoxes that result when precapitalist definitions of "virtue" come into direct conflict with the mercantilist desire for the strong (that is, wealthy) nation-state. Michael Ignatieff's brisk summary of these pre-capitalist ideologies is worth quoting here:

> In all the moral traditions that confronted the coming of capitalist modernity, the man of virtue was the man of few needs: in the Stoic discourse, the man of self-command; in the religious discourses of Calvinism and Jansenism, the

saint; in Renaissance civic humanism, the citizen; in the reveries of Scottish Lowland gentry like James Boswell, the austere, Highland chieftain.[30]

If virtue consists of few needs and even fewer desires, then it is inimicable to a commercial society that plays on and depends on the expansion of both needs and desires.[31] Thus, by most definitions of virtue available to him, Mandeville can only see modernity as a vicious contradiction that produces delicious, demystifying paradoxes. Of course, these paradoxes (also a favored mode of the greatest republican thinker of the century, Rousseau) reveal not only the limits of commercial capitalism but of precapitalist moral and political languages' own powers of description. New situations required new definitions of virtue, ones that would include the elusive image of satisfaction, and Pocock's work since *The Machiavellian Moment* has been largely dedicated to charting the intensities and the logic of these new-model versions of virtue.[32]

Pocock, because he is mostly interested in *political* theory, pays less attention than he might to the confluence of natural law moralists, Deists, and moderates of the Anglican and Presbyterian churches in the late seventeenth and early eighteenth centuries. What is so important for our purposes in figures like these is that they preserve (from the Grotian natural law tradition) the notion of a natural sociability of man; (from Neoplatonism on one hand and Newtonian thought on the other) a sense of the unity of the cosmos; and (from the critique of Hobbes) a concomitant allegiance to the pursuit of individual and general happiness. So it is that Richard Cumberland writes:

> [It] is also perfectly plain that the happiness of each person
> . . . cannot be separated from the happiness of all . . . because
> the whole is no different from the parts taken together. . . .
> There is therefore no path leading anyone to his own happiness, other than the path which leads all to the common happiness.[33]

It is significant that one of the proofs Cumberland provides for this is the ownership of property. Happiness is measured in terms of the undisturbed possession of land and one's own person.[34]

Like Cumberland, Shaftesbury posits an easy congruence between the private and the public good, between desire and duty,[35] but because he is interested in natural law, not jurisprudence (that is, the derivation of truth, not rights), he is less interested in others' rights to happiness than our own success in attaining it. In part, he is untroubled by the possible conflict here because he is able to claim, in the dialogue "The Moralists," that the universe is orderly and works by a series of ever-increasing analogies from parts to wholes.[36] This leads him to a theory of unintended effects, even though such an argument undercuts his emphasis on free will and the urgency of choosing virtue.[37]

A florilegium of happiness would also include the Newtonian Deist, Samuel Clarke, who claims that we have an obligation to promote "in general, to the utmost of our power, the welfare and happiness of all men."[38] Similarly, the influential Bishop of Durham and opponent of Deism, Joseph Butler, goes out of his way to claim that possession of property is a misleading and inadequate model for understanding the relation of interests in the world and thus discounts any notion that society constitutes a zero-sum game. He states unequivocally that "it is manifest that nothing can be of consequence to mankind or any creature, but happiness." From this he deduces that happiness "is all which any person can, in strictness of speaking, be said to have a right to. We can therefore owe no man any thing, but only to further and promote his happiness, according to our abilities."[39] The religious, the natural, and the legal obligation to see to other people's happiness is a potentially explosive one, for the demands of sociability seem to undermine the demands of commutative justice so central to the Grotian tradition of natural law and to the jurisprudential grounding of government.[40] So Butler dampens the socially unsettling implications of his argument by stressing that as we are limited by our abilities and our positions in the world, we should "behave as the respective relations require."[41] Similarly, Clarke claims that the third rule of righteousness (the second was benevolence) is that a man is "to apply himself to the business of his present station in the world, whatsoever it be, with attention and contentment."[42] So while modern virtue consists of a sensitive attention to the needs of others, it also requires that one respect the structure of existent social hierarchies.

Perhaps the most important philosopher of the first three decades of the eighteenth century for the development of later political, moral, and economic theory was Frances Hutcheson whose work, both early and late, was deeply concerned with happiness. In the early writings, he sought to quantify happiness and, in so doing, quantify virtue, both public and private.[43] Nevertheless, for all his desire to maximize happiness, he was also deeply aware of the socially disruptive potential in the promise of a happiness that had, by definition, to apply universally. In his *Short Introduction to Moral Philosophy*, Hutcheson relies on the natural jurisprudential distinction between perfect and imperfect rights. Perfect rights include the right to life, chastity, good name, liberty, and private judgment—these are rights protected and enforced by institutions of the law and government.[44] Hutcheson does not enumerate imperfect rights and concedes that though these rights

> are sometimes indeed of the greatest consequence to the happiness and ornament of society, and our obligation to maintain them, and to perform to others what they thus claim, may be very sacred: yet they are of such a nature that greater evils would ensue in society from making them matters of compulsion, than from leaving them free to each one's honour and conscience to comply with them or not.[45]

Perfect rights are those rights without which society could not function and which are therefore protected by the constitution of government. They are thus a proper motive for state compulsion; beneficence and liberality are not. One reason for this abstinence is that before one can properly honor claims of imperfect rights, one has to perform a number of complicated calculations. One has to make sure that one's charity does not hurt anyone, that it is appropriate to our fortunes and the receiver's deserts.[46] In short, perfect rights are governed by laws; imperfect rights by particular judgments.

We can find similar, perhaps more elegant moments, in Hume, but by this point my argument should be clear. For these figures, the moral legitimacy of modern commercial, fiscal-military state did not rest on the individual citizen's martial or religious virtue but on the private individual's sociability and sensitivity to the happiness of others. Furthermore, the state was built on a society in which happiness was the highest social and personal good. One could claim (and this was often claimed) that modern society had a higher degree of happiness than had yet been achieved in history. This notion underlies *The Wealth of Nations*. But the demand for happiness raises (for Butler, Clarke, Hutcheson, and others) the spectre of distributive justice, an Aristotelian holdover that Grotian jurisprudence could not eradicate.[47] These thinkers attempted to appease and control the energies inherent in a legitimation of society that was based on happiness by asserting the weakness of distributive rights or the situational nature of honoring those rights. But Hutcheson admitted that the boundaries between perfect and imperfect rights were porous and that we can arrive "at some imperfect rights so strong that they can be scarce distinguished from the perfect."[48] A space thus existed, and it was uncomfortable because infinitely negotiable, for properly distributive functions, for categories of interaction that would maintain property while seeing to needs.

If we take social and political guarantees (and pleas) for happiness seriously, we can begin to understand the adaptability and appeal of that strain of thought known to political historians (following Pocock) as "civil jurisprudential" and to literary historians as "sentimentalism." A legitimation strategy based on the *promesse de bonheur* can account for the actual existence of society in a much more graceful way than Hobbes' terrifying reduction of all human motivation to power and fear and his (counterintuitive) vision of the social contract. It turns society — and commerce — into the site of human fulfillment and relegates government to the maintenance of the laws that govern possession. It gives a moral weight to the present while also providing the basis for rather complicated ethical systems of remarkably different kinds. (One need only compare Bentham with Shaftesbury to see what I mean.) And, what is more, it allows a certain flexibility in the interrelations and boundaries between the state and civil society. Our emphasis on this legitimation strategy also allows us to sidestep the insoluble (and in the end, unuseful) problem of the etiology of sentimentalism[49] by seeing sentimentalism as an elegant answer, a constellation provided in different ways by different discursive systems, to the legitimation problems of the commercial-military state.

The hero of this narrative of intellectual history becomes Adam Smith, the premier theoretician of both commerce *and* sympathy. Teichgraeber has gone a long way towards discrediting the very terms of the so-called Adam Smith Problem. A false paradox, the Adam Smith Problem asks how it can be that the author of *The Theory of Moral Sentiments* could also have written the unsentimental

Wealth of Nations. One begins by noting that the *Theory* is a study of how people are socialized into sympathy. As Teichgraeber writes, "Smith never took sympathy to be synonymous with instinctive benevolence."[50] Rather, the scene of sympathy is the locus of a complicated transaction between a spectator who enters "the sentiments of the person principally concerned" and that person who, suffering or happy, hopes the spectator will indeed enter into those sentiments.[51] Thus the "person principally concerned" has to tailor his or her emotions to the emotions of those who watch, and has to feel no more than others can feel who are not "principally concerned."[52] So each participant in sympathetic commerce has to imagine him or herself in the other's position: each one's feelings will be calibrated against the other's capacities to feel.[53] Hence Smith's discussion of sympathy occurs under the rubric of "propriety." Sympathy depends on socially and historically derived norms and is motivated by the social sanctions that attend such norms:

> The all-wise Author of Nature has . . . taught man to respect
> the sentiments and judgements of his brethren; to be more
> or less pleased when they approve of his conduct, and to be
> more or less hurt when they disapprove of it. He has made
> man, if I may say so, the immediate judge of mankind. . . .
> (130–31)

One sympathizes because others think that it is good to do so: and if there are no others watching you, there is always the internalized voice of those others, "the jurisdiction of the man within," the impartial spectator in the imagination who "is founded altogether in the desire of praise-worthiness" (131). Our desire for praise is God-given and becomes the ground of our conscience (131).

The desire for praise and the dream of emulation also drive us to acquire wealth, even though it is an error to think that wealth's pleasures are the greatest the world has to offer. A necessary error, however, because it serves as the means by which nature itself "imposes upon us" and drives us towards ever-increasing industry (180–83). And distributive justice is best served through this imposition:

> [The rich] consume little more than the poor, and in spite of
> their natural selfishness and rapacity, though they mean only
> their own conveniency, though the sole end which they pro-

pose from the labours of all the thousands whom they
employ, be the gratification of their own vain and insatiable
desires, they divide with the poor the produce of all their
improvements. They are led by an invisible hand to make
nearly the same distributions of the necessaries of life, which
would have been made, had the earth been divided into equal
portions among all its inhabitants, and thus without intend-
ing it, without knowing it, advance the interest of the society, and afford means to the multiplication of the species.
When Providence divided the earth among a few lordly masters, it neither forgot nor abandoned those who seemed to
have been left out in the partition. These last too enjoy their
share of all that it produces. In what constitutes the real happiness of human life, they are in no respect inferior to those
who would seem so much above them. In ease of body and
peace of mind, all the different ranks of life are nearly upon a
level. . . . (184–85)

According to Smith, the rich are only slightly better off than the
poor in everything that matters and their wealth is redistributed to
the general good even when — especially when — the rich seem to
be most selfish, most self-involved. The "invisible hand" in this
passage is, of course, a precursor to the more famous invisible hand
in *The Wealth of Nations*, even though, as Smith's editors point out,
in the latter book Smith is more interested in the maximization of
the means to happiness than in its distribution (184n). Nevertheless,
maximization only underscores the strength and the weakness of
the distributive defense of the market. Smith's repetition of "nearly"
betrays a certain unease. "Nearly" is not the same as "the same": to
be almost as happy is always to be less happy. If you can show how
economic growth benefits everyone and if you can provide a blue-
print for virtually unlimited growth (as the economist Smith appears to do), then you can maintain that although the relative
shares of the national wealth remain unequal, under the system of
"natural liberty" the poor will enjoy an increasingly higher standard of living. In fact, by Smith's lights, the equitable distribution
of landed property, a system in which there was little or no division of labor, is typical of "savage nations" which are marked by
both their inhumanity (they are forced into euthanasia and infanti-
cide) and their miserable poverty.[54] Greater happiness and greater

ease are only attainable where there are concentrations of property and capital. The republican and the Christian emphases on small freeholds and frugality are shown to be misguided and ultimately misanthropic.

I thus follow Hont, Ignatieff, and Teichgraeber in seeing *The Wealth of Nations* as a defense of the commercial system against the attacks of those who would see in the great inequalities of wealth in a commercial society an indictment of that system and that society.[55] The market, once liberated from the most debilitating forms of protection, will render nugatory questions of distributive rights and equality by ensuring that the system takes care of everyone's needs. It is clear that readers of the late eighteenth and early nineteenth century saw that this was Smith's great teaching and the chief armament in political economy's legitimization of commercial society.[56] The conflicting demands of distributive and commutative justice are solved by being dissolved or rather displaced. Matters of distribution are spirited away from the realm of formal justice (the courts and the laws of the land) and placed squarely in the realm of personal relations (the market) and personal justice (ethics).[57]

Smith can therefore easily differentiate between the precise, general, and therefore universalizable rules of jurisprudence and the "loose, vague and indeterminate" dictates of ethics.[58] Although ethics and jurisprudence come from the same source (morality), they do not rely on sympathy in the same way. While sympathy is important to practical ethics, it has little if anything to do with settling the general maxims of property rights. Strictly speaking, sympathy is not necessary for the orderly workings of a wealthy economy, even though something like sympathy is at work when one is trying to establish a market price. If there were such a thing as a society whose members had no sympathy with suffering, the poorer would still benefit from the full exercise of commutative property rights. They would be fed and clothed by the circulation of capital and goods. It is an open question, however, whether such a fine mesh of interests would be a society in any sense that Smith would care to accept as a properly modern one.[59]

To see how influential Smith's elegant — though not quite stable — legitimizing solution of the conflict between perfect rights and needs was as a strategy for justifying social forms and constitutions of government, we should see it in action, that is, performing its functions in political polemic. And it is in political polemic that we can see the limitations of Smith's theory. One could say, although somewhat fancifully, that it became one of the jobs of political theory to solve the legitimation problems that economics had left. In the debate between Burke and Paine, both men rely on Smith to make what seem to be very different cases.

Early in the first part of *The Rights of Man,* Paine attacks Burke for not being Adam Smith: "Had Mr Burke possessed talents similar to the author of "On the Wealth of Nations", he would have comprehended all the parts which enter into, and by assemblage, form a constitution. He would have reasoned from minutiae to magnitude. . . ."[60] As far as Paine is concerned, Burke is a brilliant rhapsode, but rhapsodes, as we remember from the history of philosophy, usually suffer badly at the hands of rationalists. So it is with Burke. Paine claims that his antagonist is incapable of reason. Unlike the great Adam Smith, Burke doesn't know how to think, let alone argue.[61] This invocation of the spirit of Smith to attack Burke is not completely gratuitous. One of the major polemical thrusts of *The Wealth of Nations* aims squarely at the persistence of corporate monopolies, such as guilds, which stifle the "plan of natural [economic] liberty." Paine translates this argument from the realm of commerce to the realm of government. He trashes the legitimacy of the British constitution by claiming that the continued existence of an unreformed parliament with its rotten boroughs and outmoded franchise stifles political competition, participation, and natural/political liberty. Paine extends Smith's vision of a more liberal market to attack all forms of corporate privilege.

Paine, of course, scores an easy and palpable hit. Burke's *Reflections on the Revolution in France* are an unabashed defense of traditional privilege. Whereas Paine sees such traditions as promoting an illegitimate limitation of citizenship, Burke takes them as a form of possession, a hedge against governmental tyranny. But one could show just as easily that Burke is a good Smithian, perhaps a better one than Paine.

In spite of Paine's claims, Burke is as much an inductive thinker as Smith. *The Wealth of Nations* is remarkably long because Smith insists on providing the legal and economic history of every aspect of agriculture and trade since the Middle Ages. He is fascinated by the particular which may or may not fit his general observations. As Mrs. Marcet notes of the science, it is "essentially founded upon history."[62] But Smith's masses of historical detail do more than found his principles on history. They serve as an important corrective to his attempts to derive unshakable general principles in the first place. Like Burke — and this is especially visible in the sixth edition of *The Theory of Moral Sentiments* where Smith inveighs against the spirit of system in terms that would do justice to Burke[63] — Smith distrusts abstractions and is always careful to temper them with historical deviations and apparent contraventions. Hence, in Smith, as in Burke, the minutiae always qualify the magnitudes, making them provisional and conceptually flexible.

Just as Burke shares Smith's methodological tendencies, his economic prescriptions in the *Reflections* follow Smith's example. Burke's distaste for the *assignats* does not mark a hatred of paper money; rather he supports paper money on the same conditions that Smith does — that when it is based on specie, it serves in Smith's terms as "the great wheel of circulation."[64] But paper money without basis, without redeemability, marks nothing but danger. Nevertheless, Burke's affiliations with Smith are not exhausted by methods and occasional agreements over paper money.

Smith and Burke share many of the same fears and biases. It is not surprising then to find that Smith's trope of the wheel of circulation appears in the *Reflections*. In Burke's text however, the wheel is not turned by money, but by the labor of those involved "in the innumerable servile, degrading, unseemly, unmanly and often most pestiferous occupations." Burke claims that if he did not know better, he would want to liberate the laboring poor from their painful and dangerous drudgery. However, he accepts the "necessity of submitting to the yoke of luxury and the despotism of fancy, who in their own imperious way will distribute the surplus product of the soil."[65] Luxury here as in Smith is unfortunate but a deep necessity. The jobs and the markets it creates and supports distribute the wealth of land (measured here as in Smith in product, not money) most efficiently.[66]

Burke thus seems to accept Smith's defense of the division of labor while maintaining a fierce loyalty to corporate privilege and hereditary monopoly. The most lurid part of the *Reflections* remains Burke's description of the night of October 6, 1789. The most outrageous claim (to contemporary academic sensibilities at least) of the book is that the "spirit of the gentleman and the spirit of religion" are the foundations and the defenders of modern commerce and industry.[67] Paine, as we have seen, thought that such a notion was pure nonsense. Nevertheless Burke states that aristocratic manners are the basis of capitalism, not only historically, but also structurally: Do away with refined manners, he claims, and nothing of wealth or civilization will be left.[68] But why? In "Letters on a Regicide Peace," Burke writes:

> Manners are of more importance than laws. Upon them, in a great measure, the laws depend. The law touches us but here and there, and now and then. Manners are what vex or soothe, corrupt or purify, exalt or debase, barbarize or refine us, by a constant, steady, uniform insensible operation, like that of the air we breathe in.[69]

The law depends on manners. This notion can be glossed in two ways. First, quite simply: in Burke's common-law thought, as expressed in the *Reflections*, law is just the concretion of social practice, hence there is an easy transition from manners into law. This maximalist interpretation is, ironically enough, more than Burke appears to admit. Look at his hard-edged attack on outdoor relief in "Thoughts and Details on Scarcity."[70] Written in the hungry year of 1795, Burke voices a firm, free-market disapproval of both wage and price subsidies for the working poor. Labor and capital meet as equals in the marketplace, he argues. They make their bargains as free agents. The law cannot determine how they will make their agreements. If it tries to determine the cost of labor, it will infringe on the farmer's right to a profit and will harm the farmer's creation of generally beneficial wealth—beneficial because it will employ and feed more people—by tampering with his return on capital. This is a free-market Burke, as close to Smith as you could imagine him to be. So what happens to the poor laborer who cannot find sufficient work to feed himself and his family?

> Whenever it happens that a man can claim nothing according to the rules of commerce [i.e., he cannot make a contract for his labor], and the principles of justice [i.e., he cannot argue that a contract has been violated], he passes out of that department, and comes within the jurisdiction of mercy. In that province the magistrate has nothing at all to do: his interference is a violation of the property which it is his office to protect. Without all doubt, charity to the poor is a

direct and obligatory duty upon all Christians, next in order
after the payment of debts. . . .[71]

Justice here is commutative justice, the protection of goods and
property, the rule of the *suum cuique*. The government has no
means to provide for necessities, because it has only the people's
own limited wealth to draw on. It protects. It cannot redistribute,
for if it tried to remedy inequities, it would impoverish everyone.
Hence the importance of charity. But charity here is not a weak
principle. It is a close second to the payment of debt, which is an
imperative in a commercial society based on credit.

Burke proposes a very strong notion of the position of charity
in social relations. It stands just below the threshold of institutional
politics. Personal benevolence is as important to the running of the
state as fair judges. It cannot be the function of a central government to provide for the poor—this would give the government too
much power by violating property rights—so it is the function of
"society"—that is to say, the Christians of Burke's Anglican Commonwealth—to make provision for the poor. Not for nothing then
does he defend the spirit of a gentleman and the privileges of the
established Church: manners, the customs of the country, and the
cure of souls supplement the laws by taking care of physical need.
Manners in a time of scarcity take up the slack that the market can
no longer pull. Manners is the name Burke gives to Smith's "beneficence," "ethics," and "sympathy."

It is a measure of Burke's commitment to manners—that they
are not ephemeral nor the signs of privilege but rather that they
compensate for the unequal distribution of wealth in a commercial
society—that he insists in his writings of the 1790s that the purpose
of government is happiness for the governed. The modern constitution, he argues, is legitimate, not because it leads to the eternal
salvation of souls, nor because the Hanoverians have the strongest
right to the throne. Legitimacy is not a matter of religion *tout court*
nor of dynastic descent. Rather it is based on the general level of
wealth and freedom.[72] While the present institutions of government cannot provide all necessities, they can insure the conditions
in which needs can be most cheaply satisfied.

Here then Paine truly disagrees. While he accepts Burke's claim
that it is through "the revenue"—that is, public finance—that the
body politic "can act in its true genius and character . . . its collec-

tive virtue,"[73] he wants that finance to be turned to new uses. He argues that revenue should not be raised to maintain a military state overseen by a monarch to the detriment of the poor. Like Burke, he wants an "economical" government free from corruption. But Paine does not want to limit the scope of government, just to change it. Accordingly, he presents in the second part of *The Rights of Man* a plan for rationalized government spending and progressive taxation that will both be cheaper than the present system and turn funds towards social welfare by paying for education and aid for the poor.

In the same year as Burke's grim "Thoughts and Details," Paine wrote *Agrarian Justice* in which he proposed an even more wide-reaching social security system based on an inheritance tax that serves as a kind of social tithing. Paine—the Dissenting egalitarian—does not want to leave something as important as general happiness in the hands of aristocratic manners. Distributive justice should be as well codified as its commutative counterpart. The part that Burke's manners play is, in Paine's account, to be given full legal status. By subsuming distributive justice under the rubric of jurisprudence, "animal happiness" (as Burke calls it) is transformed into a universal right, governed by general maxims and thus liberated from the personal and local irregularities of taste, prejudice, and irrational desire.

If we were to keep a scorecard on Burke and Paine, we would have to see that their debate is so heated and so coherent because they argue from the same base. They both believe in a minimal state and maximal personal freedom from governmental incursion; they see liberty best defended by the workings of an ideally objective and well-codified legal procedure. They conceive of government as the outgrowth of society and envision the state as a joint-stock operation in which everyone has a share. And, most importantly, they both understand that they are living in a new economic order. Each, in his own way, tries to balance rights in things and rights to things, distribution and possession. They are firm modernists, and assume that they live in a system that has never before existed. Burke claims that commercial modernity is only humane if propped on a rigid set of traditionally grounded social expectations. Paine, on the other hand, maintains quite overtly that new forms of wealth require new forms of government. In the end, both Burke and Paine believe in the primacy of commutative rights and the distributive power of the market. They differ quite strongly on what should happen when the market does not provide the jobs or the goods that it promised, and on what should happen to people who are unassimilable to the market.

On a higher level of abstraction, we can see how Burke and Paine can create a space—or rather capitalize on a space—created by the inability of political economics to provide both a fully adequate description and an unimpeachable defense of the commercial order. Their political theory defines itself as solving problems of distribution that economics presents but cannot always solve. Of course, Burke and Paine figure the political in different ways: Burke extends to the entire field of civil society the functions of what Paine wants to ascribe to government on its own. But both agree that the discourse of politics accounts for the gaps that the market leaves. Just as government and manners step in when the market fails, so political theory will step in where political economics fails. One could argue—though gingerly and with tact—that part of the acrimony of the Revolution debate was fueled by the imperatives of system definition and maintenance.[74] Burke and Paine provide a vivid tableau of the importance of political meditation and of politics in general. The passion of their dispute shows that political theory (and the practice of politics) is so important because the stakes are so high. They thus argue not only for their positions but for the right to argue in public in the first place. Their conflict successfully articulates the relation between political economics and political theory in the public arena.

Nevertheless, the functional impetus behind the Revolutionary debate—Burke and Paine define an area of communicative turf—should not be used as a means for discounting the ideological differences between the two men. Burke's legitimation of the established constitution and Paine's legitimation of the Revolution clash on a very important issue. For Smith, as we have seen, sympathy—the basis of ethics—can only operate in situations of mutual recognition. Burke's defense of chivalry rests on the argument that feudal relations were relations of constitutive and civilizing regard. But the age of chivalry is no more, not only sundered by the Revolution but by modern commercial relations as well. Burke refuses to recognize the needs of the French mob because they do not have compassion for the suffering of the royal family. Paine, who differentiates between the sovereign and the principle of sovereignty, is less interested in the sufferings of the individual monarch than of the mass of the population whose needs were not recognized under the old monarchy. Burke and Paine are therefore arguing about who gets recognized and why. They both agree that suffering is the grounds for sympathy. They just disagree over who suffers more.

So, like Smith (especially in volume three of *The Wealth of Nations*) they tell stories to explain to their contemporaries how the world has come to this historical pass. Burke tells tales of the glorious past, of the terrifying present, and of the miserable future. Paine shows that the monarchy in England is based on theft (thus trying to ferret out the dirty secret of commutative claims from the middle ages); that the French were oppressed by their kings; that the present is wonderful and the future is one in which everything is to be hoped for. Their temporal horizons may differ, but they both justify their attempts at legitimization by appealing to histories of pain.

This aspect of sympathy is the most nauseating to good Nietzscheans because it parades unearned suffering and weakness—mere reactive positions—as forms of strength. But it is the natural result (for political thought) of the confluence of two social and historical developments: the growth of the market (with its emphasis on commutative justice) and the legitimation of that market through the appeal to that undefined but richly allusive notion of happiness. This last seems sometimes to refer to matters spiritual and frequently to matters physical. It is therefore almost always seen in distributive terms. But how can one body forth need? How can one prove that one's needs are authentic and not merely the expressions of frivolous desire? Suffering, because it establishes itself as the opposite of happiness, becomes the signal of a true lack, a real need whose claim is binding on all spectators. The realm of ethics, of sympathy, will see its most dramatic tests in the contemplation of suffering, for pain will have to be observed minutely. Like all inner states, it can be feigned: thus calculi of sufferings will be the proper response to all expressions of need, all claims on distributive justice. In such forms of justification—because one is justifying something that is not there—logos, ethos, and pathos will all collapse into each other. The truth of one's claim, one's authority to make that claim, and one's ability to move one's audience will become indistinguishable. One will have to make a spectacle of oneself in order to raise the issues of distributive justice that modern jurisprudence cannot encompass, but cannot deny.

III

It should be clearer now how it is that *Frankenstein* responds to the conflicts of eighteenth-century political and economic thought, to the shifts in English society that produced these conflicts, and to the insistence on constant justification and legitimation that these shifts made necessary. The mutual revenge, the deep incompatibility of two different modes of justice, derives from the fact that perfect rights are centrifugal in their social force and imperfect rights are centripetal. The distributive volatilizes property while the commutative solidifies it.

The personal and intellectual connections between Mary Shelley and the radical thought of the 1790s have long been established and I have only needed to allude to them here. It should be noted however that Mary and Percy were not dabbling in anachronism when at the time of Waterloo they indulged their interest in the Revolutionary decade. From their different perspectives and with different polemical axes to sharpen, E. P. Thompson, Norman Gash, and Jonathan Clark have all shown that the radicalism of the first post-Napoleonic years owed a conscious debt to the middle-class Jacobins and reformist fellow travelers of the 1790s. Thompson even goes as far as to try to trace a radical underground railroad that runs from the 1790s through the Luddites to Peterloo.[75] Clark for his part shows, with typical acerbity, that "the radicals were fighting old battles," although one could well argue with his attempt to dismiss the demystifying inflections of left-wing historiography.[76] Gash notes that through the agency of Cobbett and Cartwright, the bourgeois radicalism of the 1790s became the political program of the poorer classes by 1817. Gash suggests that this atavism might well have marked a serious category error: governmental corruption and high taxation were not to blame for social distress between 1815 and 1830 and so could not be alleviated by electoral reform. Nevertheless, the language of extra parliamentary opposition at this time was more the language of Paine than of Owen, and the language of constitutional conservatives was most often the idiom of committed anti-Jacobins.[77] In short, new struggles were being mapped onto a rather old terrain.

This mapping, however, brought out some of the more interesting contours of that terrain, for it showed the flexibility of the boundaries between distribution and protection. Burke's critique of "natural" rights — his claim that rights were historically derived and depended on the political community — obviously had an effect, for many radicals shifted their attention to the enabling fiction of a traditional, pre-Norman constitution.[78] If rights are conventional and stem from the existence of a community, then they depend not on a true understanding of the nature of the world but on a recognition of the laws which embody those rights and a recognition of others as having them. This is a rather Humean reading of Burke, an understanding of rights that highlights the necessity but also the artificiality of justice. Hume's follower, Bentham, was thus able to draw the conclusion that "right" could not be understood other than as an obligation. The claim of a right is in fact nothing more than a demand that other people recognize their obligation not to disturb you if you have acted in congruence with your own obligations. All rights are political and based on mutual recognition and restraint.[79] Thus both commutative and distributive justice depend on recognition of and identification with others either as members of a community of obligations or as sufferers of need. It is therefore important to have what in law is called "standing," to compel recognition.

We can see then that recognition becomes a positive need in a political society, not just the formal means by which needs are established and communicated. But recognition cannot be mandated by either the law or the market. Thus both Victor and the monster demand recognition and sympathy; thus their claims can overlap linguistically even though their bases might be different; thus their claims can miss each other. Similarly the radical push for political recognition, although it was limited by the circumscription of an early nineteenth-century notion of politics and government, was therefore not so much an error but an anachronistic limitation of scope. Because the underlying structures of government (as the guarantor of established justice) and the ideal of distributive justice were understood to be remarkably similar, one easily falls into the argument that recognition from one would be an important step in the achievement of the other.[80]

Such a contextualization of *Frankenstein* seeks a common horizon between this novel and the realms of political action and political theory and is thus liable to collapse the difference between

these different systems. Of course, *Frankenstein* invites this conflation through its overt thematization of problems of justice and justification. It personifies (or personalizes) problems of justice and
recognition (and therefore identity) and asks its readers to consider
the difficulty, if not the impossibility, of adjudicating conflicting
claims.[81] This personalization accounts for its difference from political theory or political economics. Where those discourses deal
in generalizations, in classes of people, the novel deals in the way
such generalizations get played out on the ground. One could
therefore say that *Frankenstein,* with its open invocation of general
norms and extenuating circumstances, is really an elegant essay not
only in forensics but in that specialized field of ethical inquiry
known as casuistry, that is, the science of complicated exceptions
to supposedly universal rules. By thematizing justice and emphasizing its limitations as an abstract problematic, *Frankenstein* approaches the environment of "modern" commercial society in a
way that differs from the methods of political economics and political theory. By emphasizing the questions of ethics, its casuistry
shows how it, as a novel, can articulate these other fields.

But the history of the interpretations of *Frankenstein* should
make us wary of any reading that wants to deny the novel's impetus towards the general. It is indeed an odd piece of casuistry that
makes us want to see its terms and solutions as universal. *Frankenstein*'s arguments in defense of the particular lead me to read the
novel as the chart of an ideological struggle between commutative
and distributive justice in an age of systemically differentiated commercial capitalism. I am therefore led to suggest that the odd dou-
blings of Frankenstein and his monster have less to do with Victor's
psychopathology than with the fact that commutative and distributive justice can overlap but are not the same, and that the principles through which the monster and his creator are constructed
will play themselves out in ways that are similar but not the same.
Others have read in this novel allegories of class struggle, of Freud-
ian family romance or patriarchal dreams of asexual creation, of
patriarchal families, or of patriarchal science. In all these cases, read
us have moved from the specificities of the text to general considerations on class, the psyche, the patriarchy, or, in my case, modern
justice. There are other readings as well; ones that in the name of
this text's difference, draw universal conclusions about language,
or literary greatness, or "the human condition."

For what reason do we feel we have to read this book this way? What in the novel leads to this reading? Let us look at the frame of this novel of frames. Percy's "Preface" to the first edition of *Frankenstein* provides a defense of the novel's gothic features:

> The event on which this fiction is founded has been supposed, by Dr Darwin and some of the physiological writers of Germany, as not of impossible occurrence. I shall not be supposed as according the remotest degree of serious faith to such an imagination; yet, in assuming it as the basis of a work of fancy, I have not considered myself as merely weaving a series of supernatural terrors. The event on which the interest of the story depends is exempt from the disadvantages of a mere tale of spectres or enchantment. It was recommended by the novelty of the situations which it developed, and however impossible as a physical fact, affords a point of view to the imagination for the delineating of human passions more comprehensive and commanding than any which the ordinary relations of existing events can yield. (57)

He justifies the novel's flights by arguing that they are based on scientific knowledge, are *conceptually* possible even if not *physically* probable. To this end, he cites unnamed German authorities and Erasmus Darwin. Thus the novel is not "merely" a series of supernatural terrors. Rather, to follow the lead of Coleridge's own description of the "Ancient Mariner," *Frankenstein* outlines a series of preternatural or hypernatural terrors.

Percy feels that he has to justify the novel's deviations from the everyday because he assumes that the reader will only take seriously that which is probable, that which is in outward agreement with the existent. So he argues that preternatural trappings of *Frankenstein* make it more serious, more like a novel, because they allow the writer to depict elemental human passions, free from the circumscription of the obvious. This novel will thus contain the same kinds of truths that more overtly pedagogical fiction does. It will also depict them more clearly and search them out more fundamentally than its main competitors. The setting and the story thus provide a dark background or foil for the play of passion and human nature. They allow human nature a specificity by situating different passions in different characters, but point beyond the individ-

ual to universal truths. In this way, Percy argues that we must read
the book as an allegory. The justification of the novel as a utilitarian form leads to the justification of this book as a figurative depiction of Truth.

But if the first paragraph of Percy's "Preface" places *Frankenstein*
in a positive relation to science and to other novels, the second paragraph tries to situate the book in a positive relation to the palladia
of literature:

> I have thus endeavoured to preserve the truth of the elemen-
> tary principles of human nature, while I have not scrupled to
> innovate upon their combinations. The *Iliad* . . . Shakespeare
> in the *Tempest* and *Midsummer Night's Dream*, and most espe-
> cially Milton in *Paradise Lost* conform to this rule; and the
> most humble novelist, who seeks to confer or receive amuse-
> ment from his labors, may, without presumption, apply to
> prose fictions a license, or rather a rule, from the adoption of
> which so many exquisite combinations of human feeling
> have resulted in the highest specimens of poetry. (57)

Frankenstein's imaginative license is merely superficial, an amusing
set of epiphenomenal variations designed to keep the reader interested. As Mrs. Barbauld noted, truth is safe in the house of fiction.
And anyone who would cavil at this surface play would have to
cavil with the established, and presumably undisputed, masters of
literature. Anyone who mistakes the novel as a lesser form has not
understood the mechanics of the higher forms of literature. Percy
legitimates *Frankenstein*, then, by claiming legitimacy for the novel
as such and for the scientific grounding for this novel's main
conceit. He goes on to claim objectivity for the truths the book
presents; to argue that the text has no polemical designs on its readers. Rather, it seeks to demonstrate what it considers to be an unpo-
lemical belief in the "amiableness of domestic affection, and the
excellence of universal virtue" (58).

Percy's defense of his wife's production indicates that the novel
does what all novels do, that it is indeed what it would become, a
"standard novel." A standard reading of a novel would then entail
a sensitivity to allegorization, a willingness to interpret characters
as typical exemplars of human nature and feeling, even though
Frankenstein goes out of its way to show how difficult exemplary
readings can be. Percy presents *Frankenstein* not as an aberrant

novel but as an essential one. Or rather, the legitimation of the novel (and the process of legitimation as a whole) works in such a way as to show that the idiosyncratic does not escape the general condition at all, but can take its place in an articulated whole.

Such appears to be the logic behind Mary's own self-presentation in the "Introduction" to the edition of 1831. She has to account for the odd fact that a young woman was able "to dilate upon so hideous an idea" (51). She explains herself to her readers even as her characters do, by telling a story about her past, by telling her past as a story and fitting that hideous idea into a chain of chronological and therefore apparently causal relations. Her tale is an appropriate frame for this novel which is at every turn a stunning dramatization of justification. And in every instance, justification entails an explanation of what does not seem at first to fit. It is a form of conceptualization understood in the Idealist sense—the subsuming of the particular under the rubric of the universal.

This same attempt to map the particular—with all its threats, its promises of freedom—marks Smithian economics. Smith's intention, of course, was to argue against the mercantilist claim that gold and wealth were the same thing. He wanted to refute the idea that a nation's economic strength depended on government supervision and that the interests of the manufacturing class were the interests of all. But in fighting over these points, Smith had to outline how personal interests *could* coincide with the general good, how the activities of individuals fit together into the well-integrated whole that is the market. The doctrine of the unintended effect, where the intentions of the individual do not coincide with the structural function of his or her activities, showed how one could map the individual onto the general, how the individual's choices had an important, if mediated, effect on the prosperity of the commonwealth. We can see in Smith's self-regulating market the traces of the Neoplatonic, Stoic, and post-Newtonian *cosmos* that in its early eighteenth-century manifestations brought "happiness" forward to English political theory in the first place. Smith's important break with this tradition, of course, was that one did not *have* to contemplate the structure of the universe in order to pursue the general good. One merely had to go about one's business and the economic growth of the nation-state would take care of itself.

One could thus argue then that political economics and the novel claim to approach the same problems from different angles and share similar assumptions and methods. They show—or so the argument goes—the relation of the part to the whole, the individual to the alien totality that appears to stand over and against that individual. Nevertheless, they are not redundant. Economics began by looking at the general and inferred the individual; the novel began with the individual and allegorized the general.

If they shared certain formal affinities, certain appeals to common norms of truthfulness, the novel and classical economics also shared with each other and with political theory a similar aim: to describe and define the limits and possibilities for the happiness that the new order promised as its horizon. And happiness entailed a constant struggle between needs and rights, between jurisprudence and commutative justice which could either be worried through systemic considerations (in economics) or on a case-by-case basis (*Frankenstein*'s promise of ethical wisdom).

For all *Frankenstein*'s distrust of the institutions of justice, it does not seem to give up on the notion of justice as such. In fact, one could claim that the tragedy of the novel, if the novel is a tragedy, lies less in the incommensurability of different ethical systems (as Hegel would have it) than in the inability of its characters to get beyond resentment and actuate true justice. *Frankenstein* could be read as an indictment of prejudice and a celebration of those amiable domestic affections that lead to universal virtue. As such, it still believes in justice (as the fulfillment of need and the protection of exclusive right) as a yet-unattained norm. The same might be true of the novel's deconstruction of exemplary readings and stable allegorizations. Such stability is a dream for the future, of a hope for reconciliation which is not quite possible now, in the time of reading and the time of writing. If the novel becomes an "allegory of reading," it might well be that it does not mourn or stubbornly face the aporias that underlie the temporality of the sign as it becomes increasingly distant from the referent it cannot encompass. Rather, it presents the shipwreck of exemplary reading and of instituted justice as a cipher of what should be. I would like to suggest that there is a deep Enlightenment core to this novel which is less a critique of utopianism than of a certain historical limitation on the imaginations of utopians as they have appeared in the world. At its base, *Frankenstein* indicates that were one to free oneself from unfounded prejudices, were one to grant the recognition that politics needs and relies on ethics to provide, the irreconcilability of rights and needs would disappear. This could be taken either in a Burkean direction or a Painean one: towards a Christian commonwealth or a welfare state. It can also be seen to be a recapitulation of Smith's main case. If the government could overcome the influence of special interests, if it would only look rationally at the laws of the market (which are as regular as hydraulics — Smith's favorite metaphor), it could benefit everybody materially while protecting property from the envy of the poor.

But *Frankenstein* seems remarkably unwilling to settle for the half-way measures of Smithian compromise, though it understands the underpinnings of the Smithian problematic. This, I think, is the lesson of the allegory of allegory, the novel's unsettling of the terms of its preface. If we can see within the book a Nietzschean critique of distributive justice (one that would draw on Nietzsche's fascinated hatred of Rousseau) and a Marxist critique of commutative justice and the exchange relations it supports, as well as a feminist critique of patriarchal relations, it is perhaps because *Frankenstein* explores the tensions of that ideology that we call liberalism. It would be tempting to see in liberalism the allegory of allegory, to see it as the ground of the aporias of representation. It might be more accurate to say, however, that the promise of happiness and the disturbing energies that promise unleashes lead to a constant — and productive — instability within the languages of liberalism, a utopian break within those idioms that serves as the engine of their ongoing critique. In this way we can reread the apparent pablum of Percy's introduction not as an indication of what is, but as a normative one, an index of what should be. Such a reading would take the amiableness of domestic affections and the excellence of universal virtue not as signs of containment, or as displacements, of utopian aspiration. Rather, these would seem to be the ends to aspire to, ends that would be socially unsettling and domestically new. So much therefore depends on complicated negotiations with the norms of commutative justice and radical recognitions of other beings of "fine sensation." The demand for happiness can let loose rapacious energies.

3

Radcliffe and Malthus in the 1790s and Beyond

In the last chapter, I suggested that the jurisprudential justification of the modern commercial order turned on the promise of happiness, a promise that could fudge the difference between commutative and distributive justice for a short time. The deficiencies of the Smithian compromise — his vision of constant growth — seemed to lead to a necessary revision of the function of government, civil society, and the intimate sphere of the family. Such an account makes it sound as if economic theory led the way and all the other discourses had to follow in its wake. This is a nice heuristic device and helps explain some of the fire in the Revolution debate, but is, of necessity, only partial. We can approach the situation in a slightly different way.

In a recent book, Charles Taylor has attempted a massive act of hermeneutic recuperation. He has tried to chart "the making of modern identity," and thus recover the discursive frameworks in which many Anglo-American political and moral assumptions were formed and developed. One can disagree with Taylor on certain points (some of his readings of the Romantics and the Modernists will seem thin to the literary critic), but one should not ignore what is perhaps the most striking aspect of his study. By stressing the importance and influence of post-Newtonian Protestant theology, he has reminded us of the extent of the debt the jurisprudential — that is, the liberal — legitimation of modernity owes to eighteenth-century theodicy. He shows how both the Lockean Deists and the followers of the Cambridge Platonists and Shaftesbury, for all their differences about the extrinsic quality of natural law, had a firm belief in the rational ordering of the universe, and the interdependency of the parts within that order.[1] He reconstructs a religious picture of "the universe as a vast interlocking order of beings, mutually subserving each other's flourishing, for whose design the architect of nature deserves our praise and thanks and admiration" (245). Such a religion will downplay mystery and grace in honor of the sheer transparency of the providence that has structured the world (245–46). God does not move in mysterious ways, His wonders to perform. Rather, He does not need to perform miracles or wonders. The laws of nature are arranged beneficently, and the cosmos is so rational that no further intervention is needed (273). All that humankind has to do is learn to see the connections, to feel or to think its way to a knowledge of the immutable laws of nature.

The notion that the universe is a regulated and rational system means that the classical hierarchy that makes contemplation the mark of the good life gives way to a natural theology that grants value to all human occupations within the economy. A legitimation of this system will thus have to show clearly the interrelation and necessity of most, if not all, human activities and spheres of activity. In *this* account, political economics does not drag the discourses of politics, ethics, and fiction behind it. They all re-orient themselves at roughly the same time and in response to each other.

But the economic system as Smith explains it does not necessarily satisfy the demands of a materialist definition of distributive justice. It will not always provide adequate satisfaction for bodily needs. Nor can it answer the Aristotelian complaint that the system is blind to virtue. It distributes its prizes to the best investor, not to the best or most honorable person. One of the tasks facing the legitimation of modernity, then, will be to provide an account of its complexity, one that gives different functions to different spheres. Furthermore, it will have to find a morality behind the facts of distribution so that it can face up to the inequalities the system produces and its failures to provide the means of happiness.

David Hume gives a classic account of the separation of the spheres.[2] After looking at his discussion in the *Enquiry Concerning the Principles of Morals*, we will move on to Malthus's first *Essay* (1798) and Radcliffe's *The Italian* (1797) to worry out the problem of ethical distribution of social goods.

Hume wants to justify the apparent coldness of commutative justice. Were we to live in a pastoral utopia in which each person's needs could be fulfilled without impinging on another's desire, or were we to live in a state of absolute scarcity, there would be no need for the institutions of justice nor for positive law.[3] Justice and law are derivations from "the nature and situation of man" (194), that is to say, from the conditions of relative scarcity in which we live, and they are instituted for the public good so that an orderly commerce (both social and economic) can take place among men. The rules of law are not the rules of benevolence: benevolence is governed by the immediate object that summons it up. It does not care about larger systems and notions of the common good (303–4). Law, on the other hand, is blind to the particular moment that might exceed its necessarily universal maxims. It establishes the rules of the social game and, for the good of the game, will not change them to conform with individual instances, no matter how much the spirit of the law might disagree with its letter. Justice only serves the good of the aggregate by creating order. It works for the general benefit (305).

Justice, then, is imperfect and a result of human circumstances. It allows the individual the freedom to pursue his or her needs and wants, but cannot fulfill them itself. Hume can only imagine two circumstances in which need or merit could be made as the criteria for the distribution and possession of property. Either the world would have to be different (abundant in its resources) or man would have to be different ("replete with friendship and generosity" [184]) for such a kingdom of benevolence to be constructed. But Hume maintains that the first is unfeasible and the second improbable. In "the present disposition of the human heart," no community can hold property in common for any amount of time except for the family (185–86). Nor could any state legislate distribution according to merit, for all claims would be infinitely disputable (193). Furthermore, all attempts to make property equal would only maintain such equality for a short time. Soon the natural difference in men's abilities would reestablish inequities (193–94).

So, benevolence is not extensive and the only community in this sublunary world which has benevolence as its base is the family. It is precisely this general lack of benevolence that renders justice and a state to administer it quite necessary. One could easily argue that Hume has an anachronistic notion of property relations within families, that wives did not have equal access to their husbands' goods in the mid-eighteenth century. But for all the blindspots of

Hume's discussion, it should be very clear that he sees benevolence and justice as separate but mutually informing virtues, each with its own space (the family and the state respectively). We can find a similar attempt to separate justice from benevolence in Burke's account of manners, which serve the distributive function that the state can, and should, not.

The separation of the spheres of benevolence and justice expresses a great fear. Their promiscuous mingling could either create tyranny by destroying the intimate sphere of personal and sexual reproduction, or anarchy by letting the logic of the intimate sphere destroy the rule of property and the sanctity of contract. We can see the prevalence of this fear in the odd fact that for both Radcliffe and Malthus, Italy seems to stand for anarchy, that place where justice falls apart. Malthus argues against Godwin's distaste for legal punishment in this manner:

> In Italy, where murderers, by flying to a sanctuary, are allowed more frequently to escape, the crime has never been held in the same detestation and has consequently been more frequent. No man, who is at all aware of the operation of moral motives, can doubt for a moment, that if every murder in Italy had been invariably punished, the use of the stiletto in transports of passion would be comparatively little known.[4]

Sanctuary thus undermines whatever justice there might be in Italy. Rather than exhibiting clemency, it only furthers crime.

Radcliffe's novel opens with a staging of the same paradox. Some English travelers visit a church near Naples. They notice the extraordinary behavior of a rather ferocious-looking gentleman who lurks, significantly enough, in the shadows. Their guide explains that the man is an assassin who has sought sanctuary in the church. Such an arrangement makes little sense to one of the Englishmen: "This is astonishing! . . . of what avail are your laws, if the most atrocious criminal may thus find shelter from them? But how does he contrive to exist here! He is, at least, in danger of being starved?"[5] The friar responds that the murderer is sustained by the charity of others who bring him food. In the face of the Englishman's mounting disbelief, another Italian tries to explain this peculiar form of charity: "If we were to shew no mercy to such unfortunate persons, assassinations are so frequent, that our cities would be half depopulated" (3). The deeply sophistic logic of "this profound remark" (3) silences the tourist who can only bow in response. The irony, of course, is plain to Radcliffe's Englishman: if there were no sanctuary, there would be fewer murders and less danger of depopulation. Charity, the individual expression of the spirit of benevolence, though perhaps a virtue in itself, can easily hobble the practice of justice and therefore lead to greater vice.

This sense of the danger of good intentions serves as the center of Malthus's attack on the Poor Laws: "The poor laws of England were undoubtedly instituted for the most benevolent purpose, but there is great reason to think that they have not succeeded in their intention" (100). They lack true humanity because they depress the cost of labor and thus deny laborers the wages they could justly demand (101). Just as important is the tyranny of the parish over the private lives of the poor, a tyranny that is "inconsistent with the genuine spirit of the constitution" (100). The pseudo-benevolence of the Poor Laws thus leads to a double injustice. It cheats workers of their economic due and of their rights as free-born Englishmen. Furthermore, the Poor Laws are unjust in that they break the very contract they establish:

> We tell the common people that if they submit to a code of tyrannical regulations, they shall never be in want. They do submit to these regulations. They perform their part of the contract, but we do not, nay cannot, perform ours, and thus the poor sacrifice the valuable blessing of liberty and receive nothing that can be called an equivalent in return. (101–2)

In this unfair exchange, two forms of liberty—economic and political—are sacrificed to the impossible aspiration of eliminating misery from the world (102). Thus benevolence destroys everything justice sets out to establish. This conclusion lies at the heart of Malthus's unpleasant paradox: to help is not to help; to feed the poor indiscriminately is to deny them the possibility of feeding themselves. Here we see Smith's notion of the unintended effect deployed with a vengeance.

Italy, for Malthus, is a sideshow, an example of how bad things could be. His polemical purpose is to engage an issue closer to home: the debate on the Poor Laws that marked the mid-1790s. He begins with two apparently self-evident postulates: that people need to eat and that they will continue to have sex at the present rate. These twin appetites lead to an untenable situation, because population increases in a geometrical ratio, while the production of food only increases arithmetically (70–72). The existence of positive (disease, war, starvation) and preventative (various forms of vice) checks keep population near or at subsistence levels (89–92). The principle of population thus serves as the outer limit of moral and social perfectibility. The system can only preserve itself through nonprocreative or extramarital sexual relations or through the misery of disease, starvation, or war. If people think they will have enough to eat, they will have children, but their rate of reproduction will outstrip the production of food and thus render them that much poorer. If people do not think they will have enough to eat, they will resort to vicious outlets for their natural appetites. There is thus no hope of ever ridding the world of poverty or of rendering society truly virtuous. Against the dream of secular progress, Malthus thus presents a vision of an eternal oscillation in the lives of the poor between vice and misery, between hunger and sin. In this light, the Poor Laws are pernicious because they encourage paupers to have more children than can be comfortably fed. Furthermore, provisions for the needy allow them to slip into indolence and drunkenness rather than helping them develop the good habits of frugality and foresight which will only help them and the common good (94–95, 98).

Malthus derives the relation between population and subsistence from Smith,[6] but with a pessimistic coloring that is alien to *The Wealth of Nations*. He disagrees with the tone and the content of Smith's defense of high wages for the laboring poor. Smith sees increases in wages as necessary and happy correlates to an insufficient supply of labor power in an expanding market. Not only do such increases signal prosperity, they will in turn stimulate population growth and bring wages back into line. It should be clear, then, that Smith takes a very long view of economic history:

> The liberal reward of labour, therefore, as it is the effect of increasing wealth, so it is the cause of increasing population. To complain of it is to lament over the necessary *effect and cause* of the greatest publick prosperity.
>
> It deserves to be remarked, perhaps, that it is in the progressive state, while the society is advancing to the further acquisition, rather than when it has acquired its full comple-

ment of riches, that the condition of the labouring poor, of the great body of the people, seems to be the happiest and most comfortable. It is hard in the stationary, and miserable in the decline state. The progressive state is in reality the cheerful and the hearty state to all the different orders of the society. The stationary is dull, the declining, melancholy.[7]

It is clear from the context of Smith's encomium to high wages that *The Wealth of Nations* is a pamphlet for the progressive state, that in that state every sector of society has the same interest, and that in that state national wealth will benefit everyone.

Malthus seems to separate the condition of the poor from the interests of the nation in such a way that for the impoverished, every state is the stationary state. Life for the poor is always melancholy. He is able to reach this conclusion by maintaining that Smith is wrong in his contention that the increase in national wealth is at the same time an increase in the wealth of the laboring poor. While manufacturing may make fortunes, it does not lift agricultural production. It only succeeds in augmenting the price of necessities through the circulation of luxuries (183–86). So Malthus is more a physiocrat than his great master in seeing true wealth only in agriculture, and he is thus even more distrustful of merchants. And, by being more of a physiocrat, he can only conceive (or present) secular progress as somewhat specious and sadly Sysiphean (199).

The arguments of Malthus's first *Essay* are determined in good part by the opponents he assails, principally William Godwin. Malthus portrays the principle of population as a natural law because, following Hume, he adheres to the notion that human society depends on orderly and impersonal institutions such as justice: "The great error under which Mr Godwin labours throughout his whole work is the attributing almost all the vices and misery that are seen in civil society to human institutions" (133). In *Political Justice*, Godwin promises the elimination of subordination in a future state by ignoring the all-important principle of scarcity on which civil jurisprudence and economics depend. He is thus free to ensure everyone will own just a modicum of property and that everyone's physical needs will be met by the just distribution of goods. By abolishing the firm distinction between mine and thine, and by stressing the predominance of distributive over commutative justice, Godwin wants to banish formal government completely.

In its place he substitutes a vastly reformed sphere of civil society which is run on the very un-Humean principle of benevolence.
Malthus will have none of this. Not only will population outgrow
the promise of plenty (139–41) but civil society without the established protection of property is inconceivable. Without the human
institutions which guard property, civil society will degenerate
into a Humean anarchy:

> All cannot share alike the bounties of nature. Were there no
> established administration of property, every man would be
> obliged to guard with force his little store. Selfishness would
> be triumphant. . . . Every individual mind would be under a
> constant anxiety about corporal support, and not a single
> intellect would be left free to expatiate in the field of thought.
> (134)

The last sentence is, of course, an attack on Godwin's relatively
labor-free republic of the mind but shows the underlying logic of
Malthus's thought: the "established administration of property"—
that is, the established administration of justice—is the necessary
precondition for all the virtues of civilized man. It is the basis for
benevolence, altruism, and the advancement of knowledge. Following in the jurisprudential mold, he argues that given the un-
avoidability of relative scarcity, the institution of property does
not immiserate mankind. It liberates it. Godwin's attempts to vola-
tilize property ("We have in reality nothing that is strictly speaking
our own. We have nothing that has not a destination prescribed to
it . . .")[8] are countered by Hume's claim that such systems that replace justice with benevolence are "really, at bottom, *impracticable*;
and were they not so, would be extremely *pernicious* to human society."[9] Pernicious, because they ignore the truth about the present
disposition of the human heart in conditions of scarcity. They thus
lead to the kind of tyranny of compassion that Hannah Arendt sin-
gled out, without much generosity, in Robespierre in particular
and in Jacobinism in general.[10]

Malthus singles out Godwin from amongst the English radicals
because Godwin projects a utopia on false principles. Malthus feels
that he cannot ignore the very presuppositions on which economic
thought is based: Society is a rational system whose laws can be
derived inductively, and mankind will never have enough of everything. In short, he falls back on the Biblical limits to utopian hope:

humans will always have to work[11] and all people definitely have to die.

Malthus calls Godwin's system an "enchanting picture" (69). It is a pleasing representation but inaccurate, because it is based on faulty reasoning. Malthus pits his own empiricist "Newtonianism" against Godwin's utopian-rationalist "Cartesianism." He claims that science must move from effects to causes, not vice versa. Hence he argues that the laws of nature are immutable because the course of experience has always shown the same effects to result from the same causes. In other words, the belief in the perfectibility of man is a false reasoning that new causes will lead to new effects. But new causes entail new laws and a break from what appears to be the established order of nature (126). Human knowledge is based on the assumption of the constancy of natural law. Without observable symptoms, we cannot predict radical change without undermining the very basis of knowledge (126–27).

Malthus's vision is thus very dark indeed. Not only does it separate justice from benevolence (thus banishing equity from considerations of commutative right) but, following Hume, he is quite clear about the conflicts between these two virtues and the spheres that encompass them. His first *Essay* can be read as a strong critique of Smithian optimism, published a year after the basically economic mutinies amongst the fleets at Spithead and Nore.[12] But although he wants to do away with radical "systems of equality," he does not want his reader to use the principle of population as a goad to despair:

> The tendency in the race of man to increase beyond the means of subsistence is one of the general laws of animated nature which we can have no reason to expect will change. Yet, discouraging as the contemplation of this difficulty must be to those whose exertions are laudably directed to the improvement of the human species, it is evident that no possible good can arise from any endeavours to slur it over or keep it in the background. . . . Independently of what relates to this great obstacle, sufficient yet remains to be done for mankind to animate us to the most unremitting exertion.
> (199)

The principle of population provides limits to human perfectibility, but it does not foreclose human activity nor human improvement.

It is at this point that Malthus launches into an interestingly heterodox theodicy, and in so doing switches registers: he returns the notion of the providential system to Providence itself. Reasoning from Nature back to God and assuming the beneficence of the Creator (202), Malthus argues that the evils and depredations of the world were created to stimulate humankind to greater exertions, to leave the animal torpor of a purely physical existence and cultivate its mind. At first blush Malthus's position sounds like the theological defenses of economic inequality that Boyd Hilton has done such an excellent job of excavating. Hilton argues that the influence of Evangelical thought in the late eighteenth and early nineteenth centuries was greater than we have realized. In his account, the evangelical use of the doctrine of atonement—that this world is a trial and a purgation in expectation of the next—was so widespread that one can call the eighty years after 1790 "the age of atonement." Malthus thus sounds like an adherent of that "moderate evangelicalism which developed after 1789" and which "represented a shift in natural religion from *evidences* to *paradoxes* . . . from examples of benign contrivance in the natural world to demonstrations of how superficial misery may work inner improvement."[13] It is not surprising therefore to find that Malthus argues that moral depravity is necessary for the free choice of moral excellence (210) and that the "sorrows of life [are] necessary to soften and humanize the heart" (209). But—and this cannot be stressed enough—he is explicitly unwilling to defend the doctrine of atonement. He does not accept the idea that this world is a trial of a species cursed with original sin (201), and he rejects the notion of the eternal vengeance of Hell as being unworthy of the Deity. Rather, he suggests that those who do not achieve moral excellence are simply extinguished:

> When we reflect on the temptations to which man must necessarily be exposed in this world, from the structure of his frame, and the operation of the laws of nature, and the consequent moral certainty that many vessels will come out of this mighty creative furnace in wrong shapes, it is perfectly impossible to conceive that any of these creatures of God's hand can be condemned to eternal suffering. Could we once admit such an idea, all our natural conceptions of goodness and justice would be completely overthrown, and

we could no longer look up to God as a merciful and right-
eous Being. (215)

If we consider that Malthus's shift in register to the theological can
be seen as an attempt to redeem the claims of distributive justice, in
that the good will receive the reward they have earned, we can see
how strong his case against Hell must be. Those who are not righ-
teous could not really help it. God has stacked the deck against
them. To punish them would be to show that the entire universe is
not only unjust but that it redoubles its apparently arbitrary injus-
tices. So, unlike the moderate evangelicals to whose number he
seems at first to belong, Malthus does not transfer the distributive
rewards to Heaven and Hell. Nor is he interested in individual salvation, the personal scorekeeping that promises to requite suffering in the hereafter.

According to Malthus, the world is not a trial but a kiln. The
mind that is stimulated out of inert material is not an individual
mind, but rather Mind in general and as such. For that reason, damnation does not make much sense. The misshapen pots constitute
the failed experiments, the clay that did not take properly. It appears that God cannot create mind all at once: He must do it over
time. He needs history to perfect humanity:

> And, unless we wish to exalt the power of God at the ex-
> pense of his goodness, ought we not to conclude that even
> to the great Creator, almighty as he is, a certain process may
> be necessary, a certain time (or at least what appears to us as
> time) may be requisite, in order to form beings with those
> exalted qualities of mind which will fit them for his high
> purposes? (201)

The doctrine of atonement requires original sin, that is, the notion
that we have fallen from the relative perfection in which we were
originally created. But according to Malthus, we have not achieved
that relative perfection yet. Paradise has not been lost. Mind has yet
to be gained.[14]

Is Malthus just rewriting Godwin? Donald Winch has written:
"Paradoxically . . . Malthus's theological commitments provide him
with a teleology of improvement that acts as the religious equivalent of the secular perfectibilism which his *Essay* set out to undermine."[15] Actually Winch does not do Malthus justice. The change

in registers makes all the difference. Godwin's perfectibilism is social and tends not only towards virtue but towards equality as well. Malthus cannot even admit equality into his theodicy: the broken pots will be discarded, not redeemed. Malthus does not devote any time to imagining a world or a heaven of pure mind. His thought does not tend to the utopian, even when contemplating the saved. Mankind will always be limited to matter and to death. And the poor, of course, will always be with us.

One has to admire the scruples behind Malthus's refusal to make the afterlife pick up the distributive slack of this one, and his refusal to make the Smithian claim that the development of mind benefits everyone either morally or materially. His refutation of the eternal sanction of damnation serves as a strong critique of that distributive principle which would seek to punish temporal evil, because, as he points out, temporal suffering is doled out so unequally. It protests against that suffering and that inequality. It also puts into question the very notion of the providential organization of the world even as it seeks to defend it. In a passage quoted above, Malthus has to choose between an all-powerful Creator or a beneficent one. He tries to split the difference, but ends up having to limit the Almighty's powers. Such a notion revises the doctrine of creation rather drastically. The world is not yet fully created. The system is not balanced at all times to ensure justice. Providence does not guarantee the benevolence of the system, but rather its efficiency as it continues its drive towards the development of mind. One could argue therefore that Malthus's theodicy, by admitting the principle of progress, does not lessen the sting of his economics but repeats it on another level. His vision of progress sacrifices all the broken pots of humanity without redeeming them or giving them much to hope for. To put it another way: the theodicy does not legitimate modern capitalism at all well. It provides nothing for the poorer classes who serve, after all, as the first *Essay*'s principle object of study and concern.

But Malthus did not stop there. In the revised quarto edition of the *Essay* of 1803, Malthus took another approach which he developed in all subsequent editions. He secularized the evangelical insistence on trial by locating the rewards of virtue in this world. By admitting that the principle of population was not inexorable, but could be turned to advantage through personal reform, Malthus argued that the market did meet the claims of distributive justice, not that it satisfied everybody's needs nor that growth would accommodate those needs. Rather, the market would reward desert, that is, proper behavior.

Of course, the notion of market discipline was hardly new to Malthus. It had been the center of the debate over the morality of commerce in the previous century. Nor can it be said that Malthus was the first to lime discipline to virtue. One can easily trace such notions back to the sixteenth century. But Malthus is important to us because he shows how the principle was successfully secularized. In the next section of this chapter, we will see how Radcliffe works with a similar set of problems. Nevertheless, I shall argue that as Radcliffe's novel does not engage the questions of production and class, those aporetic moments in Malthus, she ends up sounding interestingly anachronistic. To put it in Hilton's terms: her theodicy is more evidential than paradoxical. It does not take suffering seriously enough.

Midway through the first *Essay*, Malthus speculates on the ambiguity of all laws and virtues: "Perhaps there is no one general law of nature that will not appear, to us at least, to produce partial evil; and we frequently observe at the same time, some bountiful provision which, acting as another general law, corrects the inequalities of the first" (179). A law in itself has no basic ethical tendency. Its utility (and Malthus, with his constant appeal to the "general mass of happiness," is nothing if not a utilitarian) can only be judged by its place in a balanced system of laws and virtues.

In *The Italian* this paradigm of countervailing forces becomes the dominant model of psychology. Here is Radcliffe on the father of her ingenue hero, Vincentio di Vivaldi: "His pride of birth was equal to either [power and rank], but it was mingled with the justifiable pride of a principled mind. . . . *His pride was at once his vice and his virtue, his safeguard and his weakness*" (7; emphasis added). Pride, in itself, signals both danger and strength. Similarly, the ingenue heroine, Ellena di Roasalba, is deeply aware of the treacherous calibrations of her most virtuous tendencies:

> Her very virtues, now that they were carried to excess, seemed to her to border upon vices; her sense of dignity appeared to be narrow pride; her delicacy weakness; her moderated affection cold ingratitude; and her circumspection, little less than prudence degenerated into meanness. (180)

Her best qualities seem to have been traduced by excess, but the appearance of excess is itself an interpretation born of Ellena's fine moral sensibility. Ellena is arguing with herself about the propriety of marrying above her station. Her love for and her sense of gratitude towards Vivaldi lead her in one direction, while her sense of her own rights (the term is hers) leads her in another (181). In both the Marchese and Ellena, then, a sense of one's rights (the language of jurisprudence) becomes a vice if it overwhelms the sense of one's sociability and others' needs (the language of benevolence). Just as the novel is framed by the paradoxical nullification of justice by benevolence, its characters are defined by their own negotiations between these two principles.

If it is hard to find the right mix of virtues in *The Italian*, this is in large part due to the different versions of justice the novel presents. Radcliffe's gothics are notoriously schematic. In this one, therefore, it is quite easy to see how different characters embody — and how different strands of the plot develop — differing notions of justice. For the better part of *The Italian*, the formal institutions of justice are identified with the evil monk Schedoni and the Church. But Schedoni's notion of justice is hypocritical. He uses its universalist language to forward his private interests and ends. He convinces Vivaldi's mother that justice demands that young Ellena be murdered for the *lèse majesté* of trying to marry Vivaldi:

> "Justice does not the less exist, because her laws are
> neglected," observed Schedoni. "A sense of what she com-
> mands lives in our breasts; and when we fail to obey that
> sense, it is to weakness, not to virtue that we yield."
>
> "Certainly," replied the Marchesa, "that truth never yet
> was doubted."
>
> "Pardon me, I am not so certain as to that," said the Con-
> fessor, "when justice happens to oppose prejudice, we are apt
> to believe it virtuous to disobey her. For instance, though the
> law of justice demands the death of this girl, yet because the
> law of the land forbears to enforce it, you my daughter . . .
> would think that virtue bade her live, when it was only
> fear." (168)

In this interchange, Schedoni posits that justice is a natural feeling that can run counter to positive law. Positive law, as it happens, is equated here with a benighted and weak-willed prejudice that stands in opposition to nature. Schedoni's arguments parody Rousseau's deeply liberationist vision of conscience in *Julie* and that section of *Emile* devoted to the Curé Savoyard. They are parodic in that they are used to justify oppression and reinforce the prejudice of birth.

It would be tempting then to see Schedoni as one of Burke's revolutionaries, as a canting self-centered hypocrite. But the novel is not afraid of Rousseau. Schedoni's misappropriation of Rousseau is a parodic repetition of the ingenues' own unironic use of the language of Jacobinism. Ellena complains to Vivaldi that his parents' pride of birth is "a visionary prejudice that destroys our peace" (26). When Vivaldi's father orders the young man to break off his engagement, Vivaldi argues strenuously:

> I will defend the oppressed, and glory in the virtue, which teaches me, that it is the first duty of humanity to do so. Yes, my Lord, if it must be so, I am ready to sacrifice inferior duties [to the supposed pride of his father's house] to the grandeur of a principle which ought to expand all hearts and impel all actions. (30)

It could be argued that Vivaldi is relying here on the assumptions of benevolence ("humanity," "expand all hearts"), but he is arguing against *oppression*, that is, the subjugation of an individual in defiance of his or her rights. The jurisprudential source of Vivaldi's resistance to his father's will is made clear several pages later:

> [R]egarding his father as a *haughty oppressor* who would rob him of his most *sacred right*, and as one who did not scruple to stain the name of the innocent and defenseless, when his interest required it . . . he suffered either pity or remorse to mingle with the resolution of asserting *the freedom of his nature*. . . . (40; emphasis added)

Vivaldi's father is the familial equivalent of the absolute monarch of Whig nightmare, and against such prejudiced absolutism Vivaldi asserts the claim of what are seen quite unproblematically as his natural commutative rights to his own person.

Ellena is also quite well versed in this political idiom. When she is held against her will in a convent in the mountains because she will not submit to the social prejudice that forbids her marriage, she exclaims:

> I am prepared to meet whatever suffering you shall inflict upon me; but be assured, that my own voice never shall sanction the evils to which I may be subjected, and that the immortal love of justice, which fills all my heart, will sustain my courage no less powerfully than the sense of what is due to my own character. (84)

Natural rights stand opposed to the false pronouncements of an oppressive custom: Ellena bases her right to resistance—albeit passive resistance[16]—on the evidence and legitimacy of her emotion. The ultimately comic plot of *The Italian* which pits the unjust and unsuccessful will of fathers against the legitimate loves of their children[17] thus also *appears* to recount the struggle between a false practice of justice based on the dead hand of custom and a natural justice that is grounded in virtue and desert. Such a reading makes the novel appear to be quite radical in its argument. This provisional interpretation, based on the disposition of its main characters in the first volume (which ends on page 128 of the Oxford reprint) seems to locate injustice and inhumanity generationally and institutionally, in parents (and their surrogates), and in the Church.

But *The Italian* defeats these expectations by dividing the plot between the fortunes of Ellena, who is abducted from the altar by Schedoni's henchmen, and Vivaldi, who is brought to Rome to face the dreaded Inquisition. Ellena is rushed off to a secluded house on the coast where Schedoni is set to murder her, only to discover—erroneously, as it turns out—that she is his daughter. Paternal emotions and the considerations of self-interest make Schedoni perform an abrupt about-face. He will now try to insure that his putative daughter marries the well-placed Vivaldi. On the way to Rome to subvert his own evil designs, he deposits his daughter in the convent of the *Santa della Pieta*. We have every right to fear for Ellena's treatment here. In the other convent, she was abused and threatened with death. But the polar schematism of the plot ensures that in fact this does not happen now. Our Lady of Pity is run by a good abbess and the whole community shows "the influence, which a virtuous mind may acquire over others" (299). As it happens, this woman is tolerant and truly charitable. The convent appears "like a large family, of which the lady abbess was the mother" (300). It is, then, the seat of benevolence. The Church, so far from being unambiguously inhumane, is shown to have distinctly positive qualities. As if to underline the identification of the significantly named convent (does it refer to the Virgin Mary or to the lady abbess who runs it?), it is within the walls of Our Lady of Pity that Ellena is reunited with her overwhelmingly kind mother, a nun previously known as Olivia.

While benevolence marks the terminus of Ellena's plot, justice is the motive force behind Vivaldi's. The Inquisition serves as the focus of the third volume. At first, the Inquisition is as unjust as the first convent that Ellena visits. Its procedures are a travesty of justice: It does not seek to discover the truth but to browbeat the accused into an admission of an already-presumed guilt. As Vivaldi exclaims in disgust: "How! . . . is the tribunal at once the Prosecutor, Witness, and Judge! What can private malice wish for more, than such a court of *justice*, at which to arraign it's [sic] enemy? The stiletto of the Assassin is not so sure, or so fatal to innocence" (206). The established institution of justice is manifestly unjust, for it allows nothing but the severest punishment. It pursues not universalistic principles of the right but the private ends of vengeance. And the dilations of the plot seem designed to generate a deep anxiety that Vivaldi will indeed be done to death in the caverns of the Inquisition. But after several tense interviews with his inquisitors, some mysterious midnight meetings with what appears to be a ghost, and some surprising courtroom reversals, the Inquisition becomes a recognizable court of law (346f). It is as if Radcliffe had forgotten the schematism that separated the good convent from the bad, and incorporated both negative and positive views of the Church in her depiction of the Inquisition. Suddenly, when the Vicar-general starts cross-examining different witnesses in order to arrive at the truth, Vivaldi is overcome by admiration: "Are these the sentiments of an inquisitor! . . . can such glorious candour appear amidst the tribunal of an Inquisition!" (352) The answer of course is that it can. The tribunal of an Inquisition can become an institution of true retributive justice where the wicked are punished and the innocent saved. The Inquisition uncovers Schedoni's guilt and releases Vivaldi. It finds out the facts and requites everyone according to his deeds.

The abrupt reversal in the plot can only be meant to cause an equally abrupt reversal of affect.[18] The main source of anxiety in the second and third volumes of *The Italian* is suddenly revealed to be harmless after all. More importantly, the transvaluation of the

Inquisition serves the same purpose as the convent of the *Santa della Pieta*. It shows that social institutions themselves are not to blame for injustice and misery, in spite of the Rousseauistic indications of the first volume. The fault lies with those who run them. The viciousness displayed by the Church is really just a personnel problem. In the hands of the right abbess or Inquisitor, a convent can be truly benevolent and a court can be truly just.

If we pay attention to the meanderings of the plot of *The Italian*, we see that Radcliffe has been very careful to separate justice and benevolence and then to gender them. The plot has sifted apart what the preface had shown to be hopelessly mixed. It has restored justice and benevolence to their proper spheres and by attributing sexes to them, has rooted benevolence in the family and civil society, while leaving justice to the domain of established (male) administrative institutions. Like Malthus, who found the claims of Radicalism attractive but thoroughly misguided, Mrs. Radcliffe has capitalized on the pathos of the rhetoric of Rousseauism only to reinforce the very institutions she seemed to attack. In the end, the danger the book seems to want to assail is not the contamination of justice by prejudice, but rather the promiscuous commingling of the spheres of commutative justice and benevolence. Like Malthus, Mrs. Radcliffe stakes out a territory that is neither radical nor reactionary, one whose legitimacy seems to rest on its resolute determination to discover freedom and happiness in the division and balance of powers and principles.

Mrs. Radcliffe ends up justifying the existent. Her novel turns abruptly from critique to theodicy, much in the way that Malthus's first *Essay* does. *The Italian* is a vindication of natural religion and of providence. This can be seen in Radcliffe's most distinguishing features. Radcliffe was famous for her spectacular descriptions of landscape and for the (related) habit of invoking the supernatural only to reduce all the eerie aspects of her plots to purely human — and natural — agency. Scott writes: "A principal characteristic of Mrs. Radcliffe's romances is the rule which the author imposed upon herself, that all the circumstances of her narrative, however mysterious and superhuman, were to be accounted for on natural principles at the winding up of the story."[19] Scott goes on to note that this technique has its dangers. The natural explanations might fall short of the reader's expectations: "It is no wonder that, hemmed in by rules so strict, Mrs. Radcliffe, a mistress of the art of exciting curiosity, has not been uniformly fortunate in the mode of gratifying it."[20] Scott here echoes the sentiments of her earliest reviewers, who praised *The Italian* for its correctness, but found it less successful than her previous efforts precisely because those earlier novels had trained her readers just what to expect.[21]

The liability presented by Radcliffe's explanations—whose demystificatory impetus is further explored in *Northanger Abbey*—has itself, of course, a precursor in Clara Reeve's *Old English Baron*,[22] which in turn marketed itself as a revision of the Gothic as presented in *The Castle of Otranto*. According to Mrs. Reeve, Walpole's novel is too marvelous to keep the reader's interest: "Had the story been kept within the utmost *verge* of probability, the effect had been preserved, without losing the least circumstance that excites or detains the attention."[23] One can chart, then, a common response among certain women authors of the gothic. They take up the pen to naturalize the genre's extravagance and subdue it. It is a critical commonplace that Radcliffe wrote *The Italian* as an angry response to Lewis's exuberantly excessive *The Monk*, even though there is no explicit reference to Lewis in Mrs. Radcliffe's novel.[24] But there does not need to be. By virtue of Radcliffe's gender, the clichés of literary history can cast her effort as an attempt to reform the Gothic yet again. Female authorship in this historical construction is thus fully endued with the pathos of reform: "femininity" is a "civilizing" force. By returning its enchanted reader to the world as it really is, by restoring the everyday by anchoring it in the laws of nature, Mrs. Radcliffe socializes the "male" Gothic by making it submit to the rigors of the existent and its proprieties.

The reform of the gothic points to a desired reform in the reader. At the end of the novel, Schedoni explains to Vivaldi how he had tricked the young man by playing on his imaginative credulity. Like Radcliffe, Schedoni knows that his audience wants to believe in superstition (397–98). But the demystification that Schedoni's confession leads to must be seen in its eighteenth-century context. Like the attack on prejudice that generates the first volume of *The Italian*, the attack on superstition that gets worked out in the last volume is launched in the name of the Enlightenment and progress. Mrs. Radcliffe's critique of vulgar superstition should be read in the light of her own natural religion. She clears the lumber of archaic thought to make way for a more enlightened notion of the Godhead. Throughout the book, Ellena looks to nature as a "veil of the Deity" (see, for instance, 63) and sees in the chiaroscuro landscapes of sublimity the assurance of a true justice that will release her from male oppression (90–91). The plot of the novel shows that she is indeed correct. Not only is she freed, reunited both with her lover and her mother, but the wicked are punished as they deserve. Clara Reeve complained about the violent machinery of Walpole's supernatural interventions.[25] Radcliffe makes the machinery that attends her vision of a just, providential order all the more believable by making it all the more unobtrusive. God is the very engine of the plot itself, whose resolutions are to be taken as the mark of an enduring covenant. Once rid of superstition and mystery, one can gather direct empirical evidence of the beneficence of a transcendent Creator.

In many ways, Radcliffe's novel is a fully realized narrative depiction of the providential order of intermeshing spheres that Taylor describes and that Smith relies on. Because it is a narrative, *The Italian* shows *how* the system doles out its punishments. It also opens the temporal possibility of reform. One can amend one's behavior in order to reap one's rewards. We have seen Radcliffe's reformism in her critique of the bad Inquisition and the bad Abbey. But this reformism is personal: the fault lies with the administrators, not the institutions. She is thus most interested in psychological and moral improvement.[26]

Mrs. Radcliffe presents us with a number of morally static characters. The nature of minor agents in *The Italian* is legible from their physiognomies. Here is Spalatro, Schedoni's hired killer: "Ellena shrunk while she gazed. She had never before seen villainy and suffering so strongly pictured on the same face" (210). Spalatro's face is a *picture* of the abstract qualities of suffering and villainy: his features are so molded as to admit direct entrance into the complexities—he is both victim and oppressor—of his moral being. The same readability is also true of Schedoni: "There was something in his physiognomy extremely singular, and that can not be easily defined. It bore the traces of many passions, which seemed to fix the features they no longer animated" (35). Radcliffe is not an unsubtle psychologist and in Schedoni, as in Spalatro, she is fascinated by mixed moral personalities. Schedoni's face is interesting in that it is the ledger of old passions and previous abuse. It serves as an index of his transgressions.

Even if Radcliffe's interest in physiognomy does not always tempt her into the trap of simple characterization, it does indicate that in her psychology, the evildoers are fixed in their depravity. Hence her reduction of the Marchese di Vivaldi to the virtue and the vice of pride (7), and hence her description of the Marchesa: "She was of violent passions, haughty and vindictive, yet crafty and deceitful; patient in stratagem, and indefatigable in pursuit of vengeance, on the unhappy objects who provoked her resentment" (7). Radcliffe is able to reduce the Marchese and his wife to unwavering types, to their ruling passions. Schedoni as well is reducible to "a gloomy and ferocious disposition" (35).

Such a psychological model — that the evil personality is immediately perceivable, consistent, and passionate — leaves scope for the good. Ellena becomes the focus for a different kind of psychological investigation. She, even more than her beloved Vivaldi, is given to moral calculation. If Vivaldi wonders for a few pages about the conflicting claims of filial duty and personal happiness (28–40), Ellena spends a good portion of the book in moral interrogation and self-accusation (see, for instance, 69–70). Ellena thus presents a different kind of rationality than her elders do. While the evil characters tend to use reason instrumentally (to gain specific ends), Ellena uses reason to debate within herself the propriety of action. And she is able to change her course when she sees herself to be in the wrong.

The possibility of rational psychological reform underscores the novel's didactic project and its redemptive ending. If character were cast in adamant, and reason were only means- and not ends-oriented, then there would be no function for the exemplarity of the characters and no reason for the following moral:

> It may be worthy of observation, that the virtues of Olivia, exerted in a general cause, had thus led her unconsciously to the happiness of saving her daughter; while the vices of Schedoni had as unconsciously urged him nearly to destroy his niece, and had always been preventing, by the means they prompted him to employ, the success of his constant aim. (384)

Olivia's virtue—her selflessness and universal good will—prove in the end to work in her own interest, while the selfish Schedoni works against his own avowed ends. From this comes the rather paradoxical but standard conclusion that benevolence is in fact the best policy (with all the eighteenth-century connotations of the word). Radcliffe thus describes a world given over to a traditional notion of distributive justice, where desert (not need) is granted its secular reward. Such a vision only makes sense if one assumes one's readers, once freed from superstition, will be able to calculate their duties and interests, and will use their reason to control their passions.

The narrative of *The Italian* thus seeks to present the world as an orderly, nonhierarchical set of intermeshing spheres that are overseen by a providence whose laws, transparent and immutable as they are, serve as the best guide to the good life. One must regulate one's behavior in accordance with them, but the rewards of living "naturally" are material, spiritual, almost immediate, and do not require institutions to bestow them. They come automatically.

But the automatic quality of reward seems to unsettle the surface of the novel. When Ellena looks to the mountains and sees in their sublimity the assurance that God will visit destruction on her captors, she is flirting with the notion of an imminent, personal Deity, one who will intervene directly in the affairs of the world. Another way of approaching this odd quality of the novel is to ask if Radcliffe is successful in her extirpation of the marvelous and to question the very need for the supernatural in the first place. As we have already seen, Scott echoed her other critics in finding that the apparently supernatural marvels were more interesting to Radcliffe's readers than her sometimes slipshod "natural" explanations. While the natural reduction of the uncanny phenomena in her plots might assuage certain matters of intellectual and theological conscience, the uncanniness of the phenomena was the biggest draw of this genre and of her books. The desire for direct intervention, for a mysterious Deity different from the distant Creator of a well-regulated world, speaks to the central historical weakness in the notion of an impersonal providential order. As such an order became less evident, more paradoxical by the late 1790s, it came to seem both counterfactual and counterintuitive. We can begin to account for the odd change in the book's thematics from an apparently Jacobin attack on corrupt institutions to a celebration of those institutions in this way. *The Italian* seems to want to undo quickly what it has spent so long in cultivating. It counters the rhetoric of rights and the proto-Rousseauistic rebelliousness that it has established without really addressing the attractiveness of that rhetoric and that sense of rebellion, without really answering the charges they have brought up. The desire for intervention carries with it the implication that the system is not as efficient as advertised. The thematic anacoluthon of the story indicates that the justification of the world may not be equal to the objections against it.

But it is not merely a piece of my subtlety that finds in the thematic disjunctions of *The Italian* an implicit self-reflection or critique of its theodicy. In the twentieth letter of *The Borough* (1810), George Crabbe attacks the falsely affirmative nature of gothics such as *The Italian*:

> Time have I lent — I would their Debt were less —
> To flow'ry Pages of sublime Distress;
> And to the Heroine's soul-distracting Fears
> I early gave my Sixpences and Tears:
> Oft have I travel'd in these tender Tales
> To *Darnley-Cottages* and *Maple-Vales*,
> And watch'd the Fair-one from the first-born sigh,
> When *Henry* pass'd and gaz'd in passing by;
> Till I beheld them pacing in the Park,
> Close by a Coppice where 'twas cold and dark;
> When such Affection with such Fate appear'd,
> Want and a Father to be shunn'd and fear'd,
> Without Employment, Prospect, Cot, or Cash,
> That I have judg'd th'heroic Souls were rash.
> (29–42)[27]

It was a critical commonplace at the time that Crabbe was not particularly accurate in his grammar and this deficiency is evident in the quotation above. Nevertheless his point should be fairly clear. The material distress of the protagonists' situations did not seem to inhibit their choices or their activities. Trusting their hearts and their spiritual desert, they launched themselves onto a sea of trouble in spite of the overwhelming secular obstacles in their way. The irony is nicely borne by the tension between the brute word "Cash" and the supposedly noble ethereality of the "heroic Souls."

Nevertheless, the heroines and heroes get rewarded in the end, without any apparent detriment:

> Now should we grant these Beauties all endure
> Severest Pangs, they've still the speediest Cure;
> Before one Charm be wither'd from the Face,
> Except the Bloom, which shall again have place,
> In Wedlock ends each Wish, in Triumph each Disgrace.
>
> (113–17)

Suffering leaves no visible marks on the heroines whose looks and lives endure the greatest extremities. In fact, their lives redeem in kind whatever they have lost in either complexion or reputation. *The Italian* is not as naive as Crabbe's dismissal might indicate, but his argument has some validity. The providential gothic is *too* redemptive. Its theodicy is too pat. It dismisses suffering by redeeming it so instantaneously and so insistently. And this redemption is suspect because it requires the creaky narrative tricks of sudden and unforeseen coincidence: "Till some *strange* means afford a sudden view / Of some vile Plot, and every Woe adieu!" (111–12; emphasis added).

Crabbe's indictment of the gothic serves as an introduction to what he tropes as a tale of real suffering:

> These let us leave and at her Sorrows look,
> Too often seen, but seldom in a Book;
> Let her who felt, relate them: — on her chair
> The Heroine sits — in former Years, the Fair,
> Now ag'd and poor; but *Ellen Orford* knows,
> That we should humbly take what Heav'n bestows.
>
> (120–25)

What follows is a grim little tale of sin punished and virtue unrewarded. Now, if we bracket the fact that Crabbe is trying to win for poetry the "realism" accorded to the novel, we can see that he revises the gothic. He takes the suffering it describes quite seriously but rejects the easily redemptive providentialism to which it subscribes. What Ellen Orford (who is now old, ugly, poor and blind) *knows* is that redemption of her suffering will not occur on this side of the grave. She trusts in atonement. She will not kick against the pricks. Jerome McGann has seen in this story Crabbe's exploration of the ultimate groundlessness of the convention of religious faith.[28] I think it would be more accurate to say that Crabbe's critical intelligence is aimed at the all-too-easy secular providentialism that he finds in the gothic, at the willingness to claim that in the world spiritual worth can be translated readily into material wealth. By returning to the doctrine of atonement, Crabbe separates commutative from distributive justice and leaves the distributive in the hands of a just and merciful Lord.

Of course, one of the problems with the providential justification of a well-regulated world that one finds in the gothic — and this is particularly true of *The Italian* — is that while it is well-tuned to questions of gender (a point we shall return to in the next chapter), it is, not surprisingly, blind to questions of class. One of the reasons for the providential legitimation of the modern commercial order was that such an order had to account for its inequalities to those who suffered from them. While *The Italian* goes out of its way to assert the dignity of women in the new world order, it reduces the poor to villainy or sheer buffoonery. It also finds its virtues, as Crabbe points out above, in moral excellences that have little to do with the economy. To redeem the notion of a secular justice guaranteed by the market and based on spiritual qualities, one has to insist on market morality.

Malthus delineated such a morality in the second and all subsequent editions of his *Essay*. He added moral restraint to misery and vice as the great checks on population growth.[29] Restraint changes the whole complexion of his theory by allowing reason to counter the excesses of appetite. Evil is an instrument whereby the Creator warns us against injurious conduct, by which Malthus clearly means intemperance:

> If we are intemperate in eating and drinking, our health is disordered; if we indulge the transports of anger, we seldom fail to commit acts of which we afterwards repent; if we multiply too fast, we die miserably of poverty and contagious diseases. The laws of nature in all these cases are similar and uniform. They indicate to us that we followed these impulses too far . . . and if we heed not this admonition, we justly incur the penalty of our disobedience, and our suffering operates as a warning to others. (2:152)

Such then is secular retribution. If you follow a passion too far, you will suffer in this world. But you cannot simply eschew your desires:

It is acknowledged by all, that these desires put in motion
the greatest part of that activity, from which the multiplied
improvements and advantages of civilised life are derived;
and that the pursuit of these objects, and the gratification of
these desires, form the principal happiness of the larger half
of mankind, civilised or uncivilised, and are indispensably
necessary to the more refined enjoyments of the other half.
(2:153)

Passion is not in itself an evil, nor is the spirit of the domestic any
longer at odds with the conditions of scarcity that necessitate justice. Rather, the domestic becomes a sphere, interlocked with justice and the market, that has both a dignity and a function:

When we contemplate the constant and severe toils of the
greatest part of mankind, it is impossible not to be forcibly
impressed with the reflection, that the sources of human
happiness would be most cruelly diminished, if the prospect
of a good meal, a warm house, and a comfortable fireside in
the evening, were not incitements sufficiently vivid to give
interest and cheerfulness to the labours and privations of the
day. (2:154)

If the domestic provides a needed daily supplement to a life of
labor, if it makes that labor tolerable, it is also true, according to
Malthus, that the domestic affections serve as the basis for our
strivings, our life-plans, and therefore our future labor (2:154–55).

The domestic is the aim and the end of personal labor and the
laws of nature show us how to achieve that end:

If, for the sake of illustration, we might be permitted to
draw a picture of society, in which each individual endea-
voured to attain happiness by the strict fulfillment of those
duties, which the most enlightened of the ancient philosophers deduced from the laws of nature, and which have been
directly taught, and received such powerful sanctions in the
moral code of Christianity, it would present a very different
scene from that which we now contemplate. Every act,
which was prompted by the desire of immediate gratification, but which threatened an ultimate overbalance of pain,
would be considered as a breach of duty, and consequently
no man, whose earnings were only sufficient to maintain

two children, would put himself in a situation in which he might have to maintain four or five, however he might be prompted by the passion of love. This prudential restraint, if it were generally adopted, by narrowing the supply of labour in the market, would, in the natural course of things, soon raise its price. The period of delayed gratification would be passed in saving the earnings which were above the wants of a single man, and in acquiring habits of sobriety, industry, and economy, which would enable him in a few years to enter into the matrimonial contract without fear of its consequences. (2:160–61)

The duty of man (and he is gendered here) is therefore to understand that restraint, industry, economy, and sobriety are morally enjoined by the natural law and will be rewarded with secular happiness. Nor will this happiness be merely individual. General moral restraint and population control would increase wages in real terms. People would be able to save and abject poverty would be practically eliminated from society (2:161). Furthermore, these gains would lead to extraordinary general prosperity and practically universal peace (2:164–67).

Malthus has thus saved the utopian core of economic liberalism, has squared the circle between justice and desert and redeemed the future that he had previously foreclosed, not by asserting that one can see the providence of the present dispensation as he had tried before. Unlike Radcliffe, he does not present a theodicy of the conditions that already pertain. Rather, like Smith, he locates his theodicy in conditions that are possible but as yet untapped. Smith claimed that the "system of natural liberty"—that is, free trade—was natural in that it followed recognizable, providential laws. If one only adhered to nature, and took the restrictions off trade, commercial modernity would truly be able to fulfill its promises as well as lead to an even brighter, almost blinding, future. Malthus expands on Smith's belief that profit maximalisation is the engine of the natural economy. Malthus brings it home to the individual, showing how the individual can understand profit, not merely as money, but as a gain in a happiness that is spiritual as well as material. By emphasizing that prudence and sobriety and restraint are duties commanded by God and Nature, Malthus turns the market into a medium of traditional distributive justice where the morally

dutiful are recognized and rewarded by the goods that help under-
write the domestic.

Malthus's Enlightenment vision of a peace universal and justice
everlasting indicates that the relations both within and between
states will change with the change of markets. But that does not
tell us what the fit between the state and the market should be. It
does not indicate how the state should be constituted, who should
have political power, and who can justifiably be disenfranchised. In
the next two chapters, our attention will turn to questions of the
constitution and citizenship. But, as we shall see in the fifth chapter, the valorization of the domestic within liberal legitimation
raises interesting moral as well as political questions. Are women
citizens? And does the transformation of prudence and profit maximalisation into forms of virtue render an adequate portrait of a
properly ethical life?

4

Scott's Big Bow–Wow

The big bow-wow strain I can do myself like any now going; but the exquisite touch, which renders ordinary commonplace things and characters interesting, from the truth of the description and the sentiment, is denied me.
— SCOTT, *Journals*

We can get some insight into the political instincts behind Malthus's first *Essay* by looking at the fragments of a lost, unpublished manuscript of 1796 called *The Crisis*. Malthus's early biographer, Empson, saw the pamphlet and wrote that Malthus's "first object was, as a friend of freedom, to protest against Mr Pitt's administration. His second, as the friend of order and moderation, to arbitrate between extreme parties."[1] He opposed the war in Europe and the crush of taxes at home. But he was a moderate Whig, not a republican. He defined freedom in negative relation to Pitt's administration, not to the constitution as a whole. He wanted reform, not primarily to extend the definition of citizenship, but to bring "the country gentlemen"— the traditional hedge against executive usurpation — into a coalition that would bring its influence to bear in and on parliament.[2] Like many Whigs, he held the (by then) traditional notion that liberty lay in the balance of the constitution and that danger lurked when any sector accumulated too much power.[3] What is more, Malthus's stress on the country gentlemen and his belief, expressed in the first *Essay,* that agricultural and not manufacturing production created new wealth, showed an equally traditional "country" opposition to the pernicious effects of "the moneyed interests" on the hard-won liberties of 1688.

Malthus's attack on the tyranny of the Poor Laws in the first *Essay* expresses a deep fear of governmental encroachment. Malthus's Whiggish concern for the balance of constitutional freedom gets more pronounced in the revisions of the *Essay*. In the quarto of 1803, he warns the country gentlemen that they must be as diligent in protecting their rights from the government as they are in protecting their property from the poor, for "Government is a quarter in which liberty is not, nor cannot be, faithfully preserved."[4] Only if they reform the Poor Laws and educate the impoverished will both their property *and* their liberty be safe.

We will begin this chapter by looking at the way Malthus's economics and politics came into conflict with those of his greatest friend and antagonist, David Ricardo. I want to show how their ultimate disagreement over the Corn Laws and over methodology was essentially an argument about the nature of the constitution and the definition of (male) citizenship. I will then go on to discuss how their differences can help us understand the project and the constitutive limitations of the Waverley Novels.

I

In his judicious consideration of the benefits of lifting Britain's restrictions on the importation of foreign grain during the debate on the Corn Laws in 1814 and 1815, Malthus gives due weight to the positive gains of industrial progress:

> [Manufactures and commerce] infuse fresh life and activity into all classes of the state, afford opportunities for the inferior orders to rise by personal merit and exertion, and stimulate the higher orders to depend for distinction upon other grounds than mere rank and riches . . . and above all [they] give a new and happier structure to society, by increasing the proportion of the middle classes. . . .[5]

By the same token, the legislator must take great care that this economic improvement does not get out of hand and that manufactures do not completely outstrip agriculture:

> With a view to the permanent happiness and security from great reverses of the lower classes of people in this country, I should have little hesitation in thinking it desirable that its agriculture should keep pace with its manufactures, even at

the expense of retarding in some degree the growth of manufactures. . . . (119)

Malthus argues in this essay that such a retardation of manufacturing growth will benefit the laborers and the indigent. He maintains
that restrictive imports will help keep a balance between farming
and industry, will serve the poorer members of the population by
keeping the price of food—and therefore wages—high, and will
maintain agricultural labor as a ballast against the uncertain fluctuations in the industrial sector. But one of his chief arguments in his
Corn Law pamphlets is that the high capital investments that had
been poured into marginal farmlands during the Napoleonic wars
had to be protected. He fears that free trade in grain would annihi-
late those investments (120–21, 130, 139–45, 151–73). In other words,
Malthus wants to help every segment of the population. The interest
of the landlord is identical to the interest of the worker and the capitalist because a high price for grain protects *both* wages *and* capital.

The constitutional undercurrent to Malthus's argument is clear.
Manufactures tend by the nature of competition and their vulnerability to war and fashion to help foment social unrest.[6] Agriculture, when protected, provides stability against such unrest by
limiting the numbers involved in industry. Furthermore, tariffs
and restrictions maintain English autarchy. In times of war, agricultural self-sufficiency becomes a necessity for national security. So
Malthus argues that agriculture provides a beneficial anchor to
industry for political as well as for economic reasons. But, it does
more than this, although Malthus never admits it directly. Protection helps maintain the prosperity and importance of "the country
gentlemen." Restrictions on imports guard the balance of the constitution, and maintain the polity as it is (117). Even though Malthus believes in free markets on principle, he breaks rank by
arguing that the market must be tailored to the contours of the constitution. In other words, he wants to subordinate the economic
definition of man to what he considers the more important political definition of the citizen.

Malthus's most famous antagonist in the Corn Law debate was
his good friend, David Ricardo. Ricardo, working from the same
premises, comes to the exact opposite conclusions. Whereas Malthus maintains that the interest of the agricultural capitalist is no
different from that of the rest of the nation, Ricardo disagrees ada-

mantly and clearly: "The interest of the landlord is always opposed to the interest of every other class in the community."[7] The use of the term "class" is important, for Ricardo sees landlords not as "country gentlemen," not as a caste or a political power, but as a purely economic entity, just as he sees manufacturers and laborers defined by their positions in the market. Ricardo's real break from Malthus and from Smith lies in the fact that he sees economics not as an integral subdivision of statesmanship[8] but rather as a field unto itself. As Keith Tribe says of Ricardo: "For the first time it is possible to construct economic, rather than political, legal or even human agencies, which are derivative of a systematic analysis of production and distribution."[9] Ricardo's analysis is significant, not only because it pits the landlord against the rest of the community, but also because it deduces class interests from agents' positions in the matrix of production, not from their concrete or historical interests.[10]

By reconceiving economic actors this way, Ricardo can come to conclusions that directly contradict Malthus's. He argues that cheap food will increase workers' wealth, not decrease it. Free importations will benefit the whole community by raising real wages and freeing capital from unprofitable forms of agriculture for more profitable outlets in industry and commerce (4:35–36, 39–41). Ricardo gladly sacrifices the dream of autarchy for national growth and world trade:

> If we were left to ourselves, unfettered by legislative enactments, we should gradually withdraw our capital from the cultivation of such lands, and import the produce which is at present raised upon them. The capital withdrawn would be employed in the manufacture of such commodities as would be exported in return for the corn. Such a distribution of part of the capital of a country, would be more advantageous, or it would not be adopted. (4:32)

This notion will become Ricardo's concept of comparative advantage: every country will produce what is most profitable for it and will trade its manufactures with its neighbors for the goods it lacks. Every nation will do what it is best at, and everyone's wealth will increase. The countries of the world will be joined in an enormous mutually beneficial market based on an international division of labor (1:132–33).

This move towards globalism will entail a shift of wealth within the nation itself. The landlords' loss will lead to the "increased opulence of the commercial classes" (4:36) who are understood in terms of the market, not the state. And such a shift proves that the state's protection of the landlord is "unnatural." If landlords need to be protected, then capital is misused if it remains with them. Freedom cannot be protected by privilege. Natural liberty requires the abolition of restrictive monopolies so that capital can naturally seek the greatest profit. Protectionism is thus a form of economic conservatism that seeks to stop improvement and to limit wealth (4:41). Where Malthus sees the demands of particular interests as an integral part of the interest of the community and the state, Ricardo understands those particular interests as impediments to the good of the community, the state, and the world. Where Malthus seeks mediations between the individual and the whole—be it the nation or the world of nations—Ricardo does not seem interested in circuit breakers between the particular and the totality.

This aspect of Ricardo's thought becomes clear in his correspondence with Hutches Trower on parliamentary reform and his first (though posthumous) article on the subject. Ricardo stands against privilege and sectional interest, be they based on class or region. He is an enthusiast for that rather abstract entity, "the people": "There is no class in the community whose interests are so clearly on the side of good government as the people,—all other classes may have private interests opposed to those of the people" (7:261). "The people" turns out to be an economic class, not a political body. But because it is an amalgam that consists of all classes "excluding all those, whether high or low" whose interests are "distinct from the general interest" (5:498), it has a political position. This position is defined by its place in the state which is here conceived as an enormous market. In other words, Ricardo imagines the state conforming to the flow of production and distribution.

Trower argues with Ricardo at great length about reform and is a fierce partisan of the balanced constitution. As it happens, so is Ricardo, at least rhetorically. But where Trower is worried that the Commons will swamp the monarchy and the aristocracy, Ricardo is worried that the Commons has already been swamped. Trower wants to maintain a balance already struck, while Ricardo feels that the balance has already been lost. Trower wants to keep "opinion"— the *vox populi*—outside parliament:

In fact my fear is, that House of Commons should really become *too popular*—for, should such be the case, there is no sufficient power in the other branches of the Constitution to control it. I prefer therefore, that the public opinion upon sufficient emergencies operate from *without*, than constantly predominate *within*. (7:310)

Trower feels that Commons serves as a buffer between "the people" and the aristocracy, while Ricardo thinks that opinion, "as manifested through the means of the Press" (7:298) (and therefore mediated through the market) is the only buffer that can stop a jealous Government, which is dominated by atavistic interests.

Ricardo and Trower argue past each other, just as Ricardo and Malthus did.[11] Trower wants to make sure that all the mediations between the different branches of the constitution remain intact. His is the moderate Whig sense—shared by Malthus—that freedom is only maintained by an intricate balance between monarchy, aristocracy, and democracy. Ricardo, remarkably unimpressed by the traditional agencies of British politics, wants to remake the constitution.

It is important to note that Ricardo's reform of the constitution is meant to maintain the stability of the state. In a letter to James Mill, written not long after the epistolary debate with Trower, Ricardo makes an important claim:

Reform is the most efficacious preventative of Revolution, and may in my opinion be at all times safely conceded. The argument against reform now is that the people ask for too much, and that Revolution is really meant . . . I think the disaffected would lose all power after the concession of Reform. (8:49–50)

Notice that Ricardo does not think that reform will satisfy the disaffected. It won't, but it *will* take away their polemical power. So reform and revolution are not the same thing, for reform will bring the market and the constitution closer together and will not overturn either. Reform will not abolish private property nor will it redistribute wealth. The man who owns just a little property knows how precarious his holding is. The small-scale freeholder senses how important his freedom is both for him and for the country as a whole. Such a man, vigilant over his property, would be the last person to take another's away (8:50–51).

Now, it is hard to tell if Ricardo's economics influenced his views on the constitution or vice versa, although one has to admit that he developed his economic thought before he prepared his statements on reform. Of course, the same cannot be said of Malthus, whose written opinions on politics preceded and then accompanied his published contributions to economic theory. Thus a causal analysis would seem to falter and become rather redundant here. But the account I have given so far is not fair to Malthus. It indicates that while Ricardo was able to integrate his thought, Malthus was more than willing to sacrifice scientific rigor for political prejudice. Actually, nothing could be farther from the case. In his *Principles of Political Economy* first published in 1820, Malthus shows how rigorous his contribution actually was and how strong his differences from Ricardo could be.

One of the chief assumptions of Ricardo's theory is an axiom that has come to be known as Say's Law, that is, that production will generate exactly enough income to purchase all that has been produced and that *all* that income will be spent on that produce. There is thus no gap between demand and production. Every material good that finds its way to market will be sold. This providential view of a self-regulating market has very little place for what Smith called "unproductive" labor (labor that is devoted to services) and little tolerance for "unproductive" consumption (consumption that is not geared towards further production). Servants, musicians, preachers, magicians, and rentiers are thus drains on the wealth of a nation. They consume, but they do not add anything of material value to the commonwealth.

Malthus rejects this view. In the first edition of his *Principles* (the edition on which Ricardo commented), Malthus argues that demand is not necessarily so closely correlated to production:

It has been repeatedly conceded, that the productive classes have the power of consuming all that they produce; and, if this power were adequately exercised, there might be no occasion, with a view to wealth, for unproductive consumers. But it is found by experience that, though there may be the power, there is not the will; and it is to supply this will that a body of unproductive consumers is necessary. Their specific use in encouraging wealth is, to maintain such a balance between produce and consumption as to give the greatest exchangeable value to the results of national industry.[12]

Malthus's argument works this way. The surplus that is created by productive labor cannot be consumed by the laborers themselves, for this surplus is made possible by the fact that the product commands more than their wages can buy. We know from experience that the capitalists will not consume the surplus because they need to turn some of their revenues into capital. Thus there will always be a margin where in fact production will exceed the capacity of the productive consumers. To put it in Malthus's terms, the capitalists lack the will and the workers lack the power to consume all that is produced (2:431; see also 6:131–32). In order to grow, a market requires a class that can soak up the surplus without adding to it. It requires an unproductive class: "There must therefore be a considerable class of other consumers, or the mercantile classes could not continue extending their concerns, and realizing their profits. In this class the landlords no doubt stand pre-eminent" (2:224). Those who do not produce material value are still important for the wealth of the nation, for they provide the demand that stimulates growth. Malthus is quite clear in his firm revision of Say's law: "It is unquestionably true that wealth produces wants; but it is a still more important truth, that wants produce wealth" (2:248). Demand precedes supply and generates production and more wealth.

One can hear Ricardo spluttering in his marginalia on this argument:

> How can unproductive consumption increase profits? Commodities consumed by unproductive consumers are given to them, not sold for an equivalent. They have no price—how can they increase profits?
> Mr. Malthus has defined demand to be the will and power to consume. What power has an unproductive consumer? Will the taking 100 pieces of cloth from a clothiers [sic] manufactory, and clothing soldiers and sailors with it, add to his profits? Will it stimulate him to produce?—yes, in the same way as a fire would. (2:424–25)

As far as Ricardo is concerned, unproductive consumption cannot possibly add to wealth because it does not consume to create new value. Such consumption serves the same function as sheer destruction. By subtracting wealth and creating demand, it stimulates new production to replace the old. Ricardo is willing to grant that unproductive classes of people are "useful for other purposes but not in any degree for the production of wealth" (2:422).

One could say that the difference between Malthus and Ricardo is one of perspective, although such a judgment might diminish the real conflicts here. Ricardo, the reductionist, concentrates on production; Malthus, the statist, tries to construct a more complex map of production and consumption, and in so doing provides not only a political defense of the landed gentry but an economic grounding for that defense. Not only are the gentry and the rentier class important for the stability of the constitution; they serve as the engine of economic growth.

Of course, with hindsight (and with more than half-a-century of Keynesian economics) we can see what is at stake in Malthus's argument beyond special pleading for the "unproductive." Malthus allows respect to those elements of society whose labor and consumption are not caught in the nexus of production. He grants them an important place in both the state and the market. And his defense is not limited in theory to those men who live in the manor or the vicarage. In fact, Malthus sees further than Ricardo because he recognizes the importance of those people who do not produce value but still take part in the system. He sees that servants and middle-class women are part of the bigger picture. He wants to extend the dignity — that is the recognition and standing — of citizenship (although, as constitutional traditionalist, not the legal status) beyond the limits that even as apparently foresighted a thinker as Ricardo would cede.

To describe the market is to make points about the state; to understand the relationship between economics and politics one has to develop a definition of the citizen who appears centrally in both realms. The problems addressed in the Malthus-Ricardo debates were obviously not limited to the sphere of economic theory. To see how these considerations get reworked in the Waverley novels, let us now look at Scott's own professions of politics. After the "Peterloo massacre" of 1819, when the magistrates of Manchester sent ill-trained troops to disperse a large crowd of working class radicals, Scott wrote his antireform pamphlet, *The Visionary*. In a pseudo-Bunyanesque allegory, whose language and metaphors owe much to Hannah More's equally Burkean pamphlet, "Village Politics," Scott attacks universal suffrage as the prelude to anarchy. Although Scott claimed proudly that he once came across a laborer reading the work aloud to his mates,[13] *The Visionary* is not addressed to working men nor is it particularly kind to them. Rather, it is targeted at reform-minded Whigs who are leading the people astray by agitating them.[14] Scott sees himself engaged in a "war of opinion,"[15] a metaphor that becomes literalized as Scott's allegory progresses. A mob, excited but not controlled by a canting, hypocritical Whig, launches into a class war that ends in apocalyptic destruction, massive redistribution of wealth, grinding poverty, and, following the logic of Burke's *Reflections*, military dictatorship. Responsibility for the catastrophe does not lie with the people who cannot help being caught up in their petty interests, but with their self-appointed leaders, who mistake political reform for economic improvement. This fine categorical distinction is beyond the people who are by necessity below the threshold of politics, for they are in no position to know better, no position to know their own interests.[16]

Scott's fears that political reform will spill over into massive and destructive redistribution of property and power indicate that he adopts the division, which becomes clear in the Malthus-Ricardo debate, between political and economic definitions of the state. It is a well-established fact that Scott was deeply imbued with Scottish Enlightenment thought. It is helpful (but not necessary for our conclusions) that we can trace a direct line, not only from Burke to Scott, but also from Smith to Scott. Dugald Stewart, Smith's student, taught Scott at the University of Edinburgh in the early 1790s, and we know from the researches of Forbes, Garside, and Sutherland, that Scott was well acquainted with Smith's works.[17] But, as we have seen and will see again, this legacy is an inheritance of related problems, not solutions. For if politics and the market are to be articulated, then as economics become a social not a moral science, manners (the realm of anthropological study and political speculation) will have to take center stage in order to ensure the maintenance of equity. The ancient constitution will become even less a political lodestar and more a sociological and an interpersonal norm. At base we can see the great difficulty that this articulation entails: which should be given precedence—the constitution or the market? In the next section of this chapter, I will investigate the way that Scott, in *Waverley*, tries to negotiate these difficulties by mapping political, economic, and personal histories onto each other. Like Smith's attempt to square the circle between distributive and commutative justice, this compromise will result in a work of great persuasive power but of great instability, for the legitimating thrust of *Waverley* is to prove that economic growth, the very promise of progress, will settle all political claims.

II

It is something more than a glib commonplace to claim that *Waverley, or 'Tis Sixty Years Since*[18] is a novel obsessed with situation and distance. A narrative which lays great stress on topographical as well as historical accuracy, its first chapter plays, as is well known, with the generic ambiguity of its title and the concomitant ambiguity of the novel's own position. Neither a gothic romance nor a spicy tale of contemporary manners, the novel takes place in the middle distance of the reign of George II and is therefore both a romance and a tale of manners, or neither. It threatens, from its title on, to be a novelty—either a hybrid form (a romance of manners) or a completely new kind of book. As it turns out, this generic novelty uses that point in the middle distance to mediate between manners and romance; that is, it invokes history to subsume (or sublate) the apparent dichotomy between the fantasies of the romance and the documentary acerbities of manners.

Scott is able to find a ground that will allow manners, romance, and history to meet and cross-pollinate in the very notion of history itself. His narrator argues that the novel that follows will emphasize "the characters and passions of the actors;—those passions common to men in all *stages* of society" (35; emphasis added). Thus while manners and social customs provide a "necessary colouring" (36) to these essential passions, the colorings are nothing more than interesting epiphenomena, different hatchings within a firm outline. But Scott, by claiming that society has stages, shows that he does not see human history as a featureless continuum given to fancy dress, but rather has adopted the basic tenet of Scottish "conjectural history." The speculative historians of the Scottish Enlightenment, following the lead of Samuel Puffendorf, turned history into a science by reducing human community to the twin needs of self-preservation and self-reproduction, and then charting the development of society through four stages marked by increasingly complicated technologies for obtaining and distributing the necessities of life.[19] Smith, in his lectures on the law, is admirably succinct: "There are four distinct states which mankind passes through. 1st the age of Hunters; 2nd, the age of Shepherds; 3rd, the age of Agriculture; 4th, the age of Commerce." But Smith does not try to prove his point historically, through the marshalling of documentary evidence, but rather through a thought experiment in which "10 or 12 persons of different sexes" settle on an island. In this sociable rewriting of *Robinson Crusoe,* the castaways "naturally" move from simple hunting and gathering through increased opulence and division of labor to the sophisticated and populous age of commerce.[20] As in Book Three of *The Wealth of Nations,* the actual historical record of a given country might vary from this template, but the model itself in its reductive logic provides a way of measuring both development and deviation.

There is thus no contradiction between the deep historicism of this sociology and Scott's appeal to the unchanging nature of the human heart, of the passions, of Nature itself: "It is from the great book of Nature, the same through a thousand editions . . . that I have venturously essayed to read a chapter to the public" (36). Conjectural history is grounded on the permanence of the human drive for satisfaction and self-preservation. Thus Scott is able to maintain that there is a perfect adequation between Nature, History, and *Waverley,* for history, understood conjecturally, is based on "man's" "natural" drive for self-preservation and is plotted diachronically across different stages of development. Furthermore, *Waverley* investigates precisely the transitional moment between stages as it depicts the unnegotiable conflict between the feudal Highlanders and the solid modernity of Hanoverian society.

Early in *Waverley,* Flora Mac-Ivor expresses the hope that the Scottish country gentleman will one day be "a scholar . . . a sportsman . . . and a judicious improver." Scott's narrator, with the divine gift of hindsight, writes: "Thus did Flora prophesy a revolution, which time indeed has produced, but in a manner very different from what she had in mind" (183). Flora, as it turns out, misunderstands the revolution she predicts: it will not be political, but economic. It will not depend on the King or the Parliament, but rather on what citizens, secure in the spheres of the private and the social (that is, below the threshold of political consideration and demand) are able to make of themselves and their lives. Flora makes an important category error, for she collapses the two spheres that civic jurisprudential theory worked so hard to separate. Such a collapse and such an incomprehension, make civil war more likely and are therefore more dangerous. Modern civic jurisprudence, we should remember, was born of the experience of the confessional wars of the seventeenth century and, as we can see from Grotius on, served as a critique of warfare which (in the spirit of such critiques) sought to limit both its occurrence and its scope. The differentiation of the spheres of life and the emphasis on rights were both intended as curbs on unrest, as protections against the incursions of other individual citizens, the sovereign, or other states. It follows, then, in the logic of this thought that the transgression of the protective boundaries can only result in violent conflict, arbitrated by force, not by law. Flora does not understand modern natural law. Her sense of right is feudal-aristocratic and therefore her sense of politics is outmoded, just as the ambience she creates is atavistic. *Waverley* thus shows that the desire to fold the economic into the political is as regressive as the Jacobite cause with all its romantic trappings.

The narrator makes it a point to note in the last chapter of the novel that the infusion of wealth and the growth in commerce that followed the Jacobite uprising of 1745 have completely transformed Scotland for the better (492). But the irony of the restoration of Scotland and its country gentlemen to wealth is that it is based on the eradication of the Jacobites who, like Flora, have (mis)imagined such a restoration in the first place. The cunning of history lies in the fact that the would-be revolutionaries are shown to be the retarding force against the very change they desire. Civil war is the recourse of the anachronistic—it is an anachronism—and wipes out the anachronistic parties that foment it. Scott lists the defiant provincialism of the Jacobites, their jealous maintenance of "ancient Scottish manners," and their dislike of English company and customs (492) as necessary casualties of economic modernization. So we can say that "ancient manners" (a phrase Scott returns to more than once in the last paragraphs of his novel), like Jacobite politics, stand in opposition to progress.

The authority of the novel's narrator, that voice which occludes the difference between the subjectivity of experience and the supposed objectivity of the progress of history in the last chapter of *Waverley*, is derived from the fact that it, unlike the younger Edward and the Jacobite Flora, understands its position at the apogee of history. It shows that economic ends are not to be pursued by political means, that the dream of an arms-bearing, assertive masculinity has to be outgrown personally as well as historically. Thus one can claim that the distance between the narrator and Waverley himself, a distance vigilantly monitored by the narrator's ironies at the young man's expense, narrows by the end of the novel, thus allowing the narrator to assume an autobiographical, first-person singular in the last chapter. We can claim, therefore, that Waverley is so well assimilated to the very fabric of what the novel tropes to be history, that he, like the narrator, can assume the very position and voice of History itself.

Scott makes a similar case in *Redgauntlet* (1824), which, as Lockhart notes, was originally read as a reworking of *Waverley*.[21] Over the years, the novel's reputation has suffered from its formal oddity: it begins as an epistolary novel but switches, midstream, to the third-person narration more standard to the Waverley novels.[22] The narrative begins with an exchange between two friends, between Darsie Latimer, a rich young man of mysterious parentage and his rather staid friend, Alan Fairford. They are both supposed to be studying Scots law, but Darsie has decamped from Edinburgh in search of adventure. In the marches, in the flats that separate England from Scotland, Darsie meets and is subsequently kidnapped by his uncle, the dashing, dangerous, and monomaniacal Jacobite whose name provides the title of the novel. Darsie is very much in his uncle's thrall until the older man tries to argue him into joining the cause of the now-aging Young Pretender. Darsie refuses, and in so doing, pledges allegiance to English law and the Hanoverian succession, rather than to the outmoded, patriarchal rights of the exiled Stuarts. Whereas Alan Fairford's story has been subsumed into the general narration before this point (he has only served as a counterpoint to Darsie), Darsie has been allowed to manifest his rebellious (or aberrant) subjectivity in first-person letters and diaries. Soon after he eschews his uncle's cause, however, he too is narrated by a third person. Less a sign of novelistic incompetence than a rigorous thematic logic, this move from one mode of narration to another signals Darsie's full integration into modernity, his full understanding and acceptance of his historical situation.

We can therefore recuperate from a fierce literalism of Lukacs's notion that Scott's novels turn on their emphasis on representative men and women, people who embody in their passions the tendencies of larger sociopolitical transformations.[23] The representative position in the novel is not the passionate commitment of Fergus Mac-Ivor (which is completely out of step with the progress of the world as described by conjectural history) but the narrator's—that of a man or a woman who sees the present in its full historical determination. Or, if Waverley is the representative man, it is because he comes to understand the present through its direct confrontations with the self-destructive powers of past stages of development. One needs—whether one is the narrator, the hero, or the reader of this tale—a point in the distance so that one can measure one's progress. This image is Scott's own. Writing of the meteoric development of the Scottish economy since the '45, the narrator maintains that the transformation can easily go unnoticed:

> [T]he change, though steadily and rapidly progressive, has, nevertheless, been gradual; and like those who drift down the stream of a deep and smooth river, we are not aware of the progress we have made, until we fix our eye on the now distant point from which we have drifted. (492)

Though one would do well to remember the paroxysms that serve as the enabling condition for this peacefulness, let us note here that the drift is apparently without purpose. One literally goes with the flow. It is this lack of intention that requires the precisions of historical triangulation. The past is a necessary construct for the self-definition of the present. The poverty of *Waverley*'s Scotland is as important a reminder for the nation as "the spirited painting" of Fergus and Waverley in Highland dress, created after the defeat of the uprising and given a place of honor at Tully-Veolan, is for the Baron and for Waverley (489). The picture—an aesthetic object no less than the book in which it appears—is a timely souvenir of time itself.

The drift of economic progress is an odd image, for it seems to indicate that there is no agency involved. Economic development just happens. But behind Scott's apparent rejection of revolutionary action stands the fine Smithian conviction that the genius of the market, the movement of the now-too-famous "invisible hand," depends on a certain limitation of individual vision. The

market works best when each person works for his or her own personal gain, thus directing the flow of capital and goods in the most
efficient and efficacious way. The daily pursuit of private wealth is
the real engine of long-term growth and refinement. So, not only
is national progress the product of the energies of the social and the
private spheres, it is the *unintended* consequence of those energies.
Flora, who is remarkable for the cold firmness of her will, expresses a fine contempt for Waverley when she describes him to
Rose Bradwardine as a man less at home on the battlefield than "in
the quiet circle of domestic happiness, lettered indolence, and elegant enjoyments" (370). The accuracy of her description offsets the
scant value she places on the life of the dilettante reader and judicious improver of his property. Flora, of course, does not understand that, in terms of the conjectural history on which this novel
is based, it is the picturesque improver who is the true agent of history. He—and only he—will enact irreversible and far-reaching
change.

Of course, Scott's economic legitimation of Hanoverian rule in
the all-important postscript is relegated to the novel's frame and
cannot be incorporated into the narrative itself. While the narrative
can retail the cataclysmic moment when one stage gives way to
another (and it is significant that the change can only be imagined
as violent), it cannot actually represent the new age, except nega-
tively or rather, by contrast. The Regency present is a future that
cannot be imaged forth. We can speculate on the reason for this.
Perhaps the most significant reason, to which we shall return, lies
in the novel's inability to turn economic system into novelistic narrative, to create an adequate figure for economic man, that is, of a
spectral actor who is only conceivable as such in a complex network of other actors who are constituted by reference to an equally
abstract entity known as the market. Economic thought, even in
the case of the historical tale of the third volume of *The Wealth of
Nations*, deals with classes of people, distinguished less by anthropological peculiarities than by their speculative relations in the
nexus of production and exchange. Scott's novel, on the other
hand, has strongly political implications and centers on the pathos
of choice, not on the odd retrospective symmetries of capital flow.
Waverley is a book about the temptations of insurrection and the
lure of transition, not the glories of the market.

To understand the novel's pedagogical intent and therefore its structure, we would do well to note that it attempts to legitimize its position in the literary marketplace through the quotation from *2 Henry IV* on the title page. The *genius loci* of Scott's production is, of course, Shakespeare, who from Walpole on served as the great legitimator for oddities and excursions in the practice of the novel as well as for the very form of the novel itself. But, whereas Walpole invokes Shakespeare's tragedies as license for his gothic romance,[24] Scott summons forth the author of the *Henriad* as his tutelary spirit. Shakespeare is taken as a writer who can frame civil war with comedy, and who matches the outmoded Hotspurs, Mortimers, and Glendowers with the very image of the modern prince, Prince Hal. These cues thus provide illustrious precedent for Scott's fiction and allow us to describe *Waverley*'s plot as a comic romance in which the hero's wanderings across a Jacobite landscape find their fitting end in marriage and a title. The denouement of *Waverley* is remarkably recuperative, especially when one considers the fact that the main characters all fought on the losing side of a civil war. Of course, Fergus Mac-Ivor, the Jacobite firebrand, and his retainer, Evan Dhu, are executed. By the same token their deaths ensure that Tully-Veolan, the central piece of Lowland real estate in the tale, is restored to its rightful owner and that the depredations committed against its fabric are repaired. The recuperations of the plot require a remarkably sacrificial violence.

What is destroyed, of course, is the stuff that fills young Edward Waverley's dreams, the romance of the Highlands and its political attachments. The novel ends in Tully-Veolan, not in the sublime landscapes of Glennaquoich; but the Highland landscapes serve as the topographical center of Waverley's fantasies. Early on, Flora Mac-Ivor, apparently understanding the sensibility of her guest and her own abilities to stage the scene (177), leads the hapless Waverley into her favorite "haunt." The seduction is complete. Waverley passes into the glen "like a knight of romance" and the vista itself becomes nothing less than "the land of romance" (175). Appropriately, Flora is also framed by the language of romance:

> The wild beauty of the retreat, bursting upon him as if by magic, augmented the mingled feeling of delight and awe with which he approached her, like a fair enchantress of Boiardo or Ariosto, by whose nod the scenery around seemed to have been created, an Eden in the wilderness. (177)

In fact, as the narrator tells the reader, Flora has created this garden, but not with a nod: it has been carefully planted to appear absolutely natural (176). Waverley is blind to the wonderful manipulations of which Flora proves herself to be so very capable, for his education (or rather mis-education) in the literature of his grandfather's house has led him to aspire to the condition of romance itself.

Waverley can step into a series of scenes culled from literature, can overstep the apparent ontological threshold that distinguishes the literary from the real, because he has traveled back in time as he travels across Scotland. Because Scotland is poorer and more primitive than its southern neighbor, its politics and its social structures (as we see on the lowland estate as well as in the Highlands) are literally wonderful anachronisms. The uneven development of Britain has left the Highlands as an odd amalgam of ancient economics and feudal politics, a hold-out of chivalry in the modern world. Chivalric romance (like its correlate in this novel, the sublime) is the mark of the anachronistic. Since *Don Quixote*, of course, romance has suffered as the butt of the novel—the "untruth" of romance is as canonical a theme as one can find. In *Don Quixote*, though, the romance is not only suspect because it lacks the epistemological base of probability or truth but also because the books that Quixote reads are outdated. Chivalry (like the pastoral idylls that Cervantes parodies) belong to a different period of social development. The impoverished hidalgo's insistence that inns are castles shows to what extent the world has changed: hospitality is no longer feudal, paternalistic, and bound by codes of honor, but depends on the precisions of monetary exchange.

Accordingly, Waverley's Scotland is the site of historical regression as is Jacobitism. When Waverley meets Charles Edward Stuart, he finds that the young prince "answered his ideas of a hero of romance" (295). And it is Waverley who recognizes both the romantic and the sublime qualities of the wild scene at Glennaquoich. Of course, sublimity, by definition, depends on the viewer's response: it is a psychological reaction that is re-projected on the objects that cause it. So the play of the romantic and the sublime says as much about Edward as it does about Scotland, Charles Edward, and Flora. *Redgauntlet*'s leading ingenue, Darsie Latimer, is, as we noted above, cut from the same cloth as Waverley. When he first meets Herries of Birrenswirk, the Redgauntlet of the title, he writes to his friend that he could only see the older man in terms of "the ancient heroes, to whom I might assimilate the noble form and countenance before me."[25] But where Waverley is most fascinated by romance, Darsie is more impressed by the terrifying aspects of the sublime. Not surprisingly, Darsie always describes Redgauntlet in terms that Burke reserved for the sublime: awe, terror, delight.[26] Of course, Darsie is less willing to take on the Stuart cause. Unlike Waverley, he is not tempted to fight for the prince. Nevertheless, both novels chart the spell that an aristocratic past with Jacobite inflections can cast over a modern, commercial spirit. Furthermore, *Waverley* and *Redgauntlet* are careful to illustrate the inadequacy of this past for this present. In each one, the young hero moves from romantic-sublime reveries to a full acceptance of the course of history. It is not hard to read Waverley's realization that with his defection from the Pretender's forces "the romance of his life was ended, and that its real history had now commenced" (415) as a shift from his previous inclination to read romance in terms of wonder to his final rejection of it as anachronism. Romance — in its full flush — can, as Scott argues in an article on the subject in the *Encyclopaedia Britannica*, only grow on feudal, agricultural ground, and thus not on the ground of modernity.[27]

Why would young Waverley desire romance? One can argue, following the logic of a Lacan, that desire is maintained by the very law that seeks to banish it, by the affirmations and negations that sustain personal identity and social existence. If this is a helpful insight, then we can see that romance has a special claim on desire in that it stands as a negation of the existent, as a space where, by Dr. Johnson's account in *Rambler* 4, the probabilities of the known world are suspended. It stands as a model of the utopian, a place where the imperfections of human life are negated by both theme and form.[28] Romance thus has a psychologically regressive (and politically progressive) valency. It allows the wish to predominate over the chilling effects of the reality principle. For Scott, as Ina Ferris — following Hazlitt — has noted, romance also has a strongly historical and masculinist pull. To be enthralled by romance is to be able to imagine oneself in earlier, less civilized times, to imagine playing out one's masculinity on the aristocratic field of battle, not in the warehouse or the sitting room.[29] To desire romance is to want to overcome one's historical position, the limitations of one's gender and social situation.

Notice that in *Waverley* and *Redgauntlet* the desire entwined in romance is troped as a wish to go back in time. Unlike contemporary science fiction which often uses romance idealizations to figure possible, even desirable worlds, *Waverley* shows romance to be ineluctably regressive, a desire to break with the existent that is traduced by mistaking the unredeemable past as a redemptive future. Such a casting of romance puts the reader in an interesting if awkward position, for though Waverley serves as the novel's hermeneutic focus,[30] his romance desires are presented as being the reader's. The novel makes the romantic sublime the center of its interest.[31] In this regard, we should take seriously the fact that *Redgauntlet* bears its villain's name as its title, whereas *Waverley* boasts the name of the man whom Scott described as a "snivelling piece of imbecility." For if the romantic-sublime is the temptation for the young men whose lives the Waverley novels detail, the later novel makes the Jacobite its titular focus. Like that other Jacobite self-starter, Rob Roy, Redgauntlet carries the novel that bears his name even though he is, as Adolphus pointed out about other novels in the series, not technically the hero of the tale.[32] His sublimity is thus billed as one of the book's main attractions. Fergus Mac-Ivor, Brian de Bois Guilbert (*Ivanhoe*), Burley (*Old Mortality*), and even Ravenswood (*Bride of Lammermoor*) serve similar functions in their novels. They are romantic-sublime figures who fall victim to the plots they generate. They seem to exist to attract the reader (just as they attract the heroes) and then to die. Adolphus is quite explicit on the appeal of Scott's ill-fated conspirators: "Our affections and sympathies obstinately adhere to the falling, more especially if they fall bravely and becomingly; we are disposed, at the same time, to entertain something like contempt for the inglorious safety of those who survive the ruin."[33] If the violent, the Jacobite, the Covenanters, and their ilk serve as the affective centers of a good number of the more famous Waverley novels, then they present what would at first seem like a rather subversive charge. Coleridge certainly read them this way: "Walter Scott's novels are chargeable with ministering to the depraved appetite for excitement and . . . creating" sympathy for the vicious and infamous, solely because he is *daring*.[34] If the novels describe their young protagonists' progression away from the sublime and the romantic, they depend on their readers' ability to desire precisely those characters who embody those attributes most fully.

The sublime-romantic figures express what some of the Waverley novels take to be the reader's proscribed desire to overcome the merely existent. They provide the motor force for the action of the plots as well as objects for the reader (and the heroes) to invest in. Their eventual defeat serves as the moment of their exorcism. They are further isolated by the precise localization in times past and places distant. This moment of casting forth allows the plot to end, permits the necessary reconciliations to take place, and grants the reader free passage back to a redeemed present. Scott's novels thus bear witness to the energies that they summon up and then censor. If we read these books this way, we can begin to understand the paradox of Hazlitt's critique of Scott: "Through some odd process of servile logic, it would seem, that in restoring the claims of the Stuarts by the courtesy of Romance, the House of Brunswick are more firmly seated in point of fact."[35] Hazlitt and Coleridge note the same peculiarities in Scott's texts, but Coleridge is unwilling to credit them with the conservative force that Hazlitt, on the less victorious side, can see with greater clarity and greater bitterness.

By conflating history and psychology, *Waverley* is thus able to enact in what it projects as the reader's mind the same tale of development that it narrates on a micrological level (Waverley's own maturation) and on a macrological one (the birth pangs of Scottish modernity). It strengthens the reality principles which govern the present (the need for civility and the legitimacy of the Hanoverians) by giving voice to and negating what it takes to be the most potent of wishes. If the novel works through a series of analogies, where one realm is easily mapped onto another, it also works through a massive displacement. For the revolutionary dangers of 1814 did not lie in a resurgence of Jacobitism at all, but in Jacobinism. One consonant makes all the difference, for it allows Scott to trope all revolution as regression and all legitimacy as a question of succession.

That Scott can use the evidence of economic growth as a way of resolving what could be intransigent problems concerning the distribution of wealth and political power shows his indebtedness to the optimism of *The Wealth of Nations* which used growth as a way of settling the conflicting claims of commutative and distributive justice. But as we saw in the second chapter, Smith's argument is only convincing to those committed to long-term projections or to people thick in times of prosperity. A fluctuating market and periodic scarcity mean that the market cannot satisfy everyone's needs. And so, as we saw, Burke and Paine invoked political theory to supplement the deficiencies of political economics. And, as the debate between Ricardo and Malthus illustrates, the conflict between political theory and political economics could not be arbitrated by the players themselves. Rather, the "public" and thus other systems were granted the right to balance the antagonists' claims.

It goes without saying that the Tory Scott was closer to Burke than to Paine. But this allegiance meant that the teaching of his first novel was rather unstable. For, as the last chapter in *Waverley* maintains, there is a down side to the Scottish *Wirtschaftswunder*. By sweeping away prejudice, progress also destroys positive virtues such as "loyalty . . . old Scottish faith, hospitality, worth and honour" (492). By invoking the evanescence of manners, Scott specifically draws on the notion, central to conjectural history, that customs depend on the stage of material production that a society has reached. An economic transformation will necessarily entail a metamorphosis in manners. Thus the passing of old Scottish faith, hospitality, and honor is inevitable and regrettable. Modernity is not without its costs—a point that Smith made clear in *The Wealth of Nations*. But modernity is the natural environment for man as he is now and the costs, though high, are necessary and payable— according to the Scott who writes *Waverley*—in full.

III

The ease of *Waverley*'s Hanoverian triumphalism can be attributed to the fact that the novel was written in large part during the month of June 1814,[36] just two months after Napoleon's abdication. But the confidence born of victory and the ideological formations sufficient for that confidence were short lived. When the predicted and predictable postwar depression finally set in during the spring of 1816, it brought with it social unrest, mostly in the country.[37] Although discontent was most visible in the eastern counties and the Midlands, it was also noticeable in Scotland. Scott, writing to Morritt in May 1816, noted that the "disaffection among the common people" was becoming a "spirit of effervescence" which could well require the unfortunate necessity of "imposing military force . . . to preserve quiet."[38] In the shadow of this civil disorder, Scott composed *The Antiquary*, his third and, according to Lockhart, his

favorite novel.[39] What is striking about this work is that the breezy
reliance on an expanding market that ends *Waverley* is gone, as is
the willingness to concentrate on the permanence of nature at the
expense of the "ephemerality" of manners.

In *The Antiquary*, Scott is quite anxious about preserving *manners*. In the introduction to the first edition, he writes: "I have been
more solicitous to describe manners minutely than to arrange in
any case an artificial and combined narrative, and have but to regret
that I felt myself unable to unite these two requisites of a good
novel."[40] He here opposes the description of manners to the "artificiality" of a coherent plot and plumps down squarely on the side
of manners. If we judge *The Antiquary* by E. M. Forster's brutally
witty attack on its narrative vagaries, we can claim that Scott made
a horrendous mistake. This loose, baggy monster of a story— it
takes Forster a good eight pages to retell it— does not benefit from
the novelist's conscious attention to the minutiae of customary
behavior.

Forster complains of one of the characters in *The Antiquary* that
"she is just a comic turn—she leads nowhere, and your storyteller
is full of these turns. He need not hammer away all the time at
cause and effect."[41] According to this indictment, Scott stops his
plot—the consecutive drive of causality—to indulge in comic and
sentimental set-pieces that do not add to the story at all. In Forster's view, such "turns" are underdetermined and infect the plot
with their inconsequentiality. But Forster is judging this novel by
the wrong criteria: it does not claim to be a streamlined piece of
post-Flaubertian prose. For all its romance projections,[42] *The Antiquary* does not aspire to the condition of aesthetic autonomy. The
novel's notorious convolutions keep hammering away at a rather
limited set of topical problems, that is, at legitimacy, wealth, and
Catholicism. One need only have a limited acquaintance with the
politics of the postwar years to realize that Scott's preoccupations
in *The Antiquary* are the preoccupations of the press, parliamentary
debate, and radical agitation: the huge national debt, the return to
cash payments, Catholic emancipation, and the related bogey of
parliamentary reform. We can say then that Scott's insistent return
in *The Antiquary* to the same irritants is a sign that the plot and its
turns are not under- but overdetermined. My reading of the novel
will therefore seek to recuperate those "turns" that Forster so despised and see them as integral to the project of the novel.

We can enter the complicated skein of this text by taking up the question of legitimacy: it appears in at least two of the plot lines. It is tempting to agree with Francis Hart that Scott's novel is a "comic parable of Post-Napoleonic Legitimism"[43] but that would mean seeing legitimacy as a European problem. Alternatively, one could follow Judith Wilt's example and see legitimacy in the Waverley novels as a question of the impossible grounding of knowledge or possession.[44] But legitimacy in this novel is more British than Hart would admit and has more content and greater specificity than Wilt indicates. After all, the eponymous hero of *The Antiquary* makes much of his German Protestant ancestry—it keeps reappearing in the story—and the novel's romantic lead, Lovel, turns out to be the legitimate Protestant son of a Catholic Earl. Scott seems to be worrying and reasserting the legitimacy of the Hanoverian succession, based as it was, on the religion of the Electors of Hanover, not on their pressing claim to the British throne. In a preliminary way, we can say that Scott has moved from economics to religion as the basis for the legitimacy of the present dispensation. This points in an interesting direction which we shall follow shortly. It indicates that Scott's emphasis on legitimacy has directed his interests from economic to political, or rather, to social modes of integration.

But we need not restrict legitimation problems in *The Antiquary* to questions of sovereignty. The shift away from the economic valorization of the Hanoverian succession to a renewed interest in the importance of manners indicates that Scott was not happy with the grounds of Scottish modernity he explored at the end of *Waverley*. Specifically, Scott seems to have returned to a Burkean insistence on the primacy of customary manners for the legitimacy of a social order and its governing constitution. Whereas Scott subscribes in *Waverley* to a Smithian understanding of the socioeconomic contingency of manners, he seems in *The Antiquary* to explore the implications of Burke's attack on the basic premises of philosophical history. As J.G.A. Pocock has noted (and as we mentioned in the second chapter), Burke's account of the French Revolution is predicated on a reversal of Smith, for Burke claims that commercial capitalism depends on the spirit of the gentleman: it is derived from that spirit and is maintained by it. In other words, socioeconomic development is based on manners, not vice versa.[45]

In *The Antiquary*, Scott mines this vein in post-Smithian thought. In one of the most famous set-pieces of the novel, a sentimental

turn that does not aid the plot in any way, we read of the funeral
of Steenie Mucklebackit, a drowned fisherman. Jonathan Oldbuck, the Antiquary of the title, is expected to attend this funeral
since Steenie was one of his tenants. And Oldbuck is glad to go. As
he says:

> [T]ruly, as to this custom of the landlord attending the body
> of the peasant, I approve it. . . . It comes from ancient times,
> and was founded deep in the notions of mutual aid and de-
> pendence. . . . And herein, I must say, the feudal system — as
> also in its courtesy towards womankind, in which it exceeded
> — herein, I say, the feudal usages mitigated and softened the
> sternness of classical times. (273)

Compare the sentiment and the wording (especially the use of the
verb "mitigate") with Burke's famous encomium to that "mixed
system of opinion and sentiment" that is chivalry:

> It was this, which, without confounding ranks, had pro-
> duced a noble equality, and handed it down through all the
> gradations of social life. It was this opinion which mitigated
> kings into companions, and raised private men to be fellows
> with kings. Without force or opposition, it subdued the
> fierceness of pride and power; it obliged sovereigns to
> submit to the soft collar of social esteem, compelled stern
> authority to submit to elegance, and gave a domination,
> vanquisher of laws, to be subdued by manners.[46]

As we noted earlier, manners in Burke mitigate the realities of a
hierarchical social order by effecting a number of important chiastic reversals in everyday life. Under a strict code of inherited manners, social differentiation—which in Burke's account is necessary—does not disappear, but is rendered more palatable and more
just. Manners not only take the place of distributive justice: they
make the constitution work. They undermine its possible harsh-
ness by locating power not only in domination but also—and more
importantly—in mutual regard. Apart from Oldbuck's misogyny
and the odd (but I think explainable) reference to classical antiq-
uity, Oldbuck is working within Burke's terms and expectations.

  We should not be confused by Oldbuck's omission of Burke's
"soft collar of social esteem" into thinking that the Antiquary is
only interested in mutual dependence (an idea he does not find in

Burke) and that he does not do justice to the Burkean principle of mutual regard. At Steenie's funeral, Oldbuck offers to serve as chief pallbearer, an act which is deemed a "distinction on the part of the laird" by his tenants (289). This is quite a canny move on the landlord's part, for it wins the people's hearts:

> And such is the temper of the Scottish common people, that, by this instance of compliance with their customs and respect for their persons, Mr. Oldbuck gained more popularity than by all the sums which he had yearly distributed in the parish for purposes of private or general charity. (289)

Oldbuck's respect is an act of recognition. He gains the respect of the poor by observing their customs and their wishes. These customs are, of course, not the landlord's, for the tenants and the laird seem to be divided by more than wealth. The gulf between Mucklebackit and Oldbuck is as much a sign of anthropological and linguistic difference as it is of economic disparity. Or rather, economic disparity is understood in anthropological terms.

Oldbuck is not, however, cynically manipulating the affections of his tenants. Scott goes out of his way to show us that Oldbuck is that good eighteenth-century cliché, the Man of Feeling: The sentimental set-piece in which Scott describes the Mucklebackits' grief (chapter 31) is punctuated by the Antiquary's ill-disguised tears (287, 288; see also 309). It is for this reason, perhaps, that Lady Abercorn thought that Henry Mackenzie, author of *The Man of Feeling*, had written *The Antiquary*. Nevertheless, for all his sincerity, the good laird is well served by his respect for the poor around him. When Oldbuck asks Saunders Mucklebackit how it is that he can work on the day of his son's funeral, the fisherman answers him with a blast of caste consciousness that Virginia Woolf particularly admired: "It's weel wi' you gentles, that can sit in the house wi' handkerchers at your een when ye lose a friend; the like of us maun to our wark again, if our hearts were beating as hard as my hammer" (307). This expression of resentment betokens a special danger. The novel is supposed to take place in another period of economic depression, in 1797 and early 1798, when threats of an invasion from abroad were matched by the fears of insurrection at home. This spirit of effervescence has spread even to Scott's fictitious Scotland. The poor are vocal in their anger, and they are organized. There is a jacobin club in Fairport, the town near Oldbuck's small estate.

But Mucklebackit's anger quickly disappears when the Antiquary offers his help. In fact, Saunders gives a moving testimonial, not only to Oldbuck's kindness, but also to the precariousness of his position:

> Ye were aye kind and neighbourly . . . and I hae often said in thae times when they were ganging to raise up the puir folk against the gentles — I hae often said, ne'er a man should steer a hair touching to [Oldbuck] while Steenie and I could wag a finger; and so said Steenie too. (308)

Whenever warfare between castes has seemed imminent in the past—and notice that Mucklebackit indicates that the poor have been ready to cut their betters' throats a number of times — Oldbuck has been saved by the loyalty of his tenants. Oldbuck has good reason to speak of the "mutual dependence" that exists between landlord and peasant: his safety depends on the good will of the people.

But if manners, custom, and mutual recognition provide stability to otherwise volatile social relations, they also serve to shore up that somewhat more anonymous entity, the state. When the fears of a French invasion seem to come true, Oldbuck is surprised to see that the licensed beggar, Edie Ochiltree, is ready and willing to fight in spite of his poverty and his age. But Edie's patriotism does not depend on his possessions, and his determination pleases Oldbuck: "Bravo, bravo, Edie! The country's in little ultimate danger when the beggar's as ready to fight for his dish as the laird for his land" (401). As it happens, the general muster of volunteers brings out Edie, the pacific Oldbuck, and all the burghers of the town as well as the poor. Fairport is quite overrun with would-be soldiers. To garrison this new-model army, the magistrates decide to share their own goods with everyone who has turned out: "We have made ourselves wealthy under a free and paternal government, and now is the time to show we know its value" (406). This pledge of allegiance is greeted with "a loud and cheerful acquiescence"(406). Harry Shaw has suggested that class tensions in this novel are healed by the threat of invasion, but such a claim does limited justice to the last chapter of *The Antiquary*.[47] Paternalistic regard for the customs and the needs of others seems to be the point here. It heals the social divisions that the book has invoked. The rich insure loyalty through the largesse they provide in the name of a government which itself is "free and paternal."

Thus paternalism insures freedom as well as loyalty. It should be noted that this notion cuts in a number of ways, for liberty is guarded from the jealousy of government itself by the privileges that have been instituted in the past. Edie Ochiltree is a licensed beggar, a member of a protected and honored order of mendicants. As Lovel points out, in England, in the age of the Old Poor Law, "such a mendicant would get a speedy check" for his insubordinations; in Scotland, however, he is, as Oldbuck argues, "a sort of privileged nuisance" (35). But though his cheekiness might be a nuisance to Oldbuck at times, it is Edie's freedom and knowledge that save the day — and the course of the novel. For it is Edie who connects the different strands of the story and whose help is invaluable for the denouement. He unwittingly brings Glenallan and Oldbuck together, helps save Sir Arthur, and provides important aid in the discovery of Lovel's true identity.

Edie can be said to stand for freedom. That is, at least, his self-presentation. When he seeks to avoid questioning in court, he says:

> Sae neighbour, ye may just write down that Edie Ochiltree, the declarant, stands up for the liberty — na, I maunna say that neither, I am nae Liberty Boy; I hae fought agan them in the riots in Dublin. . . . Ay write that Edie Ochiltree, the Blue-Gown, stands up for the prerogative . . . of the subjects of the land. . . . (339)

Edie, whose freedom depends on an ancient royal patent, identifies himself not with the newfangled "Liberty Boys" (and it is worth remembering that Scott himself broke the pates of Irish Jacobins in Edinburgh in the 1790s) but with the established rights of the King's subjects, with the liberties and prerogatives that inhere in the traditions of the law. Like Darsie Latimer in *Redgauntlet*, he defines himself in terms of his rights as a free-born subject of the British crown. Just as manners are the expression of what is best for the present from the past, freedom is, as Burke would say, an inheritance, protected not by reason but by recognized and recognizable custom.

We can thus claim that the country Scott depicts is in little ultimate danger because everyone is protected by a wide variety of manners and freedom is protected by privilege. The lower castes are bound by loyalty to their betters and the burghers are loyal to a government which allows them liberty while still remaining "paternal." Manners, recognition, and respect serve as the glue that keeps the state together and binds the castes in such a way as to create a positive sense of mutual dependence. Scott describes a ladder of ascent that leads from individual interactions to the nation as a whole. As in Burke's *Reflections*, *The Antiquary* shows that we do not come immediately to our love of the state. We move from our families to our country through what Burke elsewhere calls "the analogical principle," that is, through different levels of identification until we reach the state itself, hence the importance of Scotland for Scott and the "habitual provincial connections" he associates with it. Scotland is a way-station between the individual and the Hanoverian ascendancy.

We have therefore recovered some of the urgency that Scott lends to the notion of regional manners, but have not yet discovered why manners should get in the way of the plot as much as Forster seems to think they do. If we allow a subjective reaction to serve as a foreground estimate of *The Antiquary*, we can say that while there is a fair amount of movement in the novel, very little actually happens in the book. Most of the comings and goings in the tale are actually antiquarian, or as Francis Hart has noted, retrospective.[48] It thus bears a strong relation to *The Italian*. Apart from a harrowing escape from a cliff, some dubious financial dealings, a couple of trips to an abandoned monastery, and a duel, the characters devote their time to unravelling past mysteries. The big threat of the story—the impending French invasion—never takes place, but fizzles out into a false alarm at the end. Compare the constantly anticlimactic narrative of the novel to the action in *Waverley*. Where *Waverley* relates ancient manners to rebellion and makes those manners the engine of the uprising and the plot, *The Antiquary* deploys manners against the disruptions that Scott has hitherto considered as the necessary preconditions of narrativity itself. The structure of the novel and its thematics are very close indeed.

Scott's early novels seem therefore to be caught in a tension between the seductions of economic modernization and the demands of political stability, between inoculating the reader from the seductions of anachronism and inviting the very same reader to invest in the anachronisms that maintain the British constitution. We can say, however, that *Waverley* and *The Antiquary* work in exactly the same way. They both mine the past for the fascinations it holds. They just come to value that past, those anachronisms,

differently. *Waverley* wants the reader to be an economic modern-
ist; *The Antiquary* tropes its reader as an antiquary, a political an-
thropologist. And here we can see how the novel and the study of
economics fully differentiate themselves from each other. For
Scott's novels are concerned with the way economics affect a pre-
existing polity whose stability the novelist wants to ensure. Economics and political theory serve as the "environment" and the
horizon of his texts. His novels explore what is left over by the two
other disciplines. Scott, like Malthus, is not interested in remaking
the polity in the market's image. Hence his agents are defined
socially or in terms of their anthropological peculiarities. They are
not the free actors of the Ricardian economist's abstract marketplace.

It is therefore as much an ideological imperative as a functional
one—it is hard to tell which one comes first—that in Scott's novels
economic growth can only be alluded to, can serve as a theme or an
all-important hiatus. But the traditionary notion of "manners" that
underwrites *The Antiquary*, the apparent banishment of the realm
of political economics, comes too strongly into conflict with the
Smithian (even the Burkean) historical progressivism that ani-
mates *Waverley* and *Redgauntlet*. It is, furthermore, too exclusive. We
should take seriously the relative obscurity into which *The Antiquary* has fallen, for it only partially solves the functional problems
that it sets for itself and is not successful in fulfilling the narrative
responsibilities to plot that Mrs. Barbauld as much as Forster
seemed to assume in a novel.

But Scott did not stop with *The Antiquary*. In the last part of this
chapter, I will show how Scott tries to reconceive the relation
between the nation and the state, the relation between nationality
and citizenship. To understand and account for Scott's importance,
we will turn to a book in which he tries to imagine an increasingly
inclusive national culture. To this end, we should pay special attention to the novel which, according to Ina Ferris, ensured Scott's
authority, to *Ivanhoe,* and to its remarkable anomaly—that it features Jews so prominently.

IV

There really should not be any Jews in *Ivanhoe*. After all, the novel's
first chapter, with its witty play on the differences between Norman French and blunt Anglo-Saxon, indicates that the book will

be dominated by the conflict between Norman overlord and Saxon churl, between the language of the oppressor and that of the oppressed. Interestingly enough, in the first few pages of the novel, Scott goes out of his way to offer assurances of a future reconciliation between conqueror and conquered:

> In short, French was the language of honour, of chivalry, and even of justice, while the far more manly and expressive Anglo-Saxon was abandoned to the use of rustics and hinds who knew no other. Still, however, the necessary intercourse between the lords of the soil, and whose oppressed inferior beings by whom that soil was cultivated, occasioned the gradual formation of a dialect . . . in which they could render themselves mutually intelligible to each other; and from this necessity arose by degrees the structure of our English language, in which the speech of the victors and the vanquished have been so happily blended together. . . .[49]

No sooner does the novel open than it gives as its historical horizon the eradication of the tensions that it first presents. The quotation is also odd in that it seems to align class divisions with racial and linguistic identities: Saxon is spoken by the laborers and French by their bosses. As the novel develops, however, this neat symmetry disappears. *Ivanhoe* has its share of Saxon nobles who, like Cedric, presumably speak Anglo-Saxon with each other. Scott wants to elide class differences, it would seem, or rather claim that allegiances based on language and race supersede them. In short, Jews seem to be superfluous to the early argument of *Ivanhoe*, which is bent on mapping differing indices of personal and national identity. We will have to look at Scott's (failed) attempt to perform such a mapping before we can understand just why Rebecca and Isaac are so important for *Ivanhoe*.

We might want to begin to interrogate the rather unsuccessful ease with which *Ivanhoe* solves the problems it sets itself by noting that the novel was the product of a very difficult year. It is important for the tale I have to tell that *Ivanhoe* was written in 1819, the year of Peterloo, the Six Acts, and continuing economic depression. According to Lockhart, Scott divided his time that year between illness, *Ivanhoe,* and political reaction. After the unrest of the summer and because of the threat that radical agitation would spread across Scotland, Scott spent a great part of the autumn organizing a "legion or brigade upon a large scale" to maintain order. He was finishing *Ivanhoe* that fall as well.[50] No sooner was the novel published (in December), than Scott immediately set out to work on *The Visionary* to which we have referred earlier in this chapter.

If *Ivanhoe* is in large part a meditation on national identity and social cohesion, if it is the utopian answer to the dystopic fantasies of *The Visionary*, then we should see that the space for utopian imagining is opened through an active displacement of class conflict onto racial, and ultimately, linguistic differences. This move is again glimpsed at the wedding between Ivanhoe and Rowena at the end of the novel. This union is an unsatisfying emblem of racial reconciliation, because the couple are both Saxons. Their marriage, unlike the nuptials celebrated at the end of *Waverley*, does not join the blood of two nations, does not actually point to the all-important racial mix of Norman and Saxon. There are no Normans in the wedding, but plenty of Normans at it. Furthermore, Scott cites the "universal jubilee of the lower orders" as an indication that all segments of society will indeed join in the future dispensation. Scott's narrator takes this concord between Saxon and Norman, between rich and poor, as a "pledge of the future peace and harmony" (515). The poor, who up to this point in the novel are defined by race, not economic position, suddenly reappear. It would seem that Scott's odd racialism, the apparent manifest content of his dream of the mongrelization of Saxon and Norman stock, is an uncomfortable compromise whose inadequacy is witnessed by the lopsided marriage (two Saxons) and the acclamation of the *poor*.

We can go further by noting that the plot of *Ivanhoe* does not actually depict the reconciliation it announces. Scott tells us that the final seal of the assimilation of the two races will not come until the reign of Edward III when "the mixed language, now termed English, was spoken at the court of London, and . . . the hostile distinction of Norman and Saxon seems entirely to have disappeared" (515). The narrative is thus pitched on the verge of a future that it can point to but cannot yet encompass. Scott's interest seems to lie with the moment *before* reconciliation, before the birth of the new nation.

Given the primacy of linguistic difference to Scott's presentation of the plot, given his apparent conviction that language is the seal of national identity, it is noteworthy that the novel is remarkably free of the dialects that distinguish the earlier Waverley novels. Scott is careful to point out in the "Dedicatory Epistle" and the first chapter that he cannot reproduce the breach between Norman French and Anglo-Saxon. *Ivanhoe* is therefore a work of translation: "It is necessary, for exciting interest of any kind, that the subject assumed should be, as it were, translated into the manners, as well as the language, of the age we live in" (526). The novel is not an antiquarian curiosity like Strutt's *Queen-Hoo Hall*, the novel that Laurence Templeton, Scott's narrator, is at some pains to criticize. Strutt forgets "that extensive neutral ground, the large proportion, that is, of manners and sentiments which are common to us and our ancestors" (527). The neutral ground, of course, will be constituted here, as in *Waverley*, by the constancies of human nature. But what will the language of that neutral ground sound like?

The *Monthly Review* noted that "the dialogue of 'Ivanhoe' belongs to no precise age, but bears the nearest affinity to that of Elizabeth and of Shakespeare."[51] The *langue franche* that can communicate the thirteenth to the nineteenth century is the language of the sixteenth and, most specifically, the language of Shakespeare, who not only provides epigraphs for the chapters but the very dialogue of those chapters as well. In this way, the linguistic utopia that the novel presents as a distant horizon outside its plot gets acted out by the diction of the dialogue, a diction that is authorized by the central figure of Shakespeare himself.

Shakespeare's usefulness as a mediator is a commonplace in the Waverley novels. In two of the most obvious examples, *Waverley* and *Kenilworth*, Shakespeare's texts function overtly as a common referent that transcends political party and geographical peculiarity.[52] In *Ivanhoe*, Shakespeare cannot appear except as a frame, but his role as the tutelary spirit of English is clear. *Ivanhoe*'s version of a Shakespearean *lingua franca* is by definition literary, and this quality bothered the *Eclectic Review* which complained that the novel's style had all "the awkwardness of translation."[53] Of course, the awkward historical Muzak of Scott's Shakespearean pastiche really serves Scott's purpose quite well, for it obliterates all distinctions between Saxon and Norman, churl and thane. I am therefore suggesting that the happy resolution of the struggle between Saxon and Norman is a foregone conclusion, not only because it is predicted at the beginning and the end of the novel, but also (and more importantly) because it is actually enacted by the diction of the dia-logue. *Ivanhoe*'s characters speak the language of the redemptive future, that is, of a truly English nation. We can therefore say that *Ivanhoe* worries the difficulty of creating a nation that can serve to undergird and lend legitimacy to the state. In the novel, the English state, weak because feudal and weakened further by the civil wars of the Plantagenets, is the contingent product of historical con-quest. Scott is dabbling in anachronism here. His vision of the ten-sions of colonization is born of modern, not Saxon, experience. In Scott's mind, the Great Britain of 1819, riven as it was by regional attachments and class oppositions, stood in dire need of the solidar-ities a common culture seems to bestow.

Scott was reacting to larger historical imperatives as well. Fol-lowing Ernest Gellner, we can say that the modern state, with its drive towards increased mobility and complex divisions of labor, requires a new kind of cohesion, a new notion of nationalism to replace older and more localized forms of loyalty. It has to elimi-nate regional differentiations and particularist affections, but will need to replace these with a common "culture" that can be dissem-inated through a whole range of official and nonofficial institu-tions.[54] In our economic modernity, culture becomes an object to be known and venerated, not merely the common horizon of meaning which serves as the ambient atmosphere of group interac-tions. This culture, the product of conscious re-creation and objec-tification, serves as the very ground of the "nation," of nationalist nostalgia, aspiration, and identification. Gellner thus demystifies the "nation," claiming that it stems not from immemorial custom but rather from concerted acts of will:

> The modern nationalist consciously wills his identification
> with a culture. His overt consciousness of his own culture is
> already, in historical perspective, an interesting oddity. Tra-
> ditional man revered his city or clan through its deity or
> shrine, using the one . . . as a token for the other. He lacked
> any concept of 'culture' just as he had no idea of 'prose.' He
> knew the gods of his culture, but not the culture itself. In the
> age of nationalism, all this is changed twice over; the shared
> culture is revered *directly* and not through the haze of some
> token, and the entity so revered is diffuse, internally undif-

ferentiated, and insists that a veil of forgetfulness should dis-
creetly cover obscure internal differences.[55]

Modern versions of culture are constituted by strings of artifacts,
institutions, and practices that are rendered homogeneous in order
to create the impression of a unity that the populace, now dubbed
a nation, can share and claim as their "common" heritage. "Culture" thus requires a widespread amnesia and the invention of new
forms of tradition. *Ivanhoe*, no less than *Waverley*, creates a national
past and a model for future British solidarity. It makes of its language a pseudo-tradition and establishes Shakespeare as its *genius
loci*.

It is in the light of the dream of a national culture/language that
the Jew becomes so central. For reasons we will have to investigate,
Scott's plot establishes a Jew as its focus of libidinal attention and
then banishes her to Spain. Rebecca is *Ivanhoe*'s real damsel in distress, the true heroine. Rebecca, not Rowena, serves as this very
masculine novel's main object of desire. It is for Rebecca, not Rowena, that Ivanhoe risks his life. Here is Scott's first description of
Rebecca:

> The figure of Rebecca might indeed have compared with the
> proudest beauties of England . . . her form was exquisitely
> symmetrical, and was shown to advantage by a sort of East-
> ern dress. . . . The brilliancy of her eyes, the superb arch of
> her eyebrows, her well-formed aquiline nose, her teeth as
> white as pearl, and the profusion of her sable tresses . . . — all
> these constituted a combination of loveliness which yielded
> not to the most beautiful maidens who surrounded her.
> (82–83)

Scott's narrator makes a special point—he mentions it twice in
three sentences—of claiming that Rebecca is as beautiful as any
"Western"/British woman to whom she may be compared. Nor is
she any woman's spiritual inferior. At the stake, her fortitude is as
striking as her beauty:

> She was stript of all her ornaments. . . . A coarse white dress,
> of the simplest form, had been substituted for her Oriental
> garments; yet there was such an exquisite mixture of courage

and resignation in her look that even in this garb, and with
no other ornament than her long black tresses, each eye wept
that looked upon her, and the most hardened bigot regretted
the fate that had converted a creature so goodly into a vessel
of wrath. . . . (499)

Her relative nakedness gives a nice erotic tinge to the finely sadistic
vision of her vulnerability. (One need only think of Burke's Marie
Antoinette fleeing naked in the face of her pursuers to see one of
the many gothic precedents here.) But it is Rebecca's inner strength
as much as her physical position and remarkable beauty that makes
even the most superstitious onlookers cry for her. There is thus no
doubt that the reader, like Bois-Guilbert, is meant to fall for her
instantly and completely. But interestingly enough, the reader is
also meant to see through her eyes, that is, not only to take her as
an object to be viewed, but as a subject to be viewed with. Scott's
narrator frames the ordeal of her trial at Tempelstowe by giving
her perspective literal priority: she gazes "upon the scene, which
we shall endeavour to describe in the next chapter" (409). In other
words, the reader is invited to follow her gaze; the scene that
unfolds is the scene she sees.

What does it mean to make Rebecca the novel's libidinal and hermeneutic focal point? Let us agree that we cannot begin to discuss
Rebecca without taking her father into account. We cannot speak
of the novel's depiction of what we might call "the Jew" because
Ivanhoe actually depicts *two* Jews, or rather two kinds of Jew. Isaac,
of course, is drawn directly on the model of Shylock. To make the
parallel perfectly clear, Scott prefaces chapters 5, 6, and 22 with tags
from *The Merchant of Venice*. Isaac shares Shylock's overweening
drive for profit, but lacks his taste (or perhaps just his ability) for
revenge. Nevertheless, one could be tempted to say, as Edgar Johnson has, that Scott takes great pains to mitigate Isaac's avarice, to
save him from the apparent inhumanity of Shakespeare's repellent
Jew by putting Isaac's unseemly taste for money in the context of
Jewish persecution:[56]

> The obstinacy and avarice of the Jews being thus in a mea-
> sure placed in opposition to the fanaticism and tyranny of
> those under whom they lived, seemed to increase in propor-
> tion to the persecution with which they were visited; and the
> immense wealth they usually acquired in commerce, while it

frequently placed them in danger, was at other times used to extend their influence, and to secure to them a certain degree of protection. On these terms they lived; and their character, influenced accordingly, was watchful, suspicious, and timid—yet obstinate, uncomplying, and skilful in evading the dangers to which they were exposed. (70)

Scott's defense of the Jews contains an important qualification. Jews are obstinate—he tells us that twice in this one paragraph—in part ("in a measure") because they have been treated so harshly and because of the inhumanity of the Christians among whom they live. But only in part: Scott's qualification wants to reserve for the Jews a degree of innate, intransigent obstinacy, and avarice. Isaac, of course, fits the indictment perfectly. He is indeed watchful, suspicious, and timid. He is servile and conniving. He has a share in the general "national character [of the Jews], in which there was much, to say the least, mean and unamiable" (50). Isaac's most damning moment occurs when he finds out that Rebecca has been abducted by the Templar and taken to Tempelstowe. Locksley is keen to help negotiate terms for the young woman's ransom, but Isaac wants to bargain. He only stops when Locksley rebukes him: "Good Jew—good beast—good earthworm! . . . an dost thou go on to put thy filthy lucre in the balance with thy daughter's life and honour, by Heaven, I will strip thee of every maravedi thou hast in the world before three days are out!" (371). The equation of the Jew with an earthworm is a telling joke because it tropes Isaac's miserliness as subhuman. Locksley scares Isaac into humanity by threatening the rich man's wealth. He makes Isaac an offer that the Jew cannot, given his avaricious nature, refuse.

Even if we agree with Johnson that Isaac is not Shylock, we have to admit that he is not really much better. In fact, Scott has softened Elizabethan anti-Semitism only to give it an early nineteenth-century twist. He *historicizes* the lingering hatefulness of the Jew. And in British culture of this period, this stereotype of hatefulness did indeed linger. Todd Endelman has argued that by the eighteenth century theological anti-Semitism practically disappeared in Britain, to be replaced by secular and cultural forms of anti-Jewish hostility. Apart from the agitation surrounding the Jew Bill in 1753, there was little of the political anti-Semitism that would come to mark continental thought in the next century. Rather, Jews were figures for an all-consuming, inhuman, and cut-throat economic individualism. The objections to them were "moral" not "political." They would buy anything, cheat anyone, and, if allowed too much leeway, corrupt English life with their abundance of money.[57] One can see this stereotype doing yeoman's service in Burke's *Reflections on the Revolution in France* where Jews become a collective synonym for stock-jobbers and loan sharks, and are just waiting to snap up the wealth of the Church of England.[58] Burke seems to have nothing against the Jewish religion as such, and Jews are peripheral to his real concerns. Nevertheless, the odd chance that made Dr. Price give his fateful speech at Old Jewry made it possible for Burke to connect Jews, Dissenting ministers, and philosophical speculators in a metonymic string of contempt and vituperation. The stereotype of the covetous Jew works as a kind of shorthand. As clichés of unrestrained and unrepentant economic drives, they can serve as prefigurations for the "sophisters and oeconomists" who are Burke's real targets. Burke's anti-Semitism makes his job easier. He assumes that his readers will know just how bad a Jew can be.

Thus Isaac seems to be a focus for anti-Jewish energies in *Ivanhoe*, a negative stereotype who is provided with a pretty good excuse for being both so negative and such a stereotype. Rebecca, on the other hand, is resoundingly positive, because her father serves as a lightning rod that keeps her safe for the reader's desire. Scott saves her, by undoing his racialism and splitting the Jew from herself. Jews in *Ivanhoe* are distinguished by gender. The bad Jew is male, servile, economic, and avaricious. The good Jew is female, dignified, self-denying, and generous. If Isaac stands for usurious exchange, Rebecca stands for the free distribution of accumulated goods. She gives large amounts of money away, cares for the ill, and expresses nothing but a dignified compassion.

But even the good Jew(ess) cannot stay in Norman England. Rebecca and her father flee at the end of the novel. Thus *Ivanhoe* will not include Jews in the new linguistic and cultural dispensation that it repeatedly promises to the Saxons and the Normans. The Jews are not easily assimilable to the horizon of English hope that the novel provides. Nassau Senior complained that Rebecca's love for Ivanhoe is counterintuitive: there is nothing in her background or education that would lead her to such an improbable and unsatisfiable affection.[59] While Senior's point is well taken if we read the novel for psychological verisimilitude, it misses the mark if we look at the logic of its ideological project. Rebecca has to fall in love with Ivanhoe, because she cannot love a Jew. There are no male Jews who are fit to be loved. The only appropriate mate for a good Jew(ess) is a Christian, that is, a person who is not given either innately or through persecution to extreme forms of servile selfishness.

The gendered splitting of the figure of the Jew marks an attempt to save Scott's racialism from its worst consequences, that is from the complete banishment of a population from the cultural nation. And yet, this expedient does not work. Jews present a real difficulty for the dream of a common language and culture that underwrites this novel, because Scott uses race, gender, and religion to supplement, but not to supplant, each other. It is no accident that Rebecca's main suitor is Brian de Bois-Guilbert. Brian tries to woo his captive with "the power of vengeance . . . and the prospects of ambition" (254). He tells her that the Templars form a freemasonry of unbelievers who are interested in supplanting the temporal powers of Europe (254–55). They owe allegiance to no land, to no king, and to no faith. They are nothing less than the lying, ambitious Illuminati that people the counter-revolutionary's nightmare (442).[60]

Rebecca rejects the Templar's advances, but she shares with him the anomalous situation of having no country to call her own (422). She comes from a nationless nation; her identity is based on an occult race (whose effects are undone by gender) and she has no "real" linguistic affiliation (even though she seems to have been born in York). And because her identity rests on the mysteries of this dark faith that seems to be more a race, the novel cannot allow her to convert, because conversion would not solve the problems that the grounding of identity in race or gender seem to present. Furthermore, *Ivanhoe* is obsessed with how difference is to be mediated and translated, not with how it is to be destroyed. As Templeton writes in the novel's dedicatory letter:

> Our ancestors were not more distinct from us, surely than Jews are from Christians; they had 'eyes, hands, organs, dimensions, senses, affections, passions'; were 'fed with the same food, hurt with the same weapons, subject to he same diseases' . . . as ourselves. The tenor, therefore of their

affections and feeling must have borne the same general pro-
portions to our own. (528–29)

The problem of the historical novel, Templeton claims, is similar to
the problem that faces Christians who try to understand Jews,
because the past is to the present as the Jew is to the Gentile. There
are similarities, even points of identity between them. But the
differences remain; otherwise the historical novel would not be a
problem in the first place. The search for "the same general propor-
tions" entails a recognition that the fit is not exact. For Scott, to
write historically means to write of the Jew, of something that is
confoundingly elusive yet relevant, something whose difference
cannot be overcome by sheer cultural will.

For Scott's project, the female/feminized Jew is the test case for
the cohesive power of a newly constructed, national culture and
therefore for the project of this historical novel. This Jew represents the limit and the limitation of Scott's inclusive vision of
nationalism, and the affection with which he treats Rebecca shows
how painful this limitation is. We can appeal to the complaints of
his adult "female" readers to show that Rebecca's final exile was
painful, and to Scott's response to show that he meant it to hurt. In
the introduction to the Magnum Opus edition of his works, Scott
chastises the "fair readers" for their disappointment when Rebecca
does not get to marry Ivanhoe (544). He informs them that such a
union was "almost impossible" in those days (544) and that it is
immoral to reward the virtuous with temporal goods: virtue and
self-denial should be their own rewards (545). This recourse to a
rather butch self-denial, on the part of the readers as well as the
characters of the novel, is an odd piece of sadomasochism, especially in a book whose aim is so obviously to give pleasure. The
greatest desire that *Ivanhoe* elicits in its readers, who are paradoxically posited as both male (self-denying) and female (self-indul-
gent) in their desires, it is careful to deny.

We might well want to accept the contention that the reader
desires Rebecca and her desires precisely because these desires are
prohibited, proscribed.[61] If this is indeed the case, the very impossibility of satisfaction constitutes the character's fascination for
both the writer and the reader. And so poor Rowena, whose love
for Ivanhoe turns out to be so prosaically possible, is condemned
to be, in Scott's own words, "less interesting" (544). Ironically, in

terms of its effect, *Ivanhoe* is thus a philo-Semitic work.[62] The limits the novel asserts create a demand in the reader that those limits be overcome. The separation of Jew and Christian that *Ivanhoe* insists upon makes its Christian readers want to abolish the proscriptions on the Jews. It points to a future, unrealized in Scott's time, in which the cultural segregation of the good Jews would be eliminated.

But why can Scott not figure the assimilation whose effects he seems to desire so strongly? I want to make two suggestions that dovetail into each other. The first is historically overdetermined, a sign of the year of the novel's composition. The second has to do with the function of anti-Semitism *in sensu strictu*, that is, Jew-hatred as a cultural platform, not as a religious prejudice. And so, to the first. Sander Gilman has suggested that the image of the Jew in modern European representations is always tainted by the suggestion that the Jews speak a secret, magical language that infects the language of the nation in which they live and actively undermines it.[63] It is interesting in this regard to note that Scott does not indulge in the eighteenth- and early nineteenth-century habit of having his Jews massacre English grammar and pronunciation.[64] Rather, Rebecca and Isaac display their *Yiddischkeit* through their rather extravagant and insistent use of metaphor.

To be a Jew in *Ivanhoe* is to follow the prejudices of late eighteenth-century Biblical scholars and speak the sublime language of the Old Testament, that is, in Eastern metaphor and simile. It is in these terms that Rebecca describes the battle at Torquilstone: "His high black plume floats abroad over the throng, like a raven over the field of the slain . . . God of Jacob! it is the meeting of two fierce tides — the conflict of two oceans moved by adverse winds!" (314). This is the "natural" poetry of the Bible, a sublimity that is doubly attractive to Scott because in the mouth of Rebecca, it is freed from the suspicion of ambition that it acquires in the mouth of *Old Mortality*'s canting Covenanters. But it is also the language of that part of the Bible that has been superseded by secular authority that Christian revelation wields. To put it bluntly, although the Jews can speak like the prophets or like Solomon in the "Song of Songs," they cannot be trusted because they will not swear a good Christian oath.

Ivanhoe is a novel remarkable for the sheer number of oaths, curses, and vows it contains. Gurth's first words, the first bit of speech in the novel, are a curse in the name of a Saxon saint: "The curse of Saint Withold upon these infernal porkers!" (13), and the characters in the novel proceed to call on a whole calendar of holy witnesses. The Saxons swear by Saxon saints; the Normans swear by European saints; and they all swear by Thomas á Becket. But it is less the religious than the legal aspect of the vow that seems to be important here. Oaths are particularly important in the book because they provide guarantees of future behavior in a period of civil war during which there is no recourse to a law that can make sure that promises and contracts are fulfilled. Scott thus depicts conditions in which religious oaths become a necessity, a state of nature in which only fears for one's eternal soul can curb one's destructive or self-interested inclinations. In this *bellum omnium contra omnes* oaths have little or no religious significance in themselves; their importance is social, if not political.

It would be a mistake, however, to limit *Ivanhoe's* imaginings to a historical version of Enlightenment anthropology, that is, to see the novel reckoning out what might be the minimal conditions for human society. It does this, to be sure, but it also has a more immediate object in view. Jonathan Clark has argued that "the patriarchal, hierarchical, confessional state found its . . . political language not in secret ballots, but in personal oaths."[65] Clark, like Ian Christie and Linda Colley, reminds us of the paramount importance of the Anglican church in the constitutional and ideological imagination of Britain in the century and a half before the Great Reform Act.[66] Given the identification of the church and the state, it is hardly surprising that outward professions of faith were as important to the political as to the religious life of the century. Whereas communion in the Church of England had been the passport to even minimal citizenship in the early 1700s, oaths came increasingly to take the place of more concrete acts of allegiance as the century progressed. We see this in the Catholic Relief Act (1778) and the Dissenter's Relief Act (1779).[67] When the Test and Corporation Acts were finally repealed in 1827, the sacramental tests were replaced by an oath upon the taker's "true faith as a Christian" not to injure the established church.[68]

Of course, sacramental tests and christological oaths, even if they are altered to admit Dissenters and eventually Catholics into political life, reach the limit of their effectiveness with Jews. In fact, as Todd Endelman has shown, the chief obstacles to full Jewish assimilation in this period, the chief civil disabilities under which Jews suffered, rested on the persistence and importance of such oaths and sacraments. The Jew Bill of 1753 which sought to absolve Jews from taking the sacrament before becoming naturalized was defeated.[69] Jews were not admitted to the Bar until, in 1833, the benchers of Lincoln's Inn allowed Francis Henry Goldschmid to take an oath that did not include any reference to Christ. In 1833, Parliament voted that Jews could be seated without having to take a religious oath, but the Lords blocked such a liberalization until a compromise was finally arrived at some twenty-five years later. Similarly, oaths for municipal office were not cleansed of their christological language until 1845.[70] In short, the religious oath was the *carte d'entree* to assimilation and acceptance in 1819. While Scott can imagine a Jew speaking standard English, while he can see a Jew as an object of desire and as a candidate for cultural inclusion, he cannot imagine an English state in which religious oaths are not the sign of true and public allegiance. The secret language of the Jews in this case is a form of silence; there are words they cannot say.

So, *Ivanhoe*'s imperfect resolution of the Jewish question is historically determined. Scott, a self-defined defender of the *ancien regime*, cannot follow the logic of his own utopian aspirations as rigorously as he might want to. He cannot divorce national culture from the political function of the national church. The church, as Gash and Clark note, was already beginning to fail in its cohesive function by 1819[71] and we can speculate that it is precisely this failure which made the notion of a national culture so appealing. But this explanation of the impossibility of assimilating the alien within the limits to culture set by the constitution of the *ancien regime* can only account, in part, for the failure of Scott's rigor. It cannot account for the affect that attends this failure, nor for the variety of ways that Scott has tried to overcome it, his recourse to gender being the most interesting and most salient. To recast this problem in the words of Slavoj Zizek, the explanation I have given above "is not sufficient to explain how the figure of the Jew captures our desire."[72]

Zizek has produced a wonderfully fruitful model for the social and psychological economy of anti-Semitism, an excellent revision of Horkheimer and Adorno's claim that "anti-Semitism is based on false projection" where "impulses which the subject will not admit as his own . . . are attributed to the object."[73] Zizek, whose *For*

They Know Not What They Do proves to be a brilliant recuperation
of Frankfurt School critical theory in light of Lacan, translates the
notion of projection from the field of the individual consciousness
to the realm of the social:

> [T]he stake of social-ideological fantasy is to construct a
> vision of society which . . . is not split by an antagonistic
> division, a society in which the relation between its parts is
> organic, complementary. . . . How then do we take account
> of the distance between this corporatist vision and the factual
> society split by antagonistic struggles? The answer is, of
> course, the Jew: an external element, a foreign body intro-
> ducing corruption into the sound social fabric. In short,
> "Jew" is a fetish which simultaneously denies and embodies
> the structural impossibility of "Society": it is as if in the
> figure of the Jew this impossibility had acquired a positive,
> palpable existence. . . .[74]

Fantasy, then, is the attempt to overcome social antagonisms and to
confer on a group a sense of identification that must fail because of
those very antagonisms. But it explains its failure by projecting a
false positivity, a concrete figure — in this case, the Jew — which can
explain why the identifications do not work. The "Jew" is a necessary construction, for it provides a concreteness, if not a cause, for
the ultimate impossibility of a truly cohesive society. The oppro-
brium and contempt that the narrator visits on Isaac serve to under-
score Zizek's point, but in a limited way, for Isaac is corrupt, but
not really a corrupter. Zizek's thesis is supported, rather, by the
affect that surrounds the fair Jewess. The pathos that attends
Rebecca is a mark of how badly this society is desired: the exile into
which she must go is a mark of how impossible such a society and
the culture that supposedly undergirds it really are.

In *Ivanhoe*, then, Jews serve as the limit to Scott's ability to dis-
place economic and political struggles peculiar to his period onto
the racial and linguistic antagonisms of a fiercely imagined Plantagenet England. For the exclusions that Scott wants to overcome
through his fantasy of British culture — the disenfranchisement of
the middle classes, the disenfranchisement of the Catholics and the
poor — will not go away so easily. In fact, the imaginary displacements that allow the fantasy in the first place can only transfer the
exclusion from one group to the next. They cannot do away with

the very act of exclusion itself. So the exile of the Jews in *Ivanhoe* is at best a compromise, a cipher for discrimination as a whole. The intervention of the Jews in the novel can only end by acting out the very difficulties that Scott wanted to avoid when he dreamed of his common national culture, of *Ivanhoe*. In the end, the Jew is the subject of the historical novel as Scott conceives it, for the Jew (or the Jacobite, or the Covenanter) is the figure that through its difference (or anachronism) threatens to destroy the narrative of a national history and culture. Ironically, Scott's novels, which tried (following Burke) to develop richer definitions of personal and social identity than those offered to him by the abstractions of the economic thought that had such an influence on him, could only find in those definitions resistance to the coherence of their project. One could say that Scott was more successful—cognitively speaking—in the hack work of *The Visionary* which saw present problems in terms of class, not race, nation, or language. But to say that is to dismiss the aesthetic and the fantastic as mere displacements, as diversions from the *real* thing. Such iconoclasm, such hatred of illusion, has its own Puritan dangers and blinds us to the truth of *Ivanhoe*, or rather, *Ivanhoe*'s attempt to tell its truth.

I would like to submit that the most important thing about *Ivanhoe* is not its glittering knights or clichéd money-lenders—the flummery of its ideological blind spots—but rather its uncomfortable play between its philo- and anti-Semitic leanings, its unhappily sadomasochistic rejection of Rebecca. For it is in the figure of the contemporary reaction to the Jewess's exile that we see a protest against the constraints of mere history—be it Plantagenet or Regency.

We can and perhaps should temper this utopian reading with an appeal to the systemic imperatives towards functional self-definition in which this particular novel takes its form. Scott does not rest with a historico-political definition of the citizen, as Malthus does, nor with the economic delineation of citizenship that one finds in Ricardo. Rather, he insists that the citizen be seen as a member of a linguistic culture, a culture grounded on literary artifacts, such as Shakespeare or *Ivanhoe*. Culture, not class nor clan, will determine one's place in the polity and will overcome, if not dissolve, the antagonisms generated by both class and clan. And the Waverley novel— according to Scott—will play a pivotal role in creating and sustaining that all-necessary masculine and Protestant culture.

5

Telling Time with Austen

Miss Edgeworth's novels put us in mind of those clocks and watches which are con-
demned "a double or a treble debt to pay": which besides their legitimate object, to
show the hour, tell you the day of the month or the week, give you a landscape for a
dial-plate . . . all very good things in their way; but so it is that these watches never
tell the time so well as those in which that is the exclusive object of the maker.
— ARCHBISHOP WHATELY ON AUSTEN

We have seen that in *Waverley* Scott attempted to split the important
notion of citizenship into the two conflicting ideals of political and
economic participation. Edward Waverley is seduced by the anachronistic dream of direct involvement with the destiny of the state
and learns — or is it the reader who is supposed to learn? — that he
becomes a historical actor only at that moment when he returns to
the important task of improving his estate. The narrator of *Waverley*
goes out of his way in the last chapter of that novel to stress the
civic jurisprudential point that civil society and the economy are
the true engines of historical progress.

The tensions inherent in this rejection of the political definition
of the citizen-subject became quite clear by 1816. Depression made
the easy fit between constitutional stability and economic progress
seem both obsolete and politically dangerous. Hence Scott's anthropological and historical definitions of his characters take on an
importance that is no longer either merely tragic or merely humor-
ous. *The Antiquary*, which made this shift of emphasis from the economic to the constitutional-historical quite clear, might have been
Scott's favorite of his novels, but it was not the most successful in

terms of either sales or influence. Rather, it took *Ivanhoe* to bring the ideology of progress, the ideal of citizenship, and the stability of the constitution together in a collective dream of a unified and unifying British culture. This culture, which excludes both the discourses of economics and politics from its self-definition, is overseen by Shakespeare and his novel-writing heirs. Of course, Scott's solution to the British problem created a Jewish problem of its own. It excludes Rebecca from the vision of linguistic and cultural reconciliation in which the novel places its best hopes.

In my discussion of Scott, I have emphasized Rebecca's Judaism, not her gender. But we have to pay great attention to the fact that Scott's solution to the problems presented by the conflict between politics and economics—a third way that is monitored by literature—is predicated on the exclusion not only of ethnic-religious others but also on the exclusion of a woman. And it is in large part Rebecca's gender that allows Scott to worry her exclusion, to protest against it even as he performs it.

But where should women fit in this brave new world? They surely must be eligible for cultural citizenship in that they, like culture, are not defined as economic or political actors. Here is Austen's version of inclusion, as elaborated in the final paragraph of *Persuasion*:

> Anne was tenderness itself, and she had the full worth of it in Captain Wentworth's affection. His profession was all that could ever make her friends wish that tenderness less; the dread of a future war all that could dim her sunshine. She gloried in being a sailor's wife, but she must pay the tax of quick alarm for belonging to that profession which is, if possible, more distinguished in its domestic virtues than in its national importance.[1]

This is a wonderfully complicated passage to unpack because it is so easy to read Anne as belonging to the sailor's profession: her quick alarm is the price of her husband's profession. Of course to construe this sentence in this way is to attribute to Austen a solecism that she does not normally commit. After all, it is Anne, the subject of the sentence, who pays the tax and belongs to a profession. The profession—an odd term to which we will have to return—to which Anne Wentworth belongs is that of being a sailor's wife. Hence the irony of the claim that wives are even more notable for their "domestic virtues" than for their contributions to the nation as a whole. For to lay a claim for domestic virtue in this instance is to take for granted that sailors' wives constitute an important part of the nation's defense.

What does it mean that to be a wife, a sailor's wife, is to have a profession? The professions—the clergy, the military, and the law—served as the younger son's only real hope in getting on in the world. The professions served as a middle ground between labor and land, an honorable way of *earning* money for those whose social station would not allow them to till the fields, shoe the horses, or run a shop. And yet, the word profession, with its religious heritage and etymological link to commitment, betokens a calling, a vocation with burdens and privileges that are willingly taken on. To take a profession thus has a double implication. It is to assume something that is more than a job of work and it indicates that one is male. Austen's play at the end of *Persuasion* is thus quite serious. She indicates that women (of a certain class), like men (of the same class), have professions, pay taxes, and play a vital role in the life of the state.

For Scott, citizenship beyond politics and economics entails an apparently gender-determined language, literacy, and culture. Citizenship in Austen's novel is more universal in that it does away with the gender qualification. The ironic chiasmus of the last sentence of *Persuasion,* which indicates that sailors have domestic virtue and that their wives have a national importance, makes men and women (above a certain station) not-so-separate and remarkably equal subjects of the crown. In this way, Austen supports and even makes a greater claim for women of the era between Revolution and Reform than the one Linda Colley reconstructs:

> At one and the same time, separate sexual spheres were being increasingly prescribed in theory, yet increasingly broken through in practice. The half-century after the American war would witness a marked expansion in the range of British women's public and patriotic activities, as well as changes in how those activities were viewed and legitimized. Women from different social backgrounds would take part in pro-war activism. . . . And even the most conventional British women would come to accept that formal exclusion from active citizenship did not exclude them from playing a patriotic role—and a political role of a kind.[2]

Colley argues for a more dialectical reading of the insistently re-
peated ideology of separate spheres in the latter decades of the
Georgian period. She claims that this ideology does not represent
women's conditions in the period (if it did, it would not need to
protest so much) and urges us to see that it signals a distinct but partial increase in women's power. The ideology of separate spheres is
"profoundly contractual"[3] in that it consolidates women's few rights
and establishes irrevocably their hegemony over the morality of
the nation by conceding the "political" to the men.[4] Austen pushes
this argument even further, hence the quotation marks I put around
the word political in the last sentence. The chiastic irony of Austen's
conclusion indicates the permeability of the boundaries that the
ideology of separate spheres invites and establishes. Austen can
therefore be seen to weaken the distinction between the state and
civil society (between what I called in the third chapter the principles of justice and benevolence) on which depend the ideologies of
separate spheres and of civil jurisprudence.

Or perhaps not. If we read Austen in Colley's terms — that is, as
a contemporary of Walter Scott's — then we have to concede that
the end of *Persuasion* is less a stick of dynamite under a wall than a
buttress. In Austen's account, women are to be taken as seriously as
men, but are contractually bound to keep the home fires burning
while their husbands go off to fight, to earn, and to improve. Not
surprisingly, this careful demarcation of spheres (or more properly
perhaps, of systems) has important consequences for *Persuasion*.
Even more than *Northanger Abbey*, which pits the claims of the
novel against the claims of history and allows them different functions and equal honor, *Persuasion* shows that it is more than aware
of the vast marketplace of books. It begins with the Baronetage, Sir
Walter's book of books; includes a discussion of the proper diet of
poetry (Captain Benwick indulges too much, it seems) and pays
great attention to the navy List. The novel comprehends all these
books and genres. It also supersedes them in that it can encompass
them all within its span. Just as *Persuasion* is very careful to show
how the List takes the place of (or does it supplement?) the Baronetage as an index of the nation's true petty aristocracy, so too it
points to its own practice as an index of the moral health of both
the subject and the nation.[5]

Of course, that copulation between nation and subject, that
"and" that indicates an analogy between the two, is troubling in its

ease. It shows how hard it is *not* to read *Persuasion* allegorically, or to put it more rigorously, symbolically. It is hard not to read the characters in *Persuasion* as synechdoches for class positions and general moral types. In the current standard interpretation of the text, *Persuasion* describes the shift in power in which the "professionals"—in this case, the sailors—do not so much inherit the earth as earn their place in it. Wentworth is a proper gentleman in a time which is markedly un- or rather post-feudal; a gentleman with a calling, that is, with a profession. The navy List becomes quite legitimately the book which the younger Musgroves scan with such excitement. It is a truer and more modern who's who than the Baronetage. While Claudia Johnson is most likely correct in her attempt to discourage such baldly symbolic readings of the novel when she notes that the shift in hegemony that *Persuasion* signals is not really the subject of the novel, but its backdrop, she still insists on a synechdochal reading when she argues that the novel is a meditation on "the psychological impact that [new social relations] have on women and on the apparent possibilities which 'the unfeudal tone of the present day' may hold out for them";[6] not for just one woman, please note, but for women in general.

To look for the general in each of the novel's particulars is not an accident of sloppy reading, but precisely the kind of reading the novel seems to recommend. So it is that in an all-too-famous passage, Anne extrapolates from the way the Crofts drive to the very essence of their marriage:

> But by coolly giving the reins a better direction herself [the subject here is Mrs. Croft], they happily passed the danger; and by once afterwards judiciously putting out her [again, Mrs. Croft's] hand, they neither fell into a rut, nor ran foul of a dung cart; and Anne, with some amusement at their style of driving, which she imagined no bad representation of the general guidance of their affairs, found herself safely deposited at the cottage. (90)

Anne takes Mrs. Croft's gestures very seriously indeed, just as she spends a good deal of her (and our) time weighing Frederick Wentworth's smallest moves. Just as Mrs. Radcliffe's empiricism makes the individual detail bear theological weight, Austen's last novel seems to enjoin us to see the social world symbolically. In *The Italian*, God is quite literally in the details. In *Persuasion*, with its fascination with mediation (from the insistence on the separation of spheres to its rewritten, epistolary denouement), all character and all importance are securely lodged in the most incidental of facts. Here is Anne reflecting on Mr. Elliot's character:

> She distrusted the past, if not the present. The names which occasionally dropt of former associates, the allusions to former practices and pursuits, suggested suspicions not favourable of what he had been. She saw that there had been bad habits; that Sunday-travelling had been a common thing; that there had been a period of his life (and probably not a short one) when he had been, at least, careless on all serious matters; and, though he might now think very differently, who could answer for the true sentiments of a clever, cautious man, grown old enough to appreciate a fair character? (152)

These doubts and the meditative necromancy that reinforces them prove to be extraordinarily accurate and judicious. While Mr. Elliot is a clever and a cautious man, he is not a good one, as Mrs. Smith reveals and as his own actions go on to prove.

If one can divine the whole of a character from a small detail, collapse the inner and the outer, the social and the political, it is not difficult to start reading individuals as exemplary. And of course, Anne Elliot does just this. Let us take Anne's meditation on the meaning of Mrs. Smith's good spirits:

> How could it be? — She watched — observed — reflected — and finally determined that this was not a case of fortitude or of resignation only. — A submissive spirit might be patient, a strong understanding would supply resolution, but here was something more; here was that elasticity of mind, that disposition to be comforted, that power of turning readily from evil to good, and of finding employment which carried her out of herself, which was from Nature alone. (146)

While it is worth noting that Mrs. Smith is exemplary in her acceptance, in her resolute stoicism (an exemplarity which seems quite suspect today[7]), it is more important for us to see *how* Anne Elliot reasons here. She tries to reconcile abstract universals (fortitude, resignation) and concrete cases. She attempts to read those cases in terms of those universals, and when she fails, she constructs a new norm that is extraordinary in that it cannot willfully be imitated ("that elasticity of mind . . . which was from Nature alone"). We could say that, in Kantian terms, Austen shows us the necessity of moving from reason to judgment, from the rigors of conceptual thought to aesthetic contemplation of objects which look universalizable but are decidedly and unreducibly particular. Of course, such an interpretation (influenced by disaffected post–Enlightenment philosophers such as Richard Rorty, Alasdair MacIntyre, and Martha Nussbaum), while attractive, is only partially accurate.

After all, certain characters, such as Sir Walter, Lady Russell, Mary Musgrove, and Mr. Elliot, are all easily reducible to abstractions. Sir Walter is the figure of Vanity; Lady Russell, of Prejudice; Mary Musgrove of Selfishness; and Mr. Elliot of Hypocrisy. Similarly, the plot of this novel has taught Captain Wentworth to distinguish between the steadiness of principle and the obstinacy of self-will, between the darings of heedlessness and the resolution of a collected mind (228). In short, Wentworth has learned to discriminate between abstractions, and to fit phenomena into the correct conceptual pigeonholes. He has discovered what Anne seems always to have practiced: "elasticity of mind." The posthumous title of the novel (Austen had intended to call it *The Elliots*) provides an important reading of the book in that it is an abstraction; it leads us to look for embodiments of such an abstraction in the myriad details of the plot. Furthermore, it leads its readers to ask what the grounds of persuasion might be.

Anne Elliot was originally persuaded not to marry young Wentworth because such a match would have been, by Lady Russell's lights, imprudent. In fact, it was "indiscreet, improper, hardly capable of success, and not deserving it" (31). Lady Russell, of course, was wrong, because her snobbery (and her incapacity for appreciating the intelligence of "wit") would allow her to see neither the elegance nor the genius of the man. Lady Russell, however, seems to approve of Mr. Elliot, and should she try to use her powers of persuasion to a positive end, she could talk Anne into what would turn out to be a disastrous match: "Anne could just acknowledge within herself such a possibility of having been induced to marry him, as made her shudder at the idea of the misery which must have followed. It was just possible that she might have been persuaded by Lady Russell!" (199). Psychologically, this little meditation is quite revealing. Anne does not "acknowledge" the attraction she has indeed felt for Mr. Elliot. Instead, she can only acknowledge that Lady Russell could have convinced her to marry him, could have persuaded her with relative ease. Of course, the real inducement would have been the desire to be the lady of Kellynch Hall (151–52) and thus an appeal to Anne's vanity. And such vanity would not have been adequate grounds for persuasion. Rather, the term "acknowledge" here points to what Austen seems to take as the proper basis for conviction.

One acknowledges — with difficulty — that which is true, but which one does not want to admit. Truth and its concomitant acknowledgment run against vanity of any sort. So it is with Wentworth:

> He persisted in having loved none but her. . . . Thus much indeed he was *obliged to acknowledge* — that he had been constant unconsciously, nay unintentionally; that he had meant to forget her, and believed it to be done. He had imagined himself indifferent, when he had only been angry; and he had been unjust to her merits, because he had been a sufferer from them. Her character was now fixed on his mind as perfection itself, maintaining the loveliest medium of fortitude and gentleness; but he was *obliged to acknowledge* that only at Uppercross had he learnt to do her justice, and only at Lyme had he begun to understand himself. (227–28; emphasis added)

Acknowledgment entails a form of obligation, a commitment to a truth which is seen to be objectively valid even though it constitutes a blow to one's self-regard. In fact, the very blow it delivers is the mark of its truth, its objectivity. Wentworth's self-love demanded that he forget Anne after the debacle of their engagement, that he blind himself to Anne's virtue. His sense of the truth forced him to admit that he had overvalued himself and undervalued her. He had misconceived the conceptual terms under which he should have understood her: she stands halfway between fortitude and gentleness. He can now see this with all the clarity of a chastened objectivity.

For all Austen's insistence on particularity, she is, in spite of the Aristotelian cast MacIntyre gives her, very much a product of the Enlightenment, of universalizing — that is, conceptual — and procedural thought.[8] A good part of her irony is lodged in the superior position of the narrator who is able to demolish with fine tact the pretensions of an individual who is unwilling to acknowledge his or her divergence from an objectively valid norm. Those critics who want to insist on the poetics of identification, on the great importance of individual characters, would do well to speculate on the possibility of the reader's final identification, not with any given character in Austen's novels, but with the narrator. To say this is to fly in the face of not only traditional modes of criticism but also of some rather convincing theoretical accounts of the way fiction works:

> The position of the narrator seems to provide for the reader an entry into the story, but this entry is a ruse. It is not because the reader identifies with the narrator, or takes the narrator to be his double, that he is interested in or by the story. To the extent that he identifies with the narrator he avoids being interested in the story, he avoids seeing his desire in a fiction. . . . The reader's interest in the fiction derives first from the fact that something of his, an object, is to be found therein . . .[9]

That object, of course, is a character, understood as a source of narcissistic reflection for the reader: "You read the story as if you were Dupin, as if the story were about you, not as if you were the narrator."[10] This may well be a fruitful speculation on the reader's libidinal entrance into, his or her initial investment in, a narrative. But, as we saw with Scott, the entrance and the exit are not necessarily the same.

Let us think about the privileges accorded to Austen's narrator. It is this narrator, after all, who not only grants the reader access to the given character's mind but also provides an unshakable base from which to make judgments, "objective" discriminations. This narrator seems to serve the function called the "ego-ideal" about which Freud writes:

> [W]e have ascribed to it self-observation, the moral conscience, the censorship of dreams, and the chief influence in repression. We have said that it is the heir to the original narcissism in which the childish ego enjoyed self-sufficiency; it gradually gathers up from the influences of the environment, the demands which that environment makes upon the ego and which the ego cannot always rise to. . . .[11]

The narcissistic delusions of grandeur that mark the child's early years are sacrificed to the criticism which is directed at the child by its parents.[12] But the pleasures of this narcissism do not have to be sacrificed at all, for they are reinvested in the shining example of the ego-ideal. This ego-ideal is not the same as the ideal ego, that specular image of the perfect infantile ego, that Freud describes in his article on narcissism and that Lacan recruits for his notion of the mirror-stage. Lacan is correct in his first published seminar to pay particular attention to the difference between the ideal ego and the ego-ideal.[13] As Freud argues in "Group Psychology and the Analysis of the Ego," the ego-ideal is the creation of language, of the symbolic, of the creation of identity within the social order.[14] Freud's point for us here is that the ego-ideal can itself be the locus of satisfaction. Its censure can itself become the focus of identification. Without stretching Lacan's rather stretched terminology, we can say, with Zizek, that investment in the ego-ideal is "identification with the ideal ('virtual') point *from which* the subject looks upon himself. . . ."[15] We can amend Schneiderman's argument by saying that although the character might serve as the initial interest in the narrative, in the case of Austen, the narrator serves as the most important point of identification. That narrator is most often presented as the transparent medium of truth, and so the readers take on the standpoint of that authoritative voice to judge those objects (characters) in which they would like to see themselves reflected. If such an identification with these objects is obtained, then the pleasurable, somewhat sadomasochistic censure that the narrator affords the reader must be acknowledged as well. We can approach this same phenomenon in a slightly different way, through Barthes, in one of his more Lacanian moments:

> The text is fetish-object, and this fetish desires me. The text chooses me, by a whole deployment of invisible screens . . . and lost in the middle of the text . . . there is always the other, the author. . . . I desire the author: I need its figure (which is neither its representation nor its projection) as it needs mine.[16]

The figure of the author is the figure of authority which the reader needs, which serves as the sanction for reading itself. Of course, such authority, such securely superior alterity, needs the reader as well in order to actualize itself. The fetish is the stand-in, the moment in which this mutual recognition takes place. The narrator serves as the voice and embodiment of social and epistemological authority. In Austen's novel, it is the very ground on which truth's objective abstractions, that is, the possibility of the concept, rest.

But, for all Austen's debt to Enlightenment protocols, we would do well to argue with both Marilyn Butler on the one side and Claudia Johnson on the other. Butler has on more than one occasion maintained that Austen's novels

> have the stamp of those years of strong reaction, years when the English cultural habit moved from internationalism to Francophobia, and deep-rooted popular modern Toryism was born. Among other things, Jane Austen's Toryism made it hard for her to countenance . . . Enlightenment criticism of social constraints upon women.[17]

Austen is one of Butler's reactionaries, a hidebound little Tory formed in the crucible of the 1790s. For Johnson, Austen is a late-Enlightenment figure, firmly rooted not only in the protocols of the second half of the eighteenth century but in its explicit teachings as well. To place Austen squarely in some construction of the eighteenth century is to miss the importance of her writing, especially of this, her last published novel, which was the exact contemporary of Scott's *Antiquary*. To read Austen and Scott together is to notice how her fascination with general rules and types presents a model for understanding social organizations which contrasts directly with Scott's anthropological constitutionalism. We might learn a good deal if we read Austen as as much a reductionist as Ricardo, but with one important difference. She does not reduce humanity to economic man, but to moral woman.

Austen's framing of the economic sphere in *Persuasion* within the bounds of the moral, the feminine, and the novel has interesting implications. We can begin to understand these by noting the peculiarity of her reputation. She was not the most successful female writer of her time: that title must go to Maria Edgeworth. Her success had to wait, as John Halperin has shown, until the 1860s.[18] In fact, the high cult of Austen was ushered in by Austen-Leigh's publication of his memoir of Aunt Jane in 1870 at the very moment that Scott's star began to wane.

Of course, there were dissenters from the church of Scott in the earlier decades of the century. With typically grim glee, Thomas Carlyle predicted in 1838 the neglect that awaited the Waverley novels:

> What, then, is the result of these Waverley Romances? Are they to amuse one generation only? One or more! As many generations as they can; but not all generations; ah no, when our swallow-tail has become fantastic as trunk-hose, they will cease to amuse! . . . Amusement in the way of reading can go no farther, . . .[19]

This condemnation of amusement has more than a touch of rough Calvinism to it, but is interesting in that Carlyle reduces amusement to mindless fashion and thus dismisses the unprecedented power these books had over their contemporaries as a matter of sheer contingency. But were these amusements so mindless? If we bracket Carlyle's own large investment in Scott's writing, we can say that Scott's novels had begun to lose their cognitive and their emotional interest by 1838, if only to Carlyle.

By the centenary of Scott's birth in 1871, Carlyle's prejudices had acquired a greater currency: an increasing number of critics expressed the fear that Scott had become unpopular and therefore dismissable. Hillhouse's study of the reception of the Waverley novels provides a fine summary of this turn:

> Walter Bagehot in 1858 opens his very carefully considered essay with an allusion to the passing of Scott's original popularity . . . and in 1863 another essayist declares Scott still the favorite novelist of his country, but seems doubtful of his future. . . . One of the centenary writers . . . remarks, "Scott is now somewhat faded it is common to say, and undeniably it is true to say so," and Leslie Stephen on the same occasion suspects that Scott's power is waning, "the warmth of our first love departed," and has heard whispers that he is dull.[20]

Although "neglect and indifference to Scott" was "in the atmosphere" of Victorian taste, Hillhouse is careful to show that the violent European criticism of Scott's romances had no precedent and no following in Britain.[21] This might well be the case, but Hillhouse's rearguard mission to save Scott's reputation blinds him to what might be the most damning condemnation that Scott received in the second half of the nineteenth century, the banishment to the nursery. Bagehot tells us that *Ivanhoe*, so important to Scott and to Britain in 1820, is really nothing more than (male) kids' stuff:

> The charm of *Ivanhoe* is addressed to a simpler sort of imagination, — to that kind of boyish fancy which idolises medieval society as the 'fighting time.' Everybody has heard of tournaments, and has a firm persuasion that in an age of tournaments life was thoroughly well understood. . . .[22]

Such a historical understanding, Bagehot informs us, is woefully incorrect. He discusses some of the great disadvantages of the middle ages and goes on to write:

> But these less imposing traits escape the rapid, and still more the boyish reader. His general impression is one of romance; and though, when roused, Scott was quite able to take a distinct view of the opposing faces, he likes his own mind to rest for the most part in the same pleasing illusion.[23]

Bagehot's Scott, then, is the intellectually flaccid laird that Carlyle bequeathed to the later Victorians, the untroubling purveyor of boy's-own adventures. And Bagehot's sense that Scott's works were essentially children's fiction was not uncommon.[24] The comments of a critic in the *London Review* from 1872 are typical:

> Such work as Jane Austen's and George Eliot's will grow in use and influence, and will probably reach lower and lower down the grades of society as education spreads itself; but such work cannot displace the simple healthful interest in lives of adventure, and all young people feel gratified in reading the Waverley Novels, unencumbered as those books are by any didactic or other purpose ulterior to the original nature of romance. . . .[25]

According to this reviewer, *all* the Waverley novels are especially suited to younger readers precisely because they have neither cognitive content nor didactic purpose. Unlike the novels of Austen and Brontë, Scott's romances do not solve real problems. They do not address adult interests or needs. They constitute a form of healthful exercise, a kind of muscular training.

If Scott's trajectory makes sense as the urgency of his fictions gets overtaken by the course of historical change, the mixture of subtle denigration and deification that marks Victorian Janeism is remarkable in its oddness. While it is tinged with a regressive nostalgia,[26] it is also touched with pseudoevangelical fervor, because it seems that Jane Austen always needs to be recovered from unwarranted neglect. This note, struck to a certain extent by Whately in 1821, was still sounding in the mid-1850s. A reviewer in the *New Monthly Magazine* defended writing an article devoted to Austen in 1852: "If this paper has something of the *rechauffé* odour of a 'retrospective' review, it is written not without a "prospective" purpose; the writer being persuaded that Jane Austen needs but to be more widely known to be more justly appreciated. . . . "[27] But if Austen has yet to be fully appreciated, she is, according to a series of articles from *Englishwoman's Domestic Magazine* in 1866, to be appreciated in part as a historical novelist:

> One of the greatest charms to us of Miss Austen's novels is the complete change of scene they afford: we are transferred at once to an old world which we can scarcely believe was England only half-a-century ago. . . .
> It will depend upon the taste of the reader whether the change to a different and more formal and quaint atmosphere will prove of interest to him . . . to most the accurate representation of that human nature which is never out of fashion will render these works of Miss Austen a very interesting study.[28]

This reviewer argues for Austen in much the same way that Scott argues for the historical novel in *Waverley*. If an interest in past times is not enough to hold the reader, the truth to human nature should be. But Austen is already a bit of an anachronism: she has, perhaps, not been fully appreciated, but she is already somewhat out of date.

Never of her time, it seems that Austen is really not much of a woman either. Even though the reviewer from the *Englishwoman's Domestic Magazine* makes an extra effort to argue that Austen is indeed "the most ladylike of artists" in her deep moderation, the article goes on to claim: "Miss Austen's brain does not seem to have any maternal love for its children: it treats them somewhat like a man of the world. As long as they do nothing dishonourable and make advantageous matches he is satisfied."[29] Austen is not a proper mother. She is, in fact, like a worldly or rather unsentimentally businesslike man, more interested in prudence than love. This claim, that Austen does not pay enough attention to passion or to female sensibility goes back to Scott and is frequently a stumbling-block for Victorian reviewers, such as Mrs. Oliphant.

So if Austen is ladylike in moderation, she is manly in being too *moderate*: not only does she not fit squarely into any time period, she does not fit squarely into either sex. To understand why this might be, let us consider her not only as the contemporary of Scott but of Mill as well, particularly of the Mill who argued in theory for universal (and not merely female) emancipation. We might want to take her belated canonization seriously as a sign that Austen's meaning had to wait until a later period before it became clear. To put this another way, Austen's solutions to problems of the Regency and the answers to the questions that *Persuasion* poses might not have made general sense until the middle years of Victoria's reign, but by then she was already too late. What would we gain if we read *Persuasion* in the context of *On Liberty*?

It is not quite clear, however, how we are to take Mill, who has suffered greatly in this century for the success he won in the last. When Mill is read by philosophers and political theorists, however sympathetic they may be, the arguments of *On Liberty* tend to be weighed analytically—that is to say, more or less ahistorically.[30] To readers inspired by Continental philosophy or radical political theory, Mill has been a disappointment since Nietzsche called him a blockhead (*Flachkopf*) and Marx dismissed him as a rather uninspired bourgeois ideologue.[31]

I would like to suggest against these approaches, which are all interventions in a field that Mill created, that we read *On Liberty* (published in 1859) as an intervention of its own.[32] As Mill makes very clear in his first few pages, champions of liberty in the eighteenth century located their struggles in the fight between an illegitimately authoritarian government and a legitimately resistant civil society. Such is the case no longer. Those friends of liberty won their fights, and government is now taken to be the agent of society, not its enemy (126–29). The struggle for freedom now takes place in the sphere of civil society itself where the single subject has to protect him- or herself from the impositions of a homogenizing public opinion which tries to reach into the most intimate areas of life:

In the modern world, the greater size of political communi-
ties, and above all, the separation between spiritual and
temporal authority . . . prevented so great an interference by
law in the details of private life; but the engines of moral
repression have been wielded more strenuously against
divergence from the reigning opinion in self-regarding, than
even in social matters. . . . (139)

The demarcation between the public and the private no longer lies
in the distinction between government and society. In fact, according to Mill, there is hardly any private sphere anymore. Ironically,
with the victory of civil jurisprudential theory, civil society has
extended its reach and practically obliterated the very realm it
sought to preserve. Mill is trying to alert his readers to this historical shift. He wants to signal what is a clear and present danger:

These tendencies of the times cause the public to be more
disposed than at most former periods to prescribe general
rules of conduct, and endeavour to make every one conform
to the approved standard. And that standard, express or tacit,
is to desire nothing strongly. Its ideal of character is to be
without any marked character; to maim by compression, like
a Chinese lady's foot, every part of human nature which
stands out prominently, and tends to make the person markedly dissimilar in outline to commonplace humanity. (199)

The casual reference to foot-binding forms part of Mill's larger
scheme to show that nineteenth-century Britain is in danger of
becoming the moral equivalent of the Orientalist's nightmare vision
of the stagnant "East." It is worth quoting a passage of considerable length:

The despotism of custom is everywhere the standing hin-
drance to human advancement, being in unceasing antago-
nism to that disposition to aim at something better than
customary, which is called, according to circumstances, the
spirit of liberty, or that of progress or improvement. The
spirit of improvement is not always a spirit of liberty, for it
may aim at forcing improvements on an unwilling people.
. . . The progressive principle, however, in either shape,
whether as the love of liberty or of improvement, is antago-
nistic to the sway of Custom, involving at least emancipa-

tion from that yoke; and the contest between the two constitutes the chief interest of the history of mankind. The
greater part of the world has, properly speaking, no history
because the despotism of Custom is complete. This is the
case over the whole East. Custom is there, in all things, the
final appeal; justice and right mean conform to custom. . . .
(200–201)

The spirits of liberty and progress stand in direct opposition to tradition and custom. Liberty and progress serve as the engines of all
that is valuable in human history, in fact, of history itself. The East,
bound by customs as outmoded as Sir Walter Elliot's notions of
deference, has no history to speak of, no improvement, and no liberty. The East—that vast swath of the world—is so hamstrung by
custom that no progress is possible.

Mill has thus borrowed from the economists the notion of the
stationary state, that secular eschatological horizon which served in
Malthus and Ricardo as the natural limit of human hope and distributive equity. But, as we shall see shortly, Mill takes moral stagnation, and not the eventual entropy of economic growth, as the
bogeyman of his tale. He uses the fine ideological sticks of "progress" and "Orientalism" to beat his readers out of complacency, to
show those readers that they are about to become that very thing
against which they so proudly define themselves.

Mill accepted the prospect of the economic stationary state as an
important thought experiment, a goad to a meditation on social
ends. Mill, who, as we saw in the first chapter, differentiated
strongly between art and science, ends and means, wants to think
beyond the mere laws of production:

But in contemplating any progressive movement, not in its
nature unlimited [i.e., given the limits on growth], the mind
is not satisfied with merely tracing the laws of the movement;
it cannot but ask the further question, to what goal? Towards
what ultimate point is society tending by its industrial progress? When the progress ceases, in what condition are we to
expect that it will leave mankind? (10:752)

Economic growth, therefore, is not an end in itself. Its termination
should tease us into thought about what it means to be human. But
the stationary state is not merely a speculative toy. It is a real prospect and was seen as such by Mill's forebears:

It must always have been seen, more or less distinctly, by
political economists, that the increase of wealth is not bound-
less; that at the end of what they term the progressive state
lies the stationary state, that all progress in wealth is but a
postponement of this, and that each step in advance is an
approach to it. . . . (10:752)

But Ricardo, Malthus, and McCulloch were terrified by the immi-
nence of economic stagnation, in large part because, following
Smith, they equated wealth with happiness (10:753).[33] This equation,
so important in the legitimation battles between virtue and happiness, between civil jurisprudential and civic republican thought in
the eighteenth century, had already begun to seem suspect by the
1830s.[34] Mill, in contrast to his teachers, does not see the process of
economic progress as particularly conducive to human happiness:

I confess I am not charmed with the ideal of life held out by
those who think that the normal state of human beings is
that of struggling to get on; that the trampling, crushing,
elbowing, and treading on each other's heels, which form the
existing type of social life, are the most desirable lot of
human kind, or anything but the disagreeable symptoms of
one of the phases of industrial progress. It may be a necessary stage in the progress of civilization . . . *But the best state
for human nature is that in which, while no one is poor, no one
desires to be richer,* nor has any reason to fear being thrust
back, by the efforts of others to push themselves forward.[35]

Mill is most concerned with "the best state for human nature." He
is more than willing to circumscribe the professional interests of
the economist and make that science serve a more comprehensive
notion of the general — that is, human — good. Competition between individuals is not the best state for human nature. Economic
man is not the model for moral humankind. Mill is quite explicit
on this point, for he argues that level population growth and a
small but stable margin of profits does not signal a decline in
human development or happiness. In fact, the opposite might well
be true. The economic stationary state would allow the working
classes to achieve true autonomy (10:763–64) and eliminate the
parasitism of the leisure classes. These developments would allow
capital and labor to cooperate on equal terms (10:768), although

Mill would like to retain some competition in the marketplace as a way of combatting the dangers of monopoly and bureaucratic "mental dulness" (10:795–96).

In Mill's account, the economic stationary state seems to be the prerequisite for the fulfillment of true utopian aspirations, not their limit. But the moral stationary state, the Asiatic despotism of Custom, poses a real threat to human happiness. Mill never tries to undercut the importance of physical comfort. Wealth, a condition for the good life, is clearly not its sole ingredient.

How to measure happiness and define the good life?[36] Not surprisingly, in his book on liberty Mill refers all questions back to the notion of utility: "I regard utility as the ultimate appeal on all ethical questions; but it must be utility in the largest sense, grounded on *the permanent interests of man as a progressive being*" (136; emphasis added). Utility here cannot be a simple mathematical aggregation of pleasures as Bentham might seem to suggest. Nor does Mill begin from the individual. Rather, Mill quite cannily defines utility in terms of *interests*,[37] not immediate goods or pleasures, and takes as his field a concept of humanity which is not limited to some synchronic notion of "society" but expands to a diachronic commitment to all mankind now and in the future. Progress here does not entail a genial or passive meliorism, but an orientation towards the good of all through all time to come, that is, an orientation towards posterity and not tradition.

The atomistic individual is thus not the place from which Mill starts. Individuality, which he discusses at great length in the third chapter of *On Liberty*, might well be one of the "principal ingredients of human happiness" (185), but it is not a given. Individuality is an earned autonomy, a product of education:[38]

> Nobody denies that people should be so taught and trained in youth as to know and benefit by ascertained results of human experience. But it is the *privilege and proper condition of a human being, arrived at the maturity of his faculties*, to use and interpret experience in his own way. It is for him to find out what part of recorded experience is properly applicable to his own circumstances and character. (186–87; emphasis added)

It is given to youth to be trained and educated in Custom, but it is the task of adults to judge for themselves. What is more, such judgments, such decisions are "the privilege and proper condition of a human being." The force of this statement is easy to overlook. What we take to be a social privilege is actually a privilege that distinguishes mature humans from all the animals and is nothing less than their "proper condition." Maturity, that which is the proper end of every man (and, as I shall argue, of every woman) is more than the ability to define experience. The *telos* of the human is the acquired ability to choose: "The human faculties of perception, judgment, discriminative feeling, mental activity, and even moral preference, are exercised only in making a choice" (187). Thus maturity and education are not only self-cultivation but also the very grounds of autonomy.

Mill's firm defense of the mature person's right to judge custom by his or her own experience relies on an equally firm Romantic organicism: "Human nature is not a machine to be built after a model, and set to do exactly the work prescribed for it, but a tree, which requires to grow and develop itself on all sides, according to the tendency of the inward forces which make it a living thing" (188). It would be a mistake to dismiss this metaphor of the tree as a mere residue of Mill's readings in von Humboldt whom he cites (and Schiller and Coleridge whom he does not). The rejection of mechanistic reductionism has important implications for Mill's version of utilitarianism, because his organicism makes universal education an imperative and the development of each and every person's individuality a matter of public and historical concern. In short, Mill uses the notions of development and individuality to make a claim for what the jurists called "imperfect rights," that is, the rights that appertain to distributive justice. The demand for individuality evens the score that the claims of commutative justice have skewed.

Mill's task, therefore, is to show *how* mature individuality is a public necessity, and *why* the individual's choice of a *Lebensplan* is a matter for public protection. Mill devotes the second chapter of *On Liberty* to "the Liberty of Thought and Discussion." Free speech is in the interest of society because it allows false customary opinions to be countered by the truth. It grants the truth a persuasive freshness, not by the cliché-ridden dictates of tradition, but by the superior ratio of convincing argument (141–70). More importantly, though, free discussion of free thought ensures that the partial truths by which we live can be fleshed out, made more nuanced, more true (171–75). Discussion is obviously all important here, for dialogue is the only means for supplementing knowledge and opinion. It serves as the crucible of wisdom (146). Just as critical as "the steady habit of correcting and completing [one's] own opinion by collating it with those of others" is the flexible irony and sense of fallibility that such a habit requires, an openness "to criticism of [one's] opinions and conduct" (146). Just as the individual must be willing to submit his or her opinions to stringent scrutiny, so must society: It is for the general good if a sole thinker, a Socrates perhaps, shows that prevailing dogma is nothing more than irrational prejudice.

Thus in the case of the free discussion of free thought the individual good and the public good coincide nicely. Mill's map of utility, in which the permanent interest of the person is also the permanent interest of the species, would indicate that the eighteenth-century conflation of government and society, where government could only be legitimized if it could prove itself to be representative and agent of civil society, has been superseded by a new nineteenth-century test of legitimacy. Society is more than the sum of its component parts, of its atomized participants, in that it matures as a corporate body much in the way that its constituents do. In its own way, Mill's account serves as a forebear of Habermas's attempt to correlate a Piaget-Kohlbergian model of moral development with social development as a whole. If we read *On Liberty* along these lines, we can begin to understand why Mill, who condemns the enforced "civilization" of other peoples (224), can claim that despotism is permissible in a society that is still in its nonage:

> Despotism is a legitimate mode of government in dealing with barbarians, provided the end be their improvement, and the means justified by actually effecting that end. Liberty, as a principle, has no application to any state of things anterior to the time when mankind have become capable of being improved by *free and equal discussion* . . . as soon as mankind have attained the capacity of being guided to their own improvement *by conviction or persuasion* (a period long since reached in all nations with whom we need here concern ourselves), compulsion . . . is no longer admissible as a means to their own good. . . . (136, emphasis added)

Mill's statement appears to merit its notoriety, for it seems to shoulder the white man's burden with the requisite degree of grim rectitude. But while his parenthetical qualification that his is a historical, not a geographical, argument could bear further interrogation, we should not ignore Mill's strategy. Mill does not want his readers' attention to wander away from Britain or Western Europe, whose own maturity is at stake. Mill is trying to ensure that *On Liberty* cannot be used as an imperialist tract, although it bears the scars of imperialist thought. Mill argues that history has happened (at least in the West) and that (Western) mankind is mature enough to make choices, to deliberate and decide. Paternalism cannot serve as a justification for class-based or gender-specific authoritarianism, be it legal or moral. Persuasion is all.

We have noted that Austen did not intend to call her last published novel *Persuasion* and that the title is apt in that so much of its plot turns on the rather abstract consideration of the proper grounds for making judgments. In its pages, Custom serves as a dubious model. Sir Walter in his vain stupidity and Lady Russell in her well-intentioned but crushing snobbery seem to embody the outmoded rule of traditions of thought whose anachronism makes them as laughable as they are destructive. Nor is a rigorous adherence to deductive principles a sure guide in a messily and resolutely empirical world. Wentworth is made to admit that his own convictions about strength of mind were ill founded. The narrator provides the vantage point of an ideal of truth in whose name Wentworth, like Anne, can break free from prejudice and assume a dialogic irony towards his own beliefs. In short, Mill's text can serve as a gloss on Austen's in such a way that we can begin to appreciate some of the features that have given Austen's novels their longevity.

Persuasion can also teach us something about *On Liberty*. Mill's polemic suffers from the fact that its author wants to maintain the telos of human perfection but does not want to fill that perfection with content, to foreclose it in the manner of an impatient or vulgar Hegelian. He wants, like a good Habermasian, to leave the discussion of specific ends to those who are most directly involved, that is, to maintain the importance of discussion. Thus Mill invokes principles and rules to regulate discussion. His liberalism therefore looks disappointingly like another version of the arid proceduralism that has long been felt to be liberalism's greatest weakness. Austen too is a bit of a proceduralist, worried about the intricate demands of decorum, and seems to follow Hume in conceiving manners on the model of law:

> As the mutual shocks in *society*, and the oppositions of interest and self-love have constrained mankind to establish the laws of *justice*, in order to preserve the advantages of mutual assistance and protection: in like manner, the eternal contrarieties, in *company*, of men's pride and self-conceit, have introduced the rules of Good Manners or Politeness, in order to facilitate the intercourse of minds, and an undisturbed commerce and conversation.[39]

Just as men institute justice to oversee the workings of society as a whole, so they establish good manners in the smaller spheres of friendship that Hume calls company. Note that for Hume manners are analogous to justice: they perform a similar function in a similar way for similar ends. They provide the rules for company, and like the law, they are meant to protect each member of that company from the designs of any of the others. In Mill's terms, they protect the freedom of the individual—most notably Anne's freedom—from the incursions of a painfully mediocre social totality. Hence Anne's disgust at her family's fawning attempts to gain the favor of Lady Dalrymple in whom "there was no superiority of manner, accomplishment, or understanding" (142) and for whom manners only serve as a way of asserting the authority granted her by the accident of birth. At the concert, Lady Dalrymple's company engages in what later is described as "selfish vanity":

> Upon Lady Russell's appearance soon afterwards, the whole party was collected, and all that remained, was to marshal themselves, and proceed into the concert room; and be of all the consequence in their power, draw as many eyes, excite as many whispers, and disturb as many people as they could. (175)

Their purpose is to disturb and to cut a figure, quite literally to make spectacles of themselves. On Hume's explicit and Austen's implicit definition, they do not display good manners in the slightest. They want to be regarded, but show the rest no regard. Their commotion is a sign of their power, but not necessarily of their good breeding.

Anne's kind treatment of the beleaguered Mrs. Smith serves, of course, as a direct counterpoint to the supercilious and self-seeking manners of her family and their more distant relations. Anne originally decides to see Mrs. Smith when she is assured of "the satisfaction which a visit from Miss Elliot would give" (144–45). Subsequently, when she declines the offer of a visit to the illustrious Lady Dalrymple to see her sick acquaintance (149), Sir Walter cannot believe that Anne could prefer Mrs. Smith to "her own family connections among the nobility of England and Ireland" (150). But she can and does. First of all, her good offices are part of her general commitment to the practice of benevolence and care. In addition, in keeping with her remarkably liberal interest in the good base-born men of the Navy, Anne does not care for station but for signs of intelligence and integrity. What is more, Anne is out to learn. Here is her reaction to Mrs. Smith's sole recreation of gossiping with nurse Rooke:

> Anne, far from wishing to cavil at the pleasure, replied, "I can easily believe it. Women of that class have great opportunities, and if they are intelligent may be well worth listening to. Such varieties of human nature as they are in the habit of witnessing! And not merely in its follies, that they are well read; for they see it occasionally under every circumstance that can be most interesting or affecting. . . .
> A sick chamber may often furnish the worth of volumes."
> (147–48)

When Mrs. Smith tries to disabuse Anne of this rather optimistic view, she betrays her own disappointments. Mrs. Smith cannot know that just a few paragraphs earlier, Anne found *her* an outstanding example of mental resilience and moral stature. Anne does not want to dismiss gossip as an idle pleasure but wants to see in it a very positive good, for it provides examples of both the best and the worst in human life. Not only does Anne visit Mrs. Smith out of kindness and friendship; she is also there on a fact-finding mission.

Anne is intensely interested in the way that other people live, especially if they live what seems to be the good life. As we have seen, she goes to some lengths to understand Mrs. Smith's composure and good spirits. She constantly is on the lookout for happiness. She is careful to notice it in Lyme in the "ingenious contrivances and nice arrangements" Captain Harville has concocted in his lodgings there which make those lodgings "the picture of repose and domestic happiness" (96). She subjects life at Uppercross to a rather minute inspection, but her most vivid meditations are all devoted to the Crofts:

> They brought with them their country habit of being almost always together. He was ordered to walk, to keep off the gout, and Mrs Croft seemed to go shares with him in everything, and to walk for her life, to do him good. . . . Knowing their feelings as she did, it was a most attractive picture of happiness to her. (159)

Of all the false forms of happiness associated with the Musgroves and the Elliots and of all the truer forms of happiness amongst the naval couples and Mrs. Smith, Anne and Austen pay the closest attention to the "picture of happiness" presented by the remarkably companionate marriage of Admiral and Mrs. Croft. Anne admires their "happy independence" and what appears to be the rational equality that exists between them. Or perhaps we should say, an equality based on rationality. After all, not only does Mrs. Croft participate in all conversations, but she, as a rational creature (so she argues) can participate in every aspect of the Admiral's life, even going off to sea with him (68–71).

Persuasion, like the rest of Austen's novels, is obsessed with happiness and, like the rest of those books, associates happiness with marriage. A number of feminist critics have, with some good reason, taken exception to this aspect of Austen's tales. But we should not forget that marriage is a historically determined cipher for happiness here. Apart from a life of letters (Austen's own refuge),[40] marriage constitutes a young woman's last best hope. Like Mary Shelley, Austen takes the universalism of the appeal to happiness quite seriously. She is deeply concerned with finding possible formulas for happiness for women as well as men. Now, it is true that her study of the middling classes limits her universalism in a way that has made Raymond Williams see her focus as ideological in the thickest sense, a class claim that seeks to be a universal one.[41]

But we need to interject an "and yet, and yet, and yet." If we take *Persuasion* as a parable of social change and apparent progress, of the accession of new groups to social power, then we might have to concede that *Persuasion*, even more than *Pride and Prejudice*, opens the door to an even truer universalism, a substantive—though always historically limited—vision of the good life. Austen's progressivism here makes social change normal and desirable.

Persuasion is thus a particularly interesting text in that, along with Austen's usual emphasis on female happiness, it makes a claim for female citizenship, for women having standing in the state. Her version of Britain can include women where Scott's could not because Scott, following Smith and Burke, wants to maintain a strict demarcation between society and the state. Austen, looking forward to Mill (but drawing, like him, on the teachings of the jurists), can be seen to accept the occlusion of the categorical difference between society and the state. If the state is erected upon the base of the civil society which it represents, then social power will be the most important thing. And if civil society is the domain of physical and economic reproduction, then women will have a critical place.

Of course, women are not allowed into the market in this book and therefore they can be—at best—equal but separate. Furthermore, economic reproduction is not a direct issue in the novel, although economic distribution is. As in that other romance of economic change, *Robinson Crusoe*, wealth is a kind of windfall, in this case won overseas and brought safely (and apparently bloodlessly) home. And so if my rather positive reading of *Persuasion* is to be properly nuanced, I will have to concede that the novel is Victorian in all the best and worst senses of the word. In its commitments to improvement, progress, universalism, and happiness, it displays some of the more appealing aspects of Victorian hope. On the other hand, it maps moral progress onto (bourgeois) economic success and mobility, preserves a gendered distinction between the spheres, and locates all happiness in the privacy of a moralized, feminized domestic unit which is kept apart from the very economic forces that serve as its basis.

Nevertheless, Austen was hardly blind to the economic pressures on women. As we have noted, it has been a commonplace in the criticism from Scott's review of *Emma* to the present day that Austen's heroines—and her narrator—are, if anything, too prudent, too aware of market fluctuations. What would happen if the making of wealth were to feature centrally in an Austen novel? Would it be granted the same celebration that is accorded the sudden riches and social prominence of sailors in *Persuasion*? Is it even possible that the trucking and bartering of economic man could figure in a "domestic" novel? It is hard to say, because the only one of Austen's novels, *Sanditon*, that could have begun to provide the answers to these questions remained unfinished at her death.

The engine of *Sanditon*—both the place and the novel—is speculation and many of its characters are caught up in the attempt to turn a small seaside village into a "place," a resort. Lady Denham, a major investor in the scheme, does not quite understand the way things work. She and Mr. Parker, the chief promoter of Sanditon, disagree about the usefulness to their prospects of "West Indians," that is, of the would-be nabobs of the sugar plantations of Barbados and Jamaica. Lady Denham does not approve of them on two grounds. On the one hand, their money makes them fancy themselves "equal, may be, to your old Country Families."⁴² Lady Denham's snobbery would be understandable (if reprehensible) if she herself were born to an "old Country family," whereas she was born a commoner and married her title, or rather, married for it (375–76). Nevertheless, her indictment continues. While the West Indians pose a threat to her self-esteem, their arrival will surely hurt her purse:

> "But then, they who scatter their Money so freely, never think of whether they may not be doing mischief [sic] by raising the price of Things—And I have heard that's very much the case with your West-injines—and if they come among us to raise the price of our necessaries of Life, we shall not much thank them Mr Parker."—"My dear Madam, They can only raise the price of consumable Articles, by such an extraordinary Demand for them & such a diffusion of Money among us, as must do us more Good than harm.— Our Butchers & Bakers & Traders in general cannot get rich without bringing Prosperity to *us*. If *they* do not gain, our rents must be insecure—& in proportion to their profit must be ours eventually in the increased value of our houses." "Oh!—well.—But I should not like to have Butcher's meat raised, though—& I shall keep it down as long as I can." (392–93)

Lady Denham does not understand the point that Mr. Parker makes, that the increase of money chasing the same amount of goods can only make those goods worth more at the market. And the high rents, which Lady Denham and Mr. Parker look forward to, depend directly on the increased profits of the merchants of the town. Charlotte Heywood, the ingenue heroine of Austen's tale, smiles at Lady Denham's selfish stupidity without further comment. But no further comment is needed. Lady Denham can only imagine herself as a consumer, not as a landlord. She can only think in terms of short-term costs. And Mr. Parker has already warned Charlotte of Lady Denham's "Littleness": "She cannot look forward quite as I would have her — & takes alarm at a trifling present expence without considering what returns it will make her in a year or two" (376). Lady Denham does not understand the hydraulics of distribution in the market economy as outlined by Smith, Ricardo, and Malthus. She does not see that higher prices can only serve her.

Interestingly enough, Lady Denham's fears are remarkably close to those voiced by Charlotte's father, a hail gentleman farmer who is remarkable (with his wife) for fertility. They have fourteen children, and with this burden have led a quiet life, "stationary and healthy at Willingden" (374). The elder Heywood does not care for resorts, because they are bad things "for a country; — sure to raise the price of Provisions & make the Poor good for nothing" (368). Heywood, as a farmer, stands to gain personally from a rise in the price of food, but he will only argue in terms of the national good. Prices rise and the poor get spoiled. Heywood sounds like an old-style Country Whig who mistrusts all forms of urban development and all the dangers of an urban proletariat. Parker tries to answer him on precisely this score, but falls back into the telegraphic puffery of his conversational style.

Hence *Sanditon* provides two different ways to criticize speculative development and, if the novel were completed, we could perhaps see if Austen — the great portraitist of Bath and eulogist for Lyme — had become less sanguine when dealing with resorts that had yet to be created. The reader knows that Lady Denham is a dangerously selfish fool. But the reader does not know quite how to place the firmly physiocratic Mr. Heywood. If the novel were to come down squarely with Heywood, then it would mark a distinct departure from *Persuasion* which posits a close connection between a seaside resort, new wealth, and dreams of a companionate happiness. It would seem to mitigate that novel's firm equation of moral and economic "progress" as well.

It is also hard to tell whether Austen viewed commercial speculation as the only type of modern economic relations; whether she
saw the wide diffusion of luxuries (such as those sold at Sanditon's
library) as the single signal aspect of the capitalist order. If she did
(and thus exempted the farmer from her critique and ignored the
industrialist as well), then she was returning to the language of the
Augustans. She would sound like Pope and Swift who saw the modern swerve to commercialism as a moral threat to the nation.

The Augustans, as Pocock has shown and as we mentioned in
the second chapter, distrusted the new credit-based economy because it shattered economic and moral independence while turning
value into a matter of speculative freaks and crises. Pocock has also
argued, and this is significant for our reading, that credit and credit
society were both troped as women, fragile in their stability and
vulnerable to vapors.[43] Thus the hypochondria of the goddessling
Spleen ("Pain at her Side and Megrim in her head") in "The Rape
of the Lock" is tied to the unnatural and imaginary grotesques of
her grotto ("Men prove with Child, as pow'rful Fancy works") and
to Belinda's (and the poem's) untoward fascination with commodi-
ties. In this light it is hardly surprising to read Charlotte Heywood's reaction to the supposed illness of the Misses Parker:

> It was impossible for Charlotte not to suspect a good deal of
> fancy in such an extraordinary state of health. . . . The Park-
> ers, were no doubt a family of Imagination & quick feel-
> ings — and while the eldest Brother found vent for his super-
> fluity of sensation as a Projector, the Sisters were perhaps
> driven to dissipate theirs in the invention of odd complaints.
> (412)

Charlotte equates hypochondria with speculation, although she
does not — to be fair — bind the two in a causal relation. Rather, they
are both effects of another cause — a too-ready imagination. But
Austen comes closer to her Augustan forebears in what is perhaps
the most strikingly odd aspect of the fragment, its bizarre emphasis, not on the dialogue common to all Austen novels, but to the
long linguistic riffs in which the characters indulge. The reader is
treated to long, absurd disquisitions by Sir Edward, the immoral
misreader of fiction and failed sentimental villain, and by Mr. Parker
who talks like an early nineteenth-century advertisement. They
are monomaniacs whose mania so infects and expands their speech

that they can do nothing but speak reams of cliché or "hard words." Forster's complaint about *Sanditon*, that it does not care about character, is just, but misapplied.[44] *Sanditon* does not care about character because Austen is transfixed by the degradation of language that occurs in this novel's cave of spleen, selfishness, and intrigue. No less than Pope, she makes her book a satire on the way language and speculation lead to dullness not only in the male but in the female characters as well. Charlotte Heywood hardly says a word, nor does she need to. And it might well be that she *cannot*. *Sanditon* reserves speech for those who are so captivated by their fancies that their words themselves are tainted almost beyond repair, because they reveal the basal stupidity of the place and its occupations. For Sanditon is a predatory town that dare not speak its nature; a site of a dangerously ridiculous and modern form of economic and linguistic quixotism.

To read this fragment in this way is to pit it against *Persuasion* and to counter the proleptic Victorianism I have attributed to Austen with an equally anachronistic Augustanism, in which the almost atrocious virility of the landed gentleman (fourteen children!) is contrasted with the effeminate degradation of the invalid. But we cannot leap to such conclusions, to read the novel synechdochally like *Persuasion*. To do so would be to fall into the trap that catches Sir Edward and Lady Denham so easily. The young man, who thinks himself a Lovelace, has been formed by his resolute misunderstanding of the books he has read. He concentrates too closely on "the most impassion'd, & most exceptional parts of Richardsons [novels]" (404) without realizing that they are exceptional *because* they are *not* the heart and pith of the novels in which they appear. It is also impossible to say if the much-discussed Sidney Parker, the wandering brother who never actually makes it into the book, will turn out to be a virtuous venture capitalist, an aspiring country farmer, or another speculating cad.

It is frustrating not to have more of *Sanditon*, because it seems to promise so much. It appears to engage the discourse of political economics so clearly and from such a strong moral bias. It seems to pick up where *Persuasion* left off and interrogate the very commitments that make *Persuasion* turn out as it does. But such a reading, as I began to indicate above, might also substitute our anachronisms for Austen's. While Regency critics might have faulted Austen's heroines for their rather demystified understanding of the economics of marriage, her novels are always sure to place characters who are monomaniacally self-seeking, the hypocrites like Mr. Elliot, in a terrible light. Following these clues we might ignore her contemporaries and read her, as MacIntyre does, as a communitarian. For she is both "communitarian" (and that as many critics have shown, is an awfully muddy designation) and an "individualist." She falls back on the language of the previous century because it is for her the most convenient way to attack and to broaden the reductionist self-descriptions of economic man. *Sanditon* might have looked and read differently if Austen had been able to read Mill's critique of economic and moral atomism; that is, if she had lived later and had been able to draw on a language that drew equally on utilitarian universalism and individualist defenses of liberty. But one could argue—as I think I have—that the project of Austen's six published novels was precisely to move towards an articulation of such a language, and that she makes most sense in the light of that idiom. Austen was most obviously of her time in the way that she pointed backwards and forwards anachronistically, thus creating a history for herself and a history that had to include her.

6

The Constancy of Crisis

In this study, I have claimed that the rapid growth and institutional consolidation of commercial capitalism in the eighteenth century created a demand for new descriptions of and apologias for the economy, the state, morality, and citizenship, a demand that was taken up by an increasingly rationalized public sphere which included both the field of political economics and the novel. The most successful mode of describing and defending the changing structure of Georgian Britain drew on the languages of post-Reformation civil jurisprudence and post-Newtonian liberal theology. By cross-fertilizing the notions of a providential order based on the transparency of immutable natural law and the primacy of commutative rights in the getting, keeping, and transfer of property, apologists were able to set the terms of debate and propose that happiness was the proper end of society and that virtue should be reconceived as the handmaid of that end. We can say that this sweeping project was constituted by tensions between competing principles and definitions. The tension that has served as the focus of attention for this book has been the conflict between a new emphasis on commutative justice and a more traditional fascination with distributive justice that received new energy from the normative elevation of "happiness."

In order to save *The Business of Common Life* from the abstractions of a history of ideas, I have tried to suggest that the implications of this legitimation strategy were worked out over time under the impress of immediate political problems and contemporary social questions. It should come as no surprise that the thirty-four year period between the publication of Malthus's first *Essay* and the Great Reform Act should have been the same period in which economics and the novel should have gained intellectual and critical respectability, for in this time of periodic depression and agitation for Catholic Emancipation, general constitutional reform, and the repeal of the Corn Laws, the question of the legitimacy of old and new institutions became even more compelling and more urgent.

But behind the historicism that informs the specific discussions of this book, there is also a strain of anti-historicism, of hermeneutic recuperation, even if it is more influenced by Adorno and Benjamin than by Gadamer and Jauss. For I am interested that *Frankenstein* and Austen should have retained their cultural importance to our own day, an importance visible in the remarkable half-life of Shelley's monster and in institutions such as the largely nonprofessional Jane Austen Society of North America. Similar claims could be made for Malthus, whose principle of population is alive and well on the "op ed" pages of American newspapers and in the works of environmentalists. The notion of trickle-down economics was first propounded in Smith's *Theory of Moral Sentiments* almost 225 years before Reagan championed the idea in his first term. And the ever-present political squabbles about international trade still echo the Ricardo-Malthus debate.

Furthermore, Americans might want to take seriously the fact that the definition of "liberal" has become so muddy. In the arena of political polemic, "liberal" is an epithet to describe someone motivated by the apparently suspect desire to redistribute wealth according to need (which is troped as desert). On the other hand, in the more rarified realm of political philosophy liberalism has come under a lot of fire over the last two decades for being too fascinated by individual (male) rights and prerogatives, and for not paying enough attention to the categories of community, of the feminine, and of the good. It has been the contention of this study that these views are both correct and essentially flawed. The liberal legitimation of modernity, of modern capitalism and development, has been caught in a constant dance to protect both rights and happiness, both the individual and the general good. And the dance continues to the present in both theory and practice.

This is not the forum for discussing the practical manifestations of what I have called the constitutive tension of liberalism. I do not have that expertise. But I do want to mention the implications of Michael Sandel's justly famous theoretical critique of John Rawls's influential account of justice.[1] Sandel maintains that Rawls contradicts himself, and this is a serious, if not fatal, charge to level at a writer who seeks the first principles of justice. Rawls has set out to defend each person's "inviolability founded on justice"[2] against utilitarianism which "does not take seriously the distinction between persons."[3] At the same time, however, he wants to show that "social and economic inequalities . . . are just only if they result in compensating benefits for everyone, and in particular for the least advantaged members of society."[4] Sandel demonstrates very nicely how Rawls's defense of distributive justice depends on precisely the utilitarian principles that his deontological safeguards of "the distinction between persons" try to refute.[5]

Sandel then does something very interesting. In the last paragraphs of the book, he seems to equate deontological—that is to say, individualistic—liberalism with liberalism per se in order to urge us to go beyond liberalism. But this conclusion is blind to the insight of his study: Liberalism seems to require some version of the primacy of commutative right *at the same time* that it draws on utilitarian notions of distributive justice. Rich descriptions of liberalism that take into account discourses other than that of foundational philosophy have to admit the strong insistence of both principles.

At the same time, the confrontation between Rawls and Sandel has at least one other implication. Neither Sandel nor Rawls seems quite comfortable with the tension between commutative and distributive justice. This tension is experienced as a contradiction and seems to betoken a crisis. And crisis, as Koselleck has argued, always seems to call for choice: witness Rawls's advocacy of deontological liberalism and Sandel's concomitant gestures at communitarianism.

I would like to generalize from this. One could say that since the mid-eighteenth century, Anglo-American capitalism and the states that maintain it have been caught in a constant legitimation crisis. This view takes some of the urgency out of the drive to choose between these two principles of justice. Citing Rawls as an example, we can say that such choices are self-mutilating at worst or self-delusive at best. Both commutative and distributive justice have strong critical, progressive edges—one need only look at argu-

ments for human rights or universal health care to see this. As terrifying as crisis might seem, it could well be that crisis is the
order—not the ordeal—of the day and of all our days, the order
that defines modernity's self-description.

Notes

Preface

1. In many ways one can read Anthony Arblaster, *The Rise and Decline of Western Liberalism* (Oxford: Blackwell, 1984), as a commentary on C. B. Macpherson's influential, and now dated, *The Political Theory of Possessive Individualism* (Oxford: Oxford UP, 1962).
2. Ian Shapiro, *The Evolution of Rights in Liberal Theory* (New York: Cambridge UP, 1986).
3. Gordon S. Wood, *The Radicalism of the American Revolution* (New York: Knopf, 1992).
4. Max Weber, *Economy and Society*, ed. Günther Roth and Claus Wittich (Berkeley: U of California P, 1978) 954.
5. Weber 211–13.
6. Weber 33–36, 215, 954.

CHAPTER ONE: Dialectics, Systems, and Context

1. For more recent work on seventeenth- and eighteenth-century political economics in Britain see, amongst others: Joyce Oldham Appleby, *Economic Thought and Ideology in Seventeenth Century England* (Princeton: Princeton UP, 1977); Istvan Hont and Michael Ignatieff, eds., *Wealth and Virtue* (Cambridge: Cambridge UP, 1983); S. Todd Lowry, ed., *Pre-Classical Economic Thought* (Boston: Kluwer Academic Publishers, 1987); David McNally, *Political Economy and the Rise of Capitalism*; J.G.A. Pocock, *Virtue, Commerce, and History* (Cambridge: Cambridge UP, 1985); Richard F. Teichgraeber III, *'Free Trade' and Moral Philosophy* (Durham: Duke UP, 1986).

There has been, of course, considerable work done on the etiology and the establishment of the novel in England in the last few years. I am particularly indebted to: Nancy Armstrong, *Desire and Domestic Fiction* (New York: Oxford UP, 1987); Michael McKeon, *The Origins of the English Novel 1600–1750* (Baltimore: Johns Hopkins UP, 1987); J. P. Hunter, *Before Novels* (New York: Norton, 1990).

2. For the influence of Stewart on subsequent economic theory, see Stefan Collini, Donald Winch, and John Burrow, *That Noble Science of Politics* (Cambridge: Cambridge UP, 1983) 29–64; Biancamaria Fontana, *Rethinking the Politics of Commercial Society* (Cambridge: Cambridge UP, 1985) 6–105.

3. James P. Henderson, "Just Notions of Political Economy," *Research in the History of Economic Thought and Methodology* 2 (1984): 1–20.

4. See note 2.

5. For another view of Malthus's differences with the Reviewers, see James P. Henderson, "Malthus and the *Edinburgh Review*," *Research in the History of Economic Thought and Methodology* 2 (1984): 107–24.

6. The most authoritative account of this interaction remains Boyd Hilton, *Corn, Cash and Commerce* (Oxford: Oxford UP, 1977); see also Barry Gordon, *Political Economy in Parliament* (London: Macmillan, 1976), and Gary F. Langer, *The Coming of Age of Political Economy 1815–1825* (New York: Greenwood P, 1987), especially 27–82.

7. W. D. Stockwell, "Contributions of Henry Brougham to Classical Political Economy," *History of Political Economy* 23:4 (1991): 645–73.

8. See Stewart J. Brown, *Thomas Chalmers and the Godly Commonwealth* (Oxford: Oxford UP, 1982), and Boyd Hilton, *The Age of Atonement* (Oxford: Oxford UP, 1988).

9. James P. Henderson, "The Political Economy Club," *Research in the History of Economic Thought and Methodology* 2 (1984): 77–105; see also the same author's "The Oral Tradition in British Economics," *History of Political Economy* 15:2 (1983): 149–80.

10. Victor L. Hilts, "*Aliis exterendum*," *Isis* 69 (1978): 21–43; Lawrence Goldman, "The Origins of British Social Science," *Historical Journal* 26:3 (1983): 587–611.

11. Michael Munday, "The Novel and Its Critics in the Early Nineteenth Century," *Studies in Philology* 79:2 (1982): 205–26; Ina Ferris, *The Achievement of Literary Authority* (Ithaca: Cornell UP, 1991).

12. T[heodor] W. Adorno, *Minima Moralia*, trans. E.F.N. Jephcott (London: Verso, 1978) 145.

13. See Walter Benjamin, "On Some Motifs in Baudelaire" and "The Work of Art in the Age of Mechanical Reproduction," *Illuminations*, trans. Harry Zohn (New York: Schocken, 1969) 155–200, 253–64; Richard Wolin, *Walter Benjamin* (New York: Columbia UP, 1979) 213–50; Gary Smith, ed., "Experience and Materialism in Benjamin's *Passagenwerk*," *Benjamin: Philosophy, Aesthetics, History* (Chicago: U of Chicago P, 1989) 210–27. For another approach to this same theme, see Michael Taussig, *Mimesis and Alterity* (New York: Routledge, 1993).

14. Johann Peter Eckermann, *Gespraeche mit Goethe*, ed. Fritz Bergmann (Berlin: Insel Verlag, 1955) 622–23.
15. This is a rather common argument now and, I think, an accurate one. My own contribution to thinking about thinking about the legitimacy of the humanities can be found (for what it is worth) in "The Profession of Theory," *PMLA* 106:2 (1990): 519–30.
16. In the discussion that follows, I will refer to several Adorno texts: Max Horkheimer and Theodor W. Adorno, *Dialectic of Enlightenment*, trans. John Cumming (New York: Continuum, 1986); Adorno, *Introduction to the Sociology of Music*, trans. E. B. Ashton (New York: Continuum, 1976); Adorno, *Negative Dialectics*, trans. E. B. Ashton (New York: Continuum, 1973); Adorno, "Thesen zur Kunstsoziologie," *Ohne Leitbild* (Frankfurt: Suhrkamp, 1967) 94–103; and *Hegel: Three Studies*. For the sake of speed and clarity, these texts will be referred to parenthetically within the body of my argument according to the following abbreviations: *Dialectic of Enlightenment* will appear as *DE*; *Introduction to the Sociology of Music* will appear as *ISM*; *Negative Dialectics* as *ND*; *Ohne Leitbild* will appear as *OL*; and *Hegel: Three Studies* will appear as *Hegel*.
17. Adorno, *Aesthetische Theorie* (Frankfurt: Suhrkamp, 1973) 530; a different translation can be found in *Aesthetic Theory*, trans. C. Lenhardt (London: Routledge and Kegan Paul, 1984) 489.
18. Adorno, *Hegel: Three Studies*, trans. Shierry Weber Nicholsen (Cambridge: MIT P, 1993) 57–59.
19. G.W.F. Hegel, *Phenomenology of the Spirit*, trans. A. V. Miller (New York: Oxford UP, 1977) 51.
20. Aristotle, "Categories," *The Basic Works*, trans. Richard McKeon (New York: Random House, 1941) 8:23, 25.
21. See also Adorno's seminal articles: "On the Fetish Character of Music and the Regression of Listening," in *The Essential Frankfurt School Reader*, eds. Andrew Arato and Eeike Gebhardt (New York: Continuum, 1982) 270–99, and "On Lyric and Society," *Notes to Literature*, trans. Shierry Weber Nicholsen, vol. 1 (New York: Columbia UP, 1991–92) 37–54.
22. Albrecht Wellmer, "Reason, Utopia and Enlightenment," in *Habermas and Modernity*, ed. Richard J. Bernstein (Cambridge: MIT P, 1985) 65. See also Wellmer, "Truth, Semblance, Reconciliation: Adorno's Redemption of Modernity," in *The Persistence of Modernity*, trans. David Midgley (Cambridge: MIT P, 1991) 1–35.
23. Lambert Zuidervaart, *Adorno's Aesthetic Theory* (Cambridge: MIT P, 1991) 299.
24. Luhmann has written voluminously in German and only a small amount of his work has been translated. The discussion that follows will draw mostly on three works: *The Differentiation of Society*, trans. Stephen Holmes and Charles Larmore (New York: Columbia UP, 1982); *Ecological Commu-*

nication, trans. John Bednarz, Jr. (Chicago: U of Chicago P, 1989); *Essays on Self-Reference* (New York: Columbia UP, 1990). In the notes hereafter, these books will be referred to by title only. For the primacy of communication and its relation to system, see, inter alia, *Essays on Self-Reference* 1-106 and *Ecological Communication* 28-31.

25. This point is most forcefully expressed in *Essays on Self-Reference* 1-7; see also *Ecological Communication*, passim.

26. Luhmann, *Essays on Self-Reference* 52-61; Jürgen Habermas, *The Philosophical Discourse of Modernity*, trans. Frederick Lawrence (Cambridge: MIT P, 1987) 369-70.

27. Edmund Husserl, *Cartesian Meditations*, trans. Dorion Cairns (The Hague: Martinus Nijhoff, 1977) 33.

28. Luhmann, *Differentiation of Society* 230; *Ecological Communication* 11-50.

29. *Differentiation of Society* 232-35.

30. *Differentiation of Society* 236.

31. *Ecological Communication* 48-9.

32. *Ecological Communication* 113-14.

33. *Differentiation of Society* 328.

34. *Ecological Communication* 122-26.

35. Of course, "instrumental" is the Frankfurt School's name for what Weber called "formal" reason. See Max Weber, *From Max Weber*, eds. H. H. Gerth and C. Wright Mills (New York: Oxford UP, 1946) 298-99, 331; Stephen Kalberg, "Max Weber's Types of Rationality: Cornerstones for the Analysis of Rationalization Processes in History," *American Journal of Sociology* 85.5 (1980): 1145-79.

36. *Essays on Self-Reference* 123-41; *Ecological Communication* 121-26.

37. Habermas, *Philosophical Discourse of Modernity* 368-85.

38. Keith Tribe, *Land, Labour and Economic Discourse* (London: Routledge and Kegan Paul, 1978) 10, 25, 35.

39. David Bell, *Husserl* (New York: Routledge, 1990) 160-63.

40. Habermas 359.

41. Habermas 371. His point seems well borne out by the extreme askesis of *Ecological Communication*.

42. John Stuart Mill, "*The Quarterly Review* on Political Economy," *The Collected Works of John Stuart Mill*, ed. John M. Robson, vol. 4 (Toronto: U of Toronto P, 1963-91) 26.

43. Mill 4:28.

44. Mill 4:30.

45. David Ricardo, *The Works of David Ricardo*, ed. Piero Sraffa, vol. 1 (Cambridge: Cambridge UP, 1951-73) 167.

46. V. W. Bladen, *From Adam Smith to Maynard Keynes: The Heritage of Political Economy* (Toronto: U of Toronto P, 1974) 184-86.

47. Mark Blaug, *Ricardian Economics* (New Haven: Yale UP, 1958) 32; see also

John Cunnigham Wood, ed., "David Ricardo," *David Ricardo: Critical Assessments*, vol. 1 (London: Croon Helm, 1985) 209–16. See also F. R. Kolb, "The Stationary State of Ricardo and Malthus," in Wood, 1:235–50.

48. Mill 4:309–39. All further references to this article will be included parenthetically within the body of the text.

49. Anna Laetitia Barbauld, "On the Origin and Progress of Novel-Writing," *The British Novelists*, vol. 1 (London, 1810) 1–62. All further references to this work will be included parenthetically within the body of the text.

50. See J.G.A. Pocock, *The Machiavellian Moment* (Princeton: Princeton UP, 1975) 426–32.

51. James Mill, *Elements of Political Economy*, 3rd ed. (London: Bohn, 1844) 1.

52. See Armstrong 28–95.

53. Jane Haldiman Marcet, *Conversations on Political Economy* (New York: Duyckink, 1820) 13.

54. William Hazlitt, "Standard Novels and Romances," *Collected Works*, ed. Alfred Rayney Waller and Arnold Glovers, vol. 10 (London: Dent, 1904) 25. This article was originally published in the *Edinburgh Review* in February, 1815.

CHAPTER TWO: Burke and Paine Meet *Frankenstein*

1. Mary Shelley, *Frankenstein* (Harmondsworth: Penguin Books, 1985) 255. All further references will be included parenthetically in the text.

2. Here is Paine in *The Rights of Man*: "It is their sanguinary punishments which corrupt mankind." Michael Foot and Isaac Kramnick, ed., *The Thomas Paine Reader* (Harmondsworth: Penguin Books, 1987) 213.

3. Friedrich Nietzsche, *The Will to Power*, trans. Walter Kaufmann and R. J. Hollingdale (New York: Random House, 1967) 148.

4. Nietzsche 404.

5. David Marshall, *The Surprising Effects of Sympathy* (Chicago: U of Chicago P, 1988) 178–227.

6. Lee Sterrenburg, "Mary Shelley's Monster: Politics and Psyche in *Frankenstein*," in *The Endurance of Frankenstein*, ed. George Levine and U. C. Knoepflmacher (Berkeley: U of California P, 1979) 143–71.

7. See, inter alia, Harold Bloom, "*Frankenstein*, or the Modern Prometheus," *The Ringers in the Tower* (Chicago: Chicago UP, 1971) 119–30; Leslie Tannenbaum, "From Filthy Type to Truth: Miltonic Myth in *Frankenstein*," *Keats-Shelley Journal* 26 (1977): 101–13; Sandra Gilbert and Susan Gubar, *The Madwoman in the Attic* (New Haven: Yale UP, 1979) 213–47; Paul Sherwin, "*Frankenstein*: Creation as Catastrophe," *PMLA* 96 (1981): 883–903; Mary Jacobus, "Is There a Woman in This Text?" *New Literary History* 14 (1982): 117–42; Margaret Homans, *Bearing the Word* (Chicago: Chicago UP, 1987) 100–19; Chris Baldick, *In Frankenstein's Shadow* (New York: Oxford UP,

1987) 30–62; John B. Lamb, "Mary Shelley's *Frankenstein* and Milton's Monstrous Myth," *Nineteenth-Century Literature* 47 (1992): 303–19.

8. See note 5.

9. Jerome McGann, "The Meaning of the Ancient Mariner," in *Spirits of Fire*, ed. G. A. Rosso and Daniel P. Watkins (Rutherford: Fairleigh Dickinson UP, 1990) 208–39.

10. Reinhart Koselleck, *Futures Past*, trans. Keith Tribe (Cambridge: MIT P, 1985) 23.

11. Koselleck 257.

12. Gerald MacNeice, *Shelley and the Revolutionary Idea* (Cambridge: Harvard UP, 1969) 10–41; Lee Sterrenburg, "Mary Shelley's Monster," *The Endurance of Frankenstein* 152–53.

13. Marshall 182.

14. Sterrenburg 165; see also Ronald Paulson, *Representations of Revolution* (New Haven: Yale UP, 1983) 215–47.

15. Thus Godwin: "The sum of the arguments which have been here offered amounts to a species of presumption that the term of human life may be prolonged, and that by the immediate operation of intellect, beyond any limits which we are able to assign." *Enquiry Concerning Political Justice* (Harmondsworth: Penguin Books, 1985) 776.

16. Paine 229.

17. Edmund Burke, *Reflections on the Revolution in France* (Harmondsworth: Penguin, 1968) 157. All further references to this edition will be included parenthetically in the text.

18. Paine 262.

19. *Virtue, Commerce, and History* 288.

20. For the Swiftian overtones of Burke's *Reflections*, see Paulson 57–87.

21. For Burke's understanding and defense of commercial modernity, see *Virtue, Commerce, and History* 193–212, 288; for Paine, see 288. It is worth bearing in mind that Paine's justification of revolution is based on his notion of material progress: "Agriculture, commerce, manufactures, and the tranquil arts, by which the property of Nations is best promoted, require a different system of government, and a different species of knowledge to direct its operations, than what might have been required in the former condition of the world." Paine 262.

22. See H. T. Dickinson, *Liberty and Property* (New York: Holmes and Meier, 1977), and the extraordinary collection of essays in *Wealth and Virtue*, ed. Istvan Hont and Michael Ignatieff (Cambridge: Cambridge UP, 1983).

23. J.C.D. Clark, *English Society 1688–1832* (New York: Cambridge UP, 1985); J.A.W. Gunn, *Beyond Liberty and Property* (Kingston: McGill-Queen's UP, 1983) 7–42, 120–64; Ian R. Christie, *Stress and Stability in Late Eighteenth Century Britain* (Oxford: Oxford UP, 1984); Linda Colley, *Britons: Forging a Nation 1707–1837* (New Haven: Yale UP, 1992).

24. Garry Wills, *Inventing America* (New York: Doubleday, 1978).

25. P.G.M. Dickson, *The Financial Revolution in England* (London: Macmillan, 1967); Neil McKendrick, John Brewer, and J. H. Plumb, *The Birth of a Consumer Society* (London: Hutchinson, 1982). My discussion is particularly indebted to John Brewer, *The Sinews of Power* (New York: Knopf, 1988).

26. *The Sinews of Power* 147.

27. Gunn 1–42, 88–89, 258–315; Brewer, *The Sinews of Power* 216–17.

28. Jürgen Habermas, *The Structural Transformation of the Public Sphere*, trans. Thomas Burger (Cambridge: MIT P, 1989) 28–43.

29. M. M. Goldsmith, "Liberty, luxury and the pursuit of happiness," *The Languages of Political Theory in Early-Modern Europe*, ed. Anthony Pagden (Cambridge: Cambridge UP, 1987) 225–52.

30. Michael Ignatieff, *The Needs of Strangers* (London: Chatto and Windus, 1984) 92–93.

31. Ignatieff provides the most succinct summary of the conflict between the two views of luxury. See *The Needs of Strangers* 107–31; for the classical restatement of the republican position, see *The Machiavellian Moment* 423–505.

32. See especially *Virtue, Commerce, and History* 37–50, 103–24.

33. Richard Cumberland, "De Legibus Naturae," in *British Moralists 1650–1800*, ed. D. D. Raphael, vol. 1 (Oxford: Oxford UP, 1969) 86–88.

34. Raphael 1:101–2.

35. Stanley Green, *Shaftesbury's Philosophy of Religion and Ethics* (Cincinnati: Ohio UP, 1967) 178–83; John Andrew Bernstein, *Shaftesbury, Rousseau and Kant* (Cranbury: Associated U Presses, 1980) 38.

36. Anthony Ashley Cooper, Earl of Shaftesbury, *Characteristics*, vol. 2 (London, 1915; rpt 163) 62–63, 105–7.

37. See especially Raphael's excerpts from "An Inquiry Concerning Virtue, Or Merit," 1:169–88.

38. Raphael 1:209.

39. Raphael 1:372, 375.

40. For Grotius and seventeenth-century natural law, see Richard Tuck, *Natural Rights Theories* (Cambridge: Cambridge UP, 1979).

41. Raphael 1:375.

42. Raphael 1:211.

43. For the clearest account I have been able to find, see Wills 147–69.

44. Francis Hutcheson, "A Short Introduction to Moral Philosophy," *Collected Works of Francis Hutcheson*, vol. 4 (Hildesheim: Georg Olms Verlagsbuchhandlung, 1969) 144.

45. Hutcheson 4:122.

46. Hutcheson 4:145–46.

47. See Teichgraeber's excellent summary, 23–26.

48. Hutcheson 4:122–23.

49. See, among others, R. S. Crane, "Genealogy of the 'Man of Feeling,'" *ELH*

1 (1934): 205–18; Donald Greene, "Latitudinarianism and Sensibility: The Genealogy of the 'Man of Feeling' Reconsidered," *Modern Philology* 75 (1977): 159–83; Elizabeth Duthie, "The Genuine Man of Feeling," *Modern Philology* 79 (1981): 279–85; Chester Chapin, "Shaftesbury and the Man of Feeling," *Modern Philology* 80 (1983): 47–50.

50. Teichgraeber 130.

51. Adam Smith, *The Theory of Moral Sentiments*, ed. A. L. Macfie and D. D. Raphael (Oxford: Oxford UP, 1976) 23. Further references to this book will be cited parenthetically within the text.

52. *Theory of Moral Sentiments* 22.

53. For the most exhaustive meditation on this interaction, see David Marshall, *The Figure of Theater* (New York: Columbia UP, 1986) 167–92.

54. Adam Smith, *The Wealth of Nations*, ed. W. B. Todd (Oxford: Oxford UP, 1976) 10.

55. Thus Hont and Ignatieff:

> Yet in denying that the poor's needs constituted a claim of right against the property of the rich, Smith did not exclude the question of justice from his political economy. On the contrary, he transposed the question from the terrain of jurisprudence and political theory to the terrain of political economy, using natural modelling to demonstrate that by raising the productivity of agriculture, commercial society could provide adequately for the needs of the wage-earner without having to resort to any redistributive meddling in the property rights of individuals. Growth in conditions of 'natural liberty' would explode the whole antimony between needs and rights. (24)

See also David McNally, *Political Economy and the Rise of Capitalism* (Berkeley: U of California P, 1988) 210–26; Teichgraeber 146–47.

56. Jane Haldiman Marcet, *Conversations on Political Economy* (New York: Duyckink, 1820) 22–34.

57. At the end of *The Theory of Moral Sentiments*, Smith argues that justice is the most precise subsection of morality and that morality can thus be divided into two mutually exclusive areas: ethics and jurisprudence. Casuistry is nothing more than the illegitimate crossing between the two. See 327–40.

58. *Theory of Moral Sentiments* 327. My discussion of justice in Smith is deeply indebted generally to Knud Haakonssen, *The Science of a Legislator* (Cambridge: Cambridge UP, 1981), especially 45–104.

59. Compare *Theory of Moral Sentiments* 9–16 and 227–34 to 78–79 and 86.

60. Paine 228.

61. This was a standard "Jacobin" complaint against Burke; see James T. Boulton, *The Language of Politics in the Age of Wilkes and Burke* (London: Routledge and Kegan Paul, 1963) 200–205; Marilyn Butler, ed., *Burke, Paine, Godwin and the Revolution Controversy* (Cambridge: Cambridge UP, 1984) 72–74, 91–95, as well as in the whole first part of Paine, *The Rights of Man*.

62. Marcet 15.
63. *Theory of Moral Sentiments* 230–34. This section was sent to the printer at the end of 1789—that is, well before Burke's *Reflections* were published. See "Introduction" 42–43.
64. *Reflections* 145, 357–58; *Wealth of Nations* 290–96; for the "great wheel," see 291.
65. *Reflections* 271.
66. For corn as standard measure of wealth, see *Wealth of Nations* 55–56, 206; for production as the source of wealth, see 330–49. Although Smith claims that the end of production is consumption (660), he is more critical of luxury in the *Wealth of Nations* than in the *Theory of Moral Sentiments*, though Burke may have passages in Book III in mind.
67. I am here following the lines of Pocock's argument, *Virtue, Commerce, and History* 193–214.
68. *Reflections* 174.
69. Edmund Burke, "Letters on a Regicide Peace," *The Works of the Right Honorable Edmund Burke*, vol. 5 (Boston: Little Brown, 1871) 310.
70. Edmund Burke, "Thoughts and Details on Scarcity," *The Works of the Right Honorable Edmund Burke*, vol. 5 (Boston: Little Brown, 1871) 131–69.
71. "Thoughts and Details on Scarcity" 145–46.
72. *Reflections* 233.
73. *Reflections* 351–52.
74. Pierre Bourdieu, *Language and Symbolic Power*, trans. Gino Raymond and Matthew Adamson (Cambridge: Harvard UP, 1991) 58.
75. E. P. Thompson, *The Making of the English Working Class* (New York: Random House, 1963) 451–700.
76. Clark 277–348, especially 347.
77. Norman Gash, *Aristocracy and People* (Cambridge: Harvard UP, 1979) 79–87; see also J. R. Dinwiddy, *From Luddism to the First Reform Bill* (Oxford: Basil Blackwell, 1987) 24–30.
78. Thompson 761.
79. Jeremy Bentham, "Pannomial Fragments," *The Bentham Reader*, ed. Mary Peter Mack (New York: Pegasus, 1969) 253–56.
80. See, for a similar conclusion for a different place, Gordon S. Wood, *The Radicalism of the American Revolution* (New York: Vintage Books, 1993) 5–6.
81. One could appeal to Lyotard's notion of the differend here: "As distinguished from a litigation, a differend would be a cause of conflict . . . that cannot be equitably resolved for lack of a rule of judgment applicable to both arguments." Jean-Francois Lyotard, *The Differend*, trans. Georges Van Den Abeele [Minneapolis: U of Minnesota P, 1988] xi).

CHAPTER THREE: Radcliffe and Malthus in the 1790s and Beyond

1. Charles Taylor, *Sources of the Self* (Cambridge: Harvard UP, 1989) 234–84. All further references to this work will be included parenthetically in the text.

2. One can see this separation as part of the jurisprudential rejection of patriarchal — that is, Filmerian — apologetics. If the state is not a family, then the King is not a father and sovereignty does not descend from him. Rather, it rises towards him.

3. David Hume, *Enquiries Concerning Human Understanding and Concerning the Principles of Morals* (Oxford: Oxford UP, 1975) 183–92. All future references to this work will be included parenthetically in the text. See also Haakonssen 4–41.

4. Thomas Robert Malthus, *An Essay on the Principle of Population* (Harmondsworth: Penguin, 1982) 165. All future references to this work will be included parenthetically in the text.

5. Ann Radcliffe, *The Italian* (New York: Oxford UP, 1968) 1. All further page references to this edition will be included parenthetically in the body of the text.

6. *Wealth of Nations* 96–97.

7. *Wealth of Nations* 99, emphasis added.

8. William Godwin, *Enquiry into the Principles of Political Justice* (Harmondsworth: Penguin Books, 1985) 194.

9. Hume 154, emphasis added.

10. Hannah Arendt, *On Revolution* (New York: Penguin Books, 1965) 59–114.

11. It would seem that Malthus, the ordained Anglican minister, takes seriously God's reprimands to Adam and Eve: death and work are unavoidable. In fact, work seems to be the very definition of humanity for Malthus. He attacks utopian projections in the following way:

> A writer may tell me that he thinks man will ultimately become an ostrich. I cannot properly contradict him. But before he can expect to bring any reasonable person over to his opinion, he ought to shew that the necks of mankind have been gradually elongating, that the lips have grown harder and more prominent, that the legs and feet are daily altering their shape, and that the hair is beginning to change into stubs of feathers. And till the probability of so wonderful a conversion can be shewn, it is surely lost time and lost eloquence to expatiate on the happiness of man in such a state; *to describe his powers, both of running and flying, to paint him in a condition where all narrow luxuries would be contemned, where he would be employed only in collecting the necessaries of life, and where, consequently each man's share of labour would be light, and his portion of leisure ample.* (70; emphasis mine)

In the last clauses of this sentence, mankind has no more chance of achieving Godwin's rational utopia of virtue than of becoming an ostrich. The
odd switch from running and flying to the dismissal of luxury indicates
that people are ontologically incapable of a utopia of leisure.

12. E. J. Hobsbawm, *The Age of Revolution* (London: Sphere Books, 1973) 103–4.

13. Boyd Hilton, *The Age of Atonement* (Oxford: Oxford UP, 1988) 21.

14. For the theological basis of Malthus's work, see M. B. Harvey-Phillips,
"Malthus's Theodicy: The Intellectual Background of his Contribution to
Political Economy," *History of Political Economy* 16:4 (1984): 591–608; D. L.
LeMahieu, "Malthus and the Theology of Scarcity," *Journal of the History of
Ideas* 40:3 (1979): 467–74; J. M. Pullen, "Malthus's Theological Ideas and
their Influence on the Principle of Population," *History of Political Economy*
13:1 (1981): 39–54; E. N. Santurri, "Theodicy and Social Policy in Malthus's
Thought," *Journal of the History of Ideas* 63:2 (1982): 315–36; A.M.C. Water-
man, "Malthus as Theologian," *Malthus Past and Present*, ed. J. DuPâquier
(New York: Academic P, 1983) 195–209.

15. Winch 35.

16. For the place of resistance — passive and active — in British political thought
of the eighteenth century, see H. T. Dickinson, *Liberty and Property* (New
York: Holmes and Meier, 1977) 62–65, 78–79, 131, 197–98.

17. I am here thinking of Stanley Cavell's appropriation of Northrop Frye.
Cavell sees the "comedy of remarriage" as a cross between old and new
comic plots in that it concentrates on both the personality of the hero and
the heroine. See Stanley Cavell, *Pursuits of Happiness* (Cambridge: Harvard
UP, 1981), passim.

18. It is worth noting that the early reviews of Mrs. Radcliffe's works all
stressed the reader's affect: the norms by which her novels were judged
were primarily emotional, not didactic. For a convenient collection of
these reviews, see Dan McNutt, *Eighteenth Century Gothic Novel: An Annotated Bibliography* (New York: Garland, 1975) 216–23.

19. Sir Walter Scott, "Mrs. Ann Radcliffe," *Lives of the Novelists* (London:
Oxford UP, 1906) 326–27.

20. Scott 330.

21. McNutt 221–23.

22. Clara Reeve, *The Old English Baron* (New York: Oxford UP, 1967) viii–ix.

23. Reeve 4.

24. For the relation between Lewis and Radcliffe, see Sydny M. Conger, "Sensibility Restored: Radcliffe's Answer to Lewis's *The Monk*," *Gothic Fictions:
Prohibition/Transgression*, ed. Kenneth W. Graham (New York: AMS P, 1989)
113–49.

25. Reeve 4.

26. Winch 108.

27. George Crabbe, *The Complete Poetical Works*, ed. Norma Darymple-Champneys, vol. 3 (Oxford: Oxford UP, 1988) 544–45.

28. Jerome McGann, "The Anachronism of George Crabbe," *ELH* 48 (1981): 555–72.

29. T. R. Malthus, *An Essay on the Principle of Population*, vol. 2 (London: Dent, 1973 rpt) 151. All further references will be contained parenthetically within the body of the text.

CHAPTER FOUR: Scott's Big Bow-Wow

1. Quoted by Patricia James, *Population Malthus* (London: Routledge and Kegan Paul, 1979) 50.

2. James 51.

3. H. T. Dickinson, *Liberty and Property* (New York: Holmes and Meier, 1977) 142–43, 160f, 297.

4. T. R. Malthus, *An Essay on the Principle of Population*, vol. 2 (London: Dent 1973) 189.

5. Malthus, "Observations on the Effects of the Corn Laws," *The Pamphlets of Thomas Robert Malthus* (New York: Kelley, 1970) 118. All further references will be cited parenthetically within the text.

6. *Pamphlets* 117.

7. David Ricardo, "Essay on Profits," *The Works of David Ricardo*, ed. Piero Sraffa, vol. 4 (Cambridge: Cambridge UP 1951–73) 21. All further references will be included parenthetically within the text.

8. See Biancamaria Fontana, *Rethinking the Politics of Commercial Society* (Cambridge: Cambridge UP, 1985) 77.

9. Keith Tribe, *Land, Labour and Economic Discourse* (London: Routledge and Kegan Paul, 1978) 127.

10. Tribe 127.

11. Dorfman 162–63.

12. See Ricardo, *Works* 2:435–36 for a useful edition of Malthus's *Principles* annotated by Ricardo. All further references will be included parenthetically within the text.

13. Edgar Johnson, *Walter Scott* (New York: Macmillan, 1970) 690.

14. *The Visionary* 7.

15. *The Visionary* 6.

16. For an excellent discussion of the political economics of *The Visionary*, see Fontana 165–67; for the inadequacy of the poor, see 168. For the place of the poor in liberal and not-so-liberal Tory ideology of the period, see W. R. Brock, *Lord Liverpool and Liberal Toryism 1820–1827* (Cambridge: Cambridge UP, 1941) 114–15.

17. Duncan Forbes, "The Rationalism of Sir Walter Scott," *Cambridge Journal* 7 (1953): 20–55; Peter Garside, "Scott and the Philosophical Historians," *Jour-*

nal of the History of Ideas 36:2 (1975): 497-512; Katheryn Sutherland, "Fictional Economies: Adam Smith, Walter Scott and the Nineteenth-Century Novel," *ELH* 54:1 (1987): 97-127.

18. Walter Scott, *Waverley* (Harmondsworth: Penguin, 1972). All future page references will be included parenthetically within the text.

19. For a neat florilegium of texts on this subject, see Jane Rendall, *The Origins of the Scottish Enlightenment* (London: Macmillan, 1978) 140-45. For Adam Fergusson's dissent from the Kames/Smith line, see Duncan Forbes's introduction to Adam Fergusson, *An Essay on the History of Civil Society* (Edinburgh: Edinburgh UP, 1966) xx-xxii. For Puffendorf, see Richard Tuck, "The 'Modern' Theory of Natural Law," and Istvan Hont, "The Language of Sociability and Commerce," in *The Languages of Political Theory in Early Modern Europe*, ed. Anthony Pagden (Cambridge: Cambridge UP, 1988) 99-119, 253-76. See also Duncan Forbes, *Hume's Philosophical Politics* (Cambridge: Cambridge UP, 1975) 59-90; J.G.A. Pocock, "Cambridge paradigms and Scotch philosophers," in *Wealth and Virtue*, ed. Istvan Hont and Michael Ignatieff (Cambridge: Cambridge UP, 1982) 235-52.

20. Adam Smith, *Lectures on Jurisprudence*, eds. R. L. Meek, D. D. Raphael, and P. G. Stein (Oxford: Oxford UP, 1978) 14-16.

21. John Gibson Lockhart, *The Life of Sir Walter Scott, Bart.* (London: Black, 1893) 514.

22. See David Daiches, "Scott's *Redgauntlet*," in *From Jane Austen to Joseph Conrad*, ed. Robert C. Rathburn (Minneapolis: U of Minnesota P, 1957) 46-59; Francis R. Hart, *Scott's Novels* (Charlottesville: U of Virginia P, 1965) 49f.

23. Georg Lukacs, *The Historical Novel*, trans. Hannah Mitchell and Stanley Mitchell (Lincoln: U of Nebraska P, 1983) 30-63.

24. Horace Walpole, *The Castle of Otranto* (Oxford: Oxford UP, 1969) 8-12.

25. Walter Scott, *Redgauntlet* (Oxford: Oxford UP, 1985) 40.

26. *Redgauntlet* 35, 187.

27. Walter Scott, "Essay on Romance," *The Miscellaneous Prose Works of Sir Walter Scott, Bart.*, vol. 6 (Edinburgh, 1827) 183-256.

28. Such a statement leans heavily on the aesthetics of German Idealism and the thematics of Marxist utopianism, and thus owes everything to Ernst Bloch's *The Principle of Hope*, trans. Stephen Plaice and Neville Plaice (Cambridge: MIT P, 1985). For a non-Marxist recuperation of Bloch's thematics, see Hans Robert Jauss, *Question and Answer*, trans. Michael Hays (Minneapolis: U of Minnesota P, 1989) 10-25..

29. Ina Ferris, *The Achievement of Literary Authority* (Ithaca: Cornell UP, 1991) 90-91.

30. Thus we can agree with Iser that the heroes of these tales serve as the hermeneutic focus for the reader. See Wolfgang Iser, *The Implied Reader* (Baltimore: Johns Hopkins UP, 1974) 81-100; Joseph Valente, "Upon the Braes:

History and Hermeneutics in *Waverley*," *Studies in Romanticism* 25 (1986): 251–76.

31. The classic modern study of the remarkable blankness of the nominal protagonists of the Waverley novels remains Alexander Welsh, *The Hero of the Waverley Novels* (1963; New York: Atheneum, 1968). See also Judith Wilt, *Secret Leaves* (Chicago: Chicago UP, 1985) 142–52.

32. J. L. Adolphus, *Letters to Richard Heber, Esq., MP, Containing Critical Remarks on the Series of the Novels Beginning with "Waverley"* (London, 1822) 197.

33. Adolphus 204.

34. Quoted by James T. Hillhouse, *The Waverley Novels and Their Critics* (Minneapolis: U of Minnesota P, 1936) 150.

35. William Hazlitt, *The Spirit of the Age* (London: Collins, 1969) 107.

36. Lockhart 255–56. He is quoting Scott's own letter of July 24, 1814, to Morritt.

37. See Sir Llewellyn Woodward, *The Age of Reform* (Oxford: Oxford UP, 1962) 62–64; Norman Gash, *Aristocracy and People* (Cambridge: Harvard UP, 1979) 76–79; J. E. Cookson, *Lord Liverpool's Administration* (Hamden: Archon, 1975) 90–102.

38. Sir Walter Scott, *Letters*, ed. H. H. Grierson, vol. 4 (Edinburgh: Constable, 1932) 227.

39. Lockhart 350.

40. Sir Walter Scott, *The Antiquary*, collected in *The Waverley Novels*, vol. 4 (New York: Harper Bros., nd) v.

41. E. M. Forster, *Aspects of the Novel* (New York: Harcourt Brace, 1951) 55.

42. See Welsh 1–18.

43. Hart 254.

44. Judith Wilt, *Secret Leaves* (Chicago: U of Chicago P, 1985).

45. J.G.A. Pocock, "The Political Economy of Burke's Analysis of the French Revolution," in *Virtue, Commerce, and History* (New York: Cambridge UP, 1985) 193–212.

46. Edmund Burke, *The Works of the Right Honorable Edmund Burke*, vol. 3 (Boston: Little Brown, 1871) 332.

47. Harry Shaw, *The Forms of Historical Fiction* (Ithaca: Cornell UP, 1983) 77–81.

48. Hart 251.

49. Sir Walter Scott, *Ivanhoe* (Harmondsworth: Penguin Books, 1986) 9. All future references to this edition will be included parenthetically in the text.

50. Lockhart 413.

51. Quoted by Ferris 240.

52. For a nice example of Shakespeare's function, see *Waverley* 206; see also Nicola J. Watson, "Kemble, Scott and the Mantle of the Bard," in *The Appropriation of Shakespeare*, ed. Jean L. Marsden (New York: Saint Martin's P, 1991) 73–92.

53. John O. Hayden, ed., *Scott: The Critical Heritage* (New York: Barnes and Noble, 1979) 189.

54. Here is Ernest Gellner, in *Nations and Nationalism* (Ithaca: Cornell UP, 1983): So the economy needs both the new type of central culture and the central state; the culture needs the state; and the state probably needs the homogeneous branding of its flock, in a situation in which it cannot rely on largely eroded sub-groups either to police its citizens, or to inspire them with that minimum of moral zeal and social identification without which social life becomes very difficult. . . . In brief, the mutual relationship of a modern culture and state is something quite new, and springs, inevitably from the requirements of a modern economy. (140) See also Gellner, "Nationalism and Cohesion in Complex Societies," in *Culture, Identity and Politics* (Cambridge: Cambridge UP, 1987) 6-28, especially 10.

55. Gellner, "Nationalism and Cohesion in Complex Societies," 10.

56. Johnson 743-46.

57. Todd Endelman, *The Jews of Georgian England 1714-1830* (Philadelphia: Jewish Publication Society, 1979), 86-87, 93-95, 97-101.

58. Edmund Burke, *Reflections on the Revolution in France* (Harmondsworth: Penguin Books, 1968) 138, 204.

59. Quoted Hayden 236.

60. See Burke 265.

61. See Slavoj Zizek, *For They Know Not What They Do* (New York: Verso, 1991) 9-10.

62. Of course, philo-Semitism was riven by its own evangelical, that is, anti-Jewish zeal:
English Protestantism possessed an active philo-Semitic strain generally absent on the Continent. Although philo-Semitism sought the eventual conversion of the Jews, in the short run it worked to better their status. . . . In negative terms, it meant that there was a large body of religious thought that did not identify Jewry as the embodiment of evil . . . some of the most active proponents of emancipation were philo-Semites who desired the integration of Jews into English society as a prelude to their conversion.
(From Todd M. Endelman, "The Englishness of Jewish Modernity in England," in *Toward Modernity*, ed., Jacob Katz [New Brunswick: Transaction Books, 1987] 237.)

63. Sander L. Gilman, *Jewish Self-Hatred* (Baltimore: Johns Hopkins UP, 1986) 20, 87-106, 209-69.

64. For examples of this, see Endelman, *The Jews of Georgian England* 105-6. See also Gilman 85.

65. J.C.D. Clark, *English Society 1688–1832* (Cambridge: Cambridge UP, 1985) 191–92.

66. Ian Christie investigates the reasons why England did not have a revolution in the 1790s; Colley looks to the Church, war and Empire, and concerted acts of "officially constructed patriotism" to account for the cohesion of Great Britain in the long eighteenth century. In so doing she corrects the excesses of Clark's revisionary and somewhat limiting accent on theological issues. See Ian Christie, *Stress and Stability in Late Eighteenth Century Britain* (Oxford: Oxford UP, 1984); Linda Colley, *Britons: Forging the Nation 1707–1837* (New Haven: Yale UP, 1992).

67. See E. N. Williams, *The Eighteenth Century Constitution: Documents and Commentary* (Cambridge: Cambridge UP, 1960) 344, 346.

68. Norman Gash, *Aristocracy and People: Britain, 1815–1865* (Cambridge: Harvard UP, 1979) 137.

69. Endelman, *The Jews of Georgian England* 25.

70. Endelman, "The Englishness of Jewish Modernity in England," 240–41.

71. Gash 63–69; Clark 366–408.

72. Slavoj Zizek, *The Sublime Object of Ideology* (New York: Verso, 1989) 126.

73. Max Horkheimer and Theodor W. Adorno, *Dialectic of Enlightenment*, trans. John Cumming (New York: Continuum, 1986) 187.

74. Zizek, *The Sublime Object of Ideology* 126.

CHAPTER FIVE: Telling Time with Austen

1. Jane Austen, *Persuasion* (Oxford: Oxford UP, 1971) 237. All further references to this work will be included parenthetically within the text.

2. Linda Colley, *Britons: Forging the Nation 1707–1837* (New Haven: Yale UP, 1992) 250.

3. Colley 263.

4. In this way, Claudia Johnson's incisive account of Austen, for all its refusal to satisfy radical desires in the contemporary academy (desires I in some large part share), seems to be very much on the mark. See Claudia L. Johnson, *Jane Austen: Women, Politics and the Novel* (Chicago: U of Chicago P, 1988) 2–6, 166.

5. For the important thematics of health in Austen and in *Persuasion* in particular, see D. A. Miller, "The Late Jane Austen," *Raritan* 10:1 (1990): 55–79; John Wiltshire, *Jane Austen and the Body* (New York: Cambridge UP, 1992).

6. Johnson 148.

7. For an attempt to redeem the apparent sadomasochism of this kind of stoicism, see David Kaufmann, "Law and Propriety, *Sense and Sensibility*: Austen on the Cusp of Modernity," *ELH* 59:2 (1992): 385–408.

8. Alasdair MacIntyre, *After Virtue* (Notre Dame: Notre Dame UP, 2nd ed., 1984) 226–43.

9. Stuart Schneiderman, "Fictions," in *Lacan and the Subject of Language*, ed. Ellie Ragland-Sullivan and Mark Bracher (New York: Routledge, 1991) 151.

10. Schneiderman 160.

11. Sigmund Freud, "Group Psychology and the Analysis of the Ego," *The Standard Edition of the Complete Psychological Works of Sigmund Freud*, trans. James Strachey, vol. 18 (London: Hogarth P, 1953–66) 110.

12. J. Laplanche and J. B. Pontalis, *The Language of Psychoanalysis*, trans. Donald Nicholson-Smith (New York: Norton, 1973) 143.

13. Jacques Lacan, *The Seminar of Jacques Lacan Book I: Freud's Papers on Technique*, trans. John Forrester (New York: Norton, 1988) 141–42.

14. See especially Freud 18:116.

15. Slavoj Zizek, *For They Know Not What They Do* (London: Verso, 1991) 11.

16. Roland Barthes, *Le Plaisir du Texte*, (Paris: Editions du Seuil, 1973) 45–46.

17. Marilyn Butler, *Romantics, Rebels and Reactionaries* (New York: Oxford UP, 1981) 98. This argument is an extension of Butler's *Jane Austen and the War of Ideas* (New York: Oxford UP, 1975). For the most influential accounts of Austen's conservatism (a conservatism that becomes clear when read in terms of the narratives these books tell), see Sandra Gilbert and Susan Gubar, *The Madwoman in the Attic* (New Haven: Yale UP, 1979), and Mary Poovey, *The Proper Lady and the Woman Writer* (Chicago: U of Chicago P, 1988). For attempts to counter this view, see Julia Gaily Brown, "The Feminist Depreciation of Austen," *Novel* 23:3 (1990): 303–13; Alison Sulloway, *Jane Austen and the Province of Womanhood* (Philadelphia: U of Pennsylvania P, 1989); Robin Warhol, "The Look, the Body, and the Heroine," *Novel* 26:1 (1992): 5–19.

18. John Halperin, "Jane Austen's Nineteenth-Century Critics: Walter Scott to Henry James," in *Jane Austen: Bicentenary Essays*, ed. John Halperin (Cambridge: Cambridge UP, 1975) 21–23.

19. This greatest of damnations by the faintest of praise is reprinted in John O. Hayden, *Scott: The Critical Heritage* (New York: Barnes and Noble, 1970) 366–67.

20. James T. Hillhouse, *The Waverley Novels and Their Critics* (Minneapolis: U of Minnesota P, 1936) 244.

21. Hillhouse 258–59.

22. Quoted Hayden 410.

23. Hayden 410.

24. See Hillhouse 197–99.

25. Hayden 469–70.

26. See David Kaufmann, "Law and Propriety, *Sense and Sensibility*" 407–8n.

27. B. C. Southam ed., *Jane Austen: The Critical Heritage* (New York: Barnes and Noble, 1968) 139.

28. Southam 202.

29. Southam 213.

30. This is true even of his staunchest recent defenders. See Fred R. Berger, *Happiness, Justice and Freedom* (Berkeley: U of California P, 1984); Wendy Donner, *The Liberal Self* (Ithaca: Cornell UP, 1991); John Gray, *Mill on Liberty: A Defence* (London: Routledge and Kegan Paul, 1983), and John Skorupski, *John Stuart Mill* (London: Routledge, 1989).

31. Friedrich Nietzsche, *The Will to Power*, trans. Walter Kaufmann (New York: Vintage, 1978) 21; Karl Marx, *Capital*, trans. Ben Fowkes, vol. 1 (New York: Vintage, 1977) 653–54; Graeme Duncan and John Gray, "The Left Against Mill," in *New Essays on John Stuart Mill and Utilitarianism*, ed. Wesley Cooper, Kai Nielsen, and Steven Patten, *Canadian Journal of Philosophy, Supplementary Volume 5* (1979): 203–9.

32. John Stuart Mill, *Utilitarianism and Other Writings*, ed. Mary Warnock (New York: New American Library, 1974). All further references to this work will be included parenthetically within the text.

33. I thus want to disagree sharply with Stefan Collini, Donald Winch, and John Burrow, who argue in a rather brilliant study that the breach between wealth and happiness was a feature of the Malthus-Ricardo debate. See *That Noble Science of Politics* (Cambridge: Cambridge UP, 1983) 63–90.

34. See, inter alia, Nassau William Senior, *Political Economy* (London: Griffin, rpt 1850) 1–5.

35. John Stuart Mill, *The Collected Works of John Stuart Mill*, ed. John M. Robson, vol. 10 (Toronto: U of Toronto P, 1963–91) 754, emphasis added. All further references to this work will be included parenthetically in the text.

36. By far the most nuanced discussion of happiness in Mill seems to be in Donner, *The Liberal Self*. In the paragraphs that follow, I am deeply indebted to this book, especially for its careful distinctions between quantitative and qualitative hedonism. See pages 37–65. I also refer the reader to Berger 30–64.

37. Donner 8–65.

38. "In broad brush strokes, individuality centers on the process by which each person discovers his or her own unique mix of generic capacities, talents, and abilities. Autonomy is concerned with the critical reflection, choice, and endorsement of character, projects and pursuits in harmony with one's nature." Donner 120.

39. David Hume, *Enquiry Concerning the Principles of Morals* (Oxford: Oxford UP, 1975) 261.

40. See Deborah Kaplan's excellent recent study, *Austen Amongst Women* (Baltimore: Johns Hopkins UP, 1992).

41. See *The Country and the City* (New York: Oxford UP, 1973) 112–19.

42. Jane Austen, *The Oxford Illustrated Jane Austen: Minor Works*, ed. R. W. Chapman (New York: Oxford UP, 1967) 392. All further references to this work will be included parenthetically within the body of the text.

43. J.G.A. Pocock, *Virtue, Commerce, and History* (Cambridge: Cambridge UP, 1985) 103–24.

44. E. M. Forster, *Abinger Harvest* (New York: Meridian, 1955) 146.

CHAPTER SIX: The Constancy of Crisis

1. John Rawls, *A Theory of Justice* (Cambridge: Harvard UP, 1971); Michael Sandel, *Liberalism and the Limits of Justice* (New York: Cambridge UP, 1982).

2. Rawls 3.

3. Rawls 27.

4. Rawls 14–15.

5. Sandel 66–104, 173–78.

Index